Entrepreneurship, Growth and Economic Development

Entrepreneurship, Growth and Economic Development

Frontiers in European Entrepreneurship Research

Edited by

Mário Raposo

Full Professor of Marketing and Strategy, University of Beira Interior and Scientific Coordinator of NECE, Portugal

David Smallbone

Professor of Small Business and Entrepreneurship, Small Business Research Centre, Kingston University, UK

Károly Balaton

Full Professor, Corvinus University of Budapest, Hungary

Lilla Hortoványi

Assistant Professor of Management, Corvinus University of Budapest, Hungary

IN ASSOCIATION WITH THE ECSB

Edward Elgar

Cheltenham, UK • Northampton, MA, USA

Published by
Edward Elgar Publishing Limited
The Lypiatts
15 Lansdown Road
Cheltenham
Glos GL50 2JA
UK

Edward Elgar Publishing, Inc.
William Pratt House
9 Dewey Court
Northampton
Massachusetts 01060
USA

A catalogue record for this book
is available from the British Library

Library of Congress Control Number: 2011925776

ISBN 978 0 85793 467 3

Typeset by Servis Filmsetting Ltd, Stockport, Cheshire
Printed and bound by MPG Books Group, UK

Contents

Contributors

Károly Balaton, Corvinus University of Budapest, Hungary

Katharina Becker, Swiss Institute for Entrepreneurship, University of Applied Sciences HTW Chur, Switzerland

Malin Brännback, School of Business and Economics, Åbo Akademi University, Finland

Alan Carsrud, Ted Rogers School of Management, Ryerson University, Canada and School of Business and Economics, Åbo Akademi University, Finland

Thomas M. Cooney, Dublin Institute of Technology, Ireland

Hans Crijns, Vlerick Leuven Gent Management School, Belgium

Alain Fayolle, EMLYON Business School, France

David Finn, DCU Business School, Dublin City University, Ireland

Vishal Gupta, State University of New York, Binghamton University, USA

Teresa Hogan, Dublin City University Business School, Ireland

Lilla Hortoványi, Corvinus University of Budapest, Hungary

Elaine Hutson, University College Dublin, Ireland

Kenta Ikeuchi, Graduate School of Economics, Hitotsubashi University, Tokyo, Japan

Niklas Kiviluoto, School of Business and Economics, Åbo Akademi University, Finland

Franz Kronthaler, Research Unit for Economic Policy, University of Applied Sciences HTW Chur, Switzerland

Jan Lepoutre, Vlerick Leuven Gent Management School, Belgium

Colm O'Gorman, DCU Business School, Dublin City University, Ireland

Hiroyuki Okamuro, Graduate School of Economics, Hitotsubashi University, Tokyo, Japan

Mário Raposo, University of Beira Interior, NECE Research Centre in Business Studies, Portugal

David Smallbone, Kingston University, UK

Christoph Streb, University of Groningen, The Netherlands

László Szerb, University of Pécs, Hungary

Olivier Tilleuil, Vlerick Leuven Gent Management School, Belgium

József Ulbert, University of Pécs, Hungary

Wouter Van den Berghe, Managing Director at Tilkon Consultancy, Belgium

Kerstin Wagner, Swiss Institute for Entrepreneurship, University of Applied Sciences HTW Chur, Switzerland

Friederike Welter, Jönköping University, Sweden

Olivier Witmeur, Université libre de Bruxelles, Belgium

Mirela Xheneti, Kingston University, UK

Foreword

Dear colleague,

Welcome to the latest edition of the RENT anthology based upon a selection of the best papers from the XXIII RENT conference in Budapest. This conference had the highest number of abstract submissions and conference participants in the history of the conference, which ensured that the high standard of papers and presentations that is now a feature of RENT conferences was maintained. Following your reading of this anthology, I am confident that you will agree that the excellence of research that is featured in this book reflects the increased quality of the work currently being undertaken by entrepreneurship academics across Europe.

The European Council for Small Business (ECSB) has been a constant driving force over the past two decades in the move to raise the standards of research, publications and teaching in the field of entrepreneurship. The RENT conference has become a landmark occasion each year for entrepreneurship academics and researchers, but the event has expanded to include workshops, seminars and other related events targeted at particular groups within our network. The Doctoral Colloquium is now over-subscribed each year as we seek to develop the work of our younger researchers, while the Post-Doctoral Roundtable has quickly established itself as an opportunity for recent PhD graduates to receive mentoring on the next steps of their careers. Meanwhile the Policy Forum has become a biannual event and case writing workshops are being hosted throughout the year and are also available by webinar.

The anthology is not the only publication that arises from the RENT conference as ECSB also produces an online publication called 'Inter-RENT' which is targeted at researchers who are developing their journal writing skills. This is a mentored programme that helps young researchers who have presented papers with good potential to improve the paper to a standard that warrants publication in our online journal. The anthology and Inter-RENT demonstrate ECSB's commitment to improving the quality of journal article writing within the field and to showcasing the best talents within our network.

ECSB is more than just the RENT conference as we offer a wide range of services and events throughout the year. I would strongly recommend that you visit our website at www.ecsb.org and that you join us in our work. I wish you insightful and beneficial reading and I trust that you will find it beneficial towards your own publication goals.

Thomas M. Cooney
President, ECSB

1. Introduction: entrepreneurship, growth and economic development

Mário Raposo, David Smallbone, Károly Balaton and Lilla Hortoványi

INTRODUCING RENT XXIII

The Research in Entrepreneurship and Small Business (RENT) conference is an annual international event, organized by the European Council for Small Business (ECSB) in collaboration with the European Institute for Advanced Studies in Management (EIASM). It represents one of the most significant international meetings of researchers in the field of entrepreneurship. This book comprises a selection of ten of the best papers from the 148 accepted for presentation at RENT XXIII, held in Corvinus University Budapest, Hungary in November 2009. The overarching theme of the 2009 conference was the title 'Entrepreneurial growth of the firm' and the papers selected for inclusion in this volume cover a range of topics related to the broad theme of entrepreneurship, growth and economic development. Entrepreneurship is a key source of dynamism in the European economy, enabling it to adjust to structural changes, converting challenges into opportunities. Both the causes and consequences of entrepreneurship are matters of extensive scientific debate as well as of great potential policy significance. The entrepreneur is a key change agent in a market economy, promoting the efficient use of resources and introducing new products, processes and organizational structures. A high level of entrepreneurial activity contributes to economic growth, innovative activities, competition, job creation and local development. The selection of papers included in this volume demonstrates the role of entrepreneurship in relation to growth and economic development in a variety of different contexts.

In recent decades, the world economy has seen a radical transformation of the factors that determine the competitiveness of countries. Indeed economic integration, globalization, rapid technological change and more recently the economic crisis have changed the traditional patterns of competitiveness. The new competitive model is now based in the knowledge economy, which represents a means of introducing continuous innovation through the creation of new ventures.

The contribution of entrepreneurship to economic competitiveness is related to its impact on productivity, which in turn is affected by the process of competition between firms' innovation. The process involves an increase in the supply of better products and services at lower prices to society.

The evidence shows that some new firms are dynamic, making an important contribution to economic development in three ways: first, as a channel to convert innovative ideas into market opportunities; secondly, by stimulating competitiveness by increasing productivity; and thirdly through the supply of new jobs. Alongside its contribution to economic competitiveness, the European Union regards entrepreneurship as a contributor to social inclusion and to reducing unemployment.

INTRODUCING THE CHAPTERS

The idea that entrepreneurship is the engine that stimulates economic *growth*, employment and *competitiveness* in global markets is supported by various research evidence. However, measuring firm success, performance and growth is a complex task and a potential source of frustration. In this context, Chapter 2, by Niklas Kiviluoto, Malin Brännback and Alan Carsrud, reviews existing literature in order to understand better how growth, performance and profitability are measured at the firm level, in what contexts, and what the differences are between the three concepts. They review empirical articles published between 1981 and 2009 in five top-tier journals, three specializing in the field of entrepreneurship (*Entrepreneurship: Theory & Practice, Journal of Business Venturing, Journal of Small Business Management*); and two general business and management journals (*Strategic Management Journal* and *Academy of Management Journal*).

The selection of articles was made by searching articles with the key words 'growth and profitability' or 'growth and performance' from the Harzing database 'Publish or Perish'. A final sample of 118 empirical articles was chosen for the review. Then articles were read and relevant data was extracted from the articles with respect to the dependent variables, independent variables and control variables, final sample size and firm characteristics, industry type, growth measures, performance measures and the growth–performance relationship. The results show a fragmented field of research where little consensus seems to exist in determining what performance is. The three most common dependent variables are growth (49.2 per cent), performance (44.9 per cent) and profitability (17.8 per cent). In a total of 49 studies (41.5 per cent) where only one performance measure is used, more than 53 per cent assess a firm's performance solely based on sales growth.

Based on the findings from this study, the authors argue that growth and performance *are essentially the same*. Most studies concerned with performance actually refer to growth, and more specifically to sales growth. Surprisingly, perhaps, this is often the only measure used when assessing a firm's performance. However, from a broader perspective, the answer is that growth and performance are not the same. Performance is most commonly seen as firm success, and assessing a firm's success solely based on growth only tells part of the story.

Chapter 3 also focuses on growth at the individual business level, where the role of entrepreneurial ventures in job generation is emphasized. Entrepreneurial IT services firms (EISFs) are chosen to develop and test a typology of growth strategies. This exploratory study by Olivier Witmeur and Alain Fayolle is concerned with the business-to-business activities of this type of firm for two reasons. First, EISFs face three traditional growth options that are not mutually exclusive: gaining more customers in the same market with the same or deepening provision of services; extending to new territories (internationalization) and/or developing a new service offering (diversification). Secondly, their strategic challenge is augmented by a possible evolution from a service- to a software-business model. The study builds a typology of strategic configurations for EISFs, with a description of individual growth stages, as suggested in stage models specific for hi-tech ventures.

The research employs a multiple case study, qualitative methodology, applied to four Belgian EISFs. For each of these firms, a single open-ended interview (for a minimum of one hour) was conducted with the founder/manager, and secondary corporate data (annual report, press releases, and so on) were also analysed, in order to identify both major events and strategy changes.

Analysis of the four case studies led to four propositions. First, 'willingness to grow' is more often associated with moves towards product configurations. Secondly, service configurations are driven by 'market acceptance' while early product configurations need 'investor acceptance' because of the existence of a prototyping stage before reaching the market. Thirdly, organizational structuring does not appear to be relevant at the outset for both service and product configurations, but is critical during later stages. Fourthly, although strategic planning is only relevant in the later stage for firms adopting service configurations, it is more constantly important in product configurations. Overall, a 'willingness to grow' and 'market acceptance' seem to be the most important processes.

The study proposes a systematic approach to testing the typology, as well as offering middle-range theory that provides insights into the conditions and implications of growth strategies available to entrepreneurial ventures. On a practical level, the typology indicates, and the cases confirm, that beyond the entrepreneur's profile and willingness to grow, the adoption of strategies such as deepening, diversification and internationalization must be associated with different sets of activities, market conditions, resources endowment and organizational challenges.

The lack of a well-developed venture capital market has long been viewed as a major barrier to the emergence and growth of New Technology Based Firms (NTBFs). In this context, Chapter 4 by Teresa Hogan and Elaine Hutson analyse the relationships between the key events in the start-up phase of NTBFs in venture capital-backed and non-venture capital-backed firms in the software sector. In particular, the study analyses the impact of product lead times and the availability of finance from consulting activities on the financing patterns of both cohorts at start-up.

Software is the dynamo of the Information Communication Technology (ICT) sector as it provides the code that enables hardware products to function. Low barriers to entry have provided the opportunity for NTBF formation in the software sector. Using various sources, a database of all software product firms in Ireland was compiled for this study. Having extracted a sample of 257 independent software product firms, a postal survey was administered to the company founders. In terms of responses, 110 provided information on the timing and sequencing of key events in the formation process. The number of venture capital-backed and non-venture capital-backed firms in the study is similar.

The findings show that overall product lead times in the software product sector are relatively short, with firms typically developing their first prototypes within a year of formation. In addition the evidence suggests that product lead times are not significantly longer in venture capital-backed than non-venture capital-backed firms in the sector. This is an important finding as it suggests that product lead times may not have the same impact on funding in software firms as in the case of firms in other sectors. Second, although product lead times in venture capital and non-venture capital-backed software product firms are not significantly different, the analysis reveals fundamental differences in the funding of prototype development within the two subgroups. The non-venture capital-backed cohort relies largely on internal funding for product development, whilst the venture capital-backed firms are more likely to access external funding prior to completing the process. Third, revenue from consulting is an important source of funding for prototype development in both venture capital-backed and non-venture capital-backed firms. Short product lead times facilitate a self-funding strategy which is enabled by a 'soft start' business model whereby consulting revenues are employed to fund prototype development, limiting the need for external sources of funding. The evidence confirms that while some firms can self-finance the product development process, fewer firms can fund prototype development solely from external sources of financing.

It is increasingly recognized that entrepreneurship education is a key factor influencing the entrepreneurial orientation of a population and thus ultimately the role of entrepreneurship in economic development. At the same time, there are different approaches to stimulating entrepreneurship through education at different stages of human development. Chapter 5, by Jan Lepoutre, Wouter Van den Berghe, Olivier Tilleuil and Hans Crijns, assesses whether entrepreneurship education programmes have an effect on the entrepreneurial intent, creativity and attitude towards entrepreneurship among secondary school pupils. Their literature review suggested that entrepreneurship education programmes have a significant positive impact on various proxies for entrepreneurship, including entrepreneurial intentions, the desirability and feasibility of entrepreneurial ventures, and various competencies that are associated with entrepreneurship.

The empirical study was conducted among pupils that participated in 21 entrepreneurship education programmes, implemented in the Flemish part of Belgium. The authors asked programme coordinators to submit a survey to the pupils after the programme was finished. After data cleaning, 2160 responses were retained and the results analysed using various multivariate statistical packages. The results confirmed that entrepreneurial intentions change significantly as a result of entrepreneurship education programmes. The data reinforce the notion that entrepreneurship programmes also have a significant effect on the self-perceived feasibility to start up a company. Furthermore, the study also found confirmation of the impact of entrepreneurship education programmes on the perceived desirability of starting a business. As entrepreneurship is increasingly recognized as an important vehicle for economic and social prosperity in our societies, entrepreneurship education programmes in secondary schools offer a means of influencing entrepreneurial attitudes and competencies among pupils at a young age. This research demonstrates that not only are such programmes effective, but also that their effect depends on the intensity and experience of the programme itself and how it is evaluated by the pupils.

New business start-ups increase innovation as well as the level of competition, and also create employment, thereby contributing to national and regional economic development. In Chapter 6, Kenta Ikeuchi and Hiroyuki Okamuro investigate the impact of regional human capital structure on the start-up ratio, using Japanese data at the prefecture level. Differentiating between independent start-ups and new subsidiaries of existing firms, they compare the effects of regional human capital structure on entry across different industry sectors. With regard to labour force structure, their literature review reveals numerous studies focusing on the effects of the qualitative and quantitative composition of the regional labour force, as well as the impact of the employment situation on the start-up ratio. The qualitative composition denotes the endowment of a highly educated or skilled labour force, while the quantitative composition is mainly measured by the age structure of the labour force. Based on data describing the regional workforce and stock of establishments from 47 Japanese prefectures over four observation periods, the study estimates the impact of various regional factors on the entry rate of independent start-ups and new subsidiaries for each industry sector. The authors employ SUR regression, which assumes correlation between the error terms of two regression models, because variables affecting the entries of both independent businesses and subsidiaries might be omitted.

The estimation results show considerable differences in the impact of regional factors between independent start-ups and subsidiaries as well as among different industries. First, the ratio of college graduates is negatively correlated with independent start-ups, but positively with the entry of subsidiaries. Second, the ratio of professional and technical workers positively affects independent start-ups but not the entry of subsidiaries. Third, the relationships between regional human capital structure and the entry of independent start-ups and new subsidiaries are different across industries. The results suggest that regional policies to activate business start-ups should recognize the differences between encouraging local entrepreneurship and attracting new subsidiaries. These differences may vary, even within the service sector, according to technological intensity or innovativeness.

Increasing cross-border cooperation between firms in border regions may be viewed as a form of internationalization, as well as a potential stimulus to economic development in typically disadvantaged peripheral regions. In this context, Chapter 7, by David Smallbone, Mirela Xheneti and Friederike Welter, investigates cross-border cooperation between enterprises as a form of international entrepreneurship, using empirical data from two contrasting regions: Florina, which is a Greek region with a 'hard', external EU border with the Former Yugoslav Republic of Macedonia (FYROM); and Görlitz, which is a German region with a 'soft' internal EU border with Poland.

The international entrepreneurship literature incorporates a number of specific approaches, including the resource-based approach, the network approach and the strategic choice approach. The study assesses the extent to which existing theories are appropriate to explain cross-border cooperation between enterprises. This is explored empirically by examining entrepreneurs' rationale for entering the cross-border region, their motivations for taking such a decision, their subsequent experience and the ways they interact with both the domestic and international environment. A semi-structured schedule was used as a basis for the interviews in order to gather data from the cross-border firms, which were mainly qualitative in nature.

As by definition border regions are at the periphery of their countries, the evidence shows that cross-border cooperation with foreign enterprises may offer firms a means of compensating for their peripherality. The evidence also demonstrates how the nature, extent and direction of cross-border entrepreneurial activity is affected by the respective development levels on the two sides of the border. This affects both market opportunities on the demand side and (indirectly) the capacity of firms to take advantage of them on the supply side. The empirical data also point to the role of network links as resources for cross-border cooperation to develop and a basis for the type of trust-based relationships to evolve that can be so important in facilitating effective inter-enterprise cooperation. In terms of the relevance of theories of internationalization, the analyses demonstrate a need for eclecticism, providing evidence to support several theoretical perspectives. Of particular relevance are the incremental, resource-based and network approaches, with aspects of a strategic choice perspective helpful in conceptualizing the drivers.

The identification of variables in regions with high and low entrepreneurship potential is an important aspect in the formulation of policy recommendations to foster entrepreneurial activity at the regional level. In this context, Chapter 8, by Katharina Becker, Franz Kronthaler and Kerstin Wagner, examines the conditions for new venture creation in Swiss regions, including the resources, structural characteristics and abilities of regions to generate new firms.

Theoretical and empirical literature on entrepreneurship suggests there are numerous factors which can impact on start-up activities. These include those influencing the demand and supply sides for entrepreneurship as well as urbanization and localization effects. The demand side for entrepreneurship refers to the opportunities to create a venture, influenced by the market demand for new goods and services. The supply side deals with the endogenous potential of the regional population to create new firms. This includes factors such as the size and structure of the population, employment structure, age structure, human capital and share of immigrants. Urbanization and localization economies both belong to the broader concept of agglomeration economies, in which firms are said to benefit from spatial concentration, leading to advantages associated with market size, spillovers, synergies and labour market effects.

The study aims to cluster regions according to their entrepreneurial potential at the spatial level of 106 Swiss MS (*mobilité spatiale*) regions, in order to compare regions according to their structural potential for new venture creation and to identify the strengths and weaknesses of regions with regard to their entrepreneurial activity. Cluster analysis is used to identify 10 clusters with different entrepreneurial potential. Based on factors established in the literature, it was suggested that each regional cluster was distinctive with regard to its potential for venture creation. With these results it is possible to discuss different strategies for fostering entrepreneurial activity for the respective regions. The results provide a means of benchmarking regions, in the sense that regions can compare their specific characteristics with other regions and clusters. Furthermore, the results can assist decision-makers to evaluate projects to establish whether or not they are in line with regional policy strategy.

The existence of a competitive and innovative SME sector is an important element for enhancing entrepreneurial activity and providing the necessary dynamism for economic growth. In this context, Chapter 9 is concerned with the development of a theoretical model of competitiveness and its application to the SME sector in Hungary. The study, by László Szerb and József Ulbert, develops a conceptual model containing 21 individual variables and seven pillars to determine and examine the competitiveness of small businesses. The resource-based view (RBV) and Dennis Miller's configuration theory serve as a basis for constructing the seven-pillar model of competitiveness.

While most competitiveness research focuses on identifying the key factors of competitiveness, Szerb and Ulbert view competitiveness from a system perspective, showing how the different elements of competitiveness can be recognized and combined by applying a unique methodology called the penalty for bottleneck (PFB). The PFB argument is based on the theories of constraint and weakest link. Bottlenecks are defined as the lowest value factor out of the seven pillars of competitiveness. Each pillar value is related to the weakest pillar, and penalized for differences. The calculation of the competitiveness points of individual firms is a distinctive approach in competitiveness research.

A survey of Hungarian SMEs involving 695 Hungarian businesses is used to present the empirical applicability of the conceptual model and the PFB methodology. The results show that innovation is typically the weakest aspect in the businesses surveyed, followed by networking and human resources. The implication is that public policy-makers should aim to improve the competitiveness of Hungarian SMEs by paying more attention to improving these aspects. The cluster analysis shows great differences between the seven groups of businesses in terms of competitiveness, with each cluster representing a dominant competitive strategy of Hungarian SMEs.

Chapter 10, by David Finn and Colm O'Gorman, is concerned with how innovation leads to the emergence of new industries and, in particular, with the processes by which individuals create commercially successful innovations. The authors emphasize how new knowledge-based innovations are important, not just to individual firms, but also to regional and national economies. The research approach starts with an empirical description of the radio frequency identification (RFID) industry. In collecting data they focused on two potential generative mechanisms. First, the emergence of the industry is described in terms of the evolution of RFID technology, and more particularly, the evolution of a syringe-implantable identification transponder. Second, they describe the industry in terms of the evolution of entrepreneurial firms that were involved in developing and exploiting RFID technology. Their findings have important implications for the study of the emergence of new organizations in contexts characterized by technological uncertainty; by the absence of established market mechanisms; and by the absence of institutional support for emerging organizational forms. Such contexts are important, as many policy-makers seek to stimulate economic growth through investment in science, which they expect will lead to the 'birth' of new industries. The authors argue that a core generative process in the emergence of a new industry is knowledge spillover. In their study, the discovery, evaluation and exploitation of opportunities by individuals was the result of knowledge spillovers that resulted from extensive social interactions.

The managerial implications of this research are that entrepreneurs in knowledge-driven industries need to think differently about the mechanisms which lead to knowledge spillover and the challenges of managing people and business relationships in an emerging industry. For public policy practitioners several aspects of this research offer hope to regions that lag in terms of knowledge creation through investments by government and large firms in scientific research.

The final chapter, by Christoph Streb and Vishal Gupta, has a different purpose from the other chapters, as it focuses on research methodology. It presents new methodological approaches for the study of process-intensive, context-rich, temporally oriented entrepreneurial phenomena. The study provides a summary of the radical subjectivist paradigm with regard to research methodology issues, based on a review of publications in six top entrepreneurship journals, in order to identify those using a qualitative approach, which is usually associated with a more subjectivist paradigm. The authors seek to discover the extent to which a radical subjectivist approach is represented in the current literature. By introducing a hermeneutical research approach, they offer suggestions for qualitative approaches to entrepreneurship research that takes the unique multilevel nature of entrepreneurial phenomena into account and is consistent with the radical Austrian paradigm's subjectivist ontological and epistemological assumptions.

Hermeneutics is a linguistic methodology that focuses on questions of how people interpret and understand texts. Hermeneutics suggests that the various participants in a conversation jointly produce the understanding and meaning of a text. It recognizes the existence of several different worldviews (or vantage points), which can differ to a greater or lesser degree from one another. Thus, the understanding of entrepreneurship is mutually constructed in conversations between entrepreneurs, lay people, media, commentators, and any other social participants who choose to join this conversation.

Three additional issues deserve mention. First, a hermeneutic understanding of any text involves relating unique instances and occurrences found in this text to ideas and concepts that apply to multiple situations. Secondly, hermeneutics recognizes that preconceptions, assumptions and prejudices are inherent in any understanding of a text. Thirdly, hermeneutics encourages one to be suspicious of any text and to 'dig beneath' the surface to unveil and retrieve those meanings that often lie hidden.

This chapter analyses publications in six leading entrepreneurship research journals between 2000 and 2008 with regard to their methodological orientations and relevance to the emerging disequilibrium paradigm according to Ludwig Lachmann. The key findings of this chapter suggest that Lachmann's work represents a fundamental shift in entrepreneurship research: from the objectively anchored economic paradigms of Joseph Schumpeter and Israel Kirzner to a thoroughly subjectivist paradigm based on the radical subjectivist notion of subjective ontology and epistemology. Not surprisingly, such a radical paradigm shift indicates new methodological directions, encouraging process-related, multi-level and historical research. Significantly, however, they find that appropriate methodological rigour is often lacking. This chapter thus proposes hermeneutics as an exemplary approach that could address these deficiencies via narrative and pattern-matching strategies, while rejecting variance-theoretic models.

2. Are firm growth and performance the same or different concepts in empirical entrepreneurship studies? An analysis of the dependent and independent variables

Niklas Kiviluoto, Malin Brännback and Alan Carsrud

INTRODUCTION

Entrepreneurship is generally associated with growth and seen as the engine of economic development and private wealth creation (Schumpeter, 1934; Gartner, 1988; Low and MacMillan, 1988; Stevenson and Jarillo, 1990; Storey, 1994; Delmar, 1997; Dess et al., 1997, Shane and Venkataraman, 2000). Some researchers have even argued that entrepreneurship is growth and vice versa (Davidsson et al., 2002). Research has even shown that small start-up firms create the majority of net new jobs (Birch, 1987; Kirchhoff, 1994; Aldrich, 1999; Autio, 2005; 2007). While firm growth is generally considered good and important, it is, however, rare (Shane, 2003; Autio, 2005). Moreover, entrepreneurial growth is problematic as the phenomenon can be assessed and measured in many ways (Brush and Vanderwerf, 1992; Fischer and Reuber, 2003; Davidsson et al., 2009; Shepherd and Wiklund, 2009). When measured in terms of employment (or any other dimension), however, the phenomenon remains rare, with fewer than 10 per cent of firms growing at all during their lifetime (Reynolds and White, 1997; Aldrich, 1999; Shane, 2003). Only 6.5 per cent of start-up entrepreneurs expect to create more than 20 new jobs within five years and only 1.7 per cent expect to grow beyond 100 employees within five years (Autio, 2007). Fewer than 3 per cent expect to ever grow beyond 100 employees (Reynolds and White 1997; Aldrich, 1999; Shane, 2003). Yet, as shown by Autio (2005; 2007) new firms are expected to create nearly 50 per cent of all new jobs. That is, nearly 90 per cent of all new jobs are expected to be created by fewer than 25 per cent of nascent and new entrepreneurs.

Growth is also closely associated with business success. It is generally assumed that growth is a necessity for successful business performance. In fact, for the past two decades, larger, established firms have operated under growth imperatives, in other words, a necessity to pursue growth rates that exceed consensus forecasts to satisfy shareholders' expectations (Christensen and Raynor, 2003). Reasons for the existence of these growth imperatives can be many; in a recent article Levie and Lichtenstein (2010) criticize the stages models, which build on the assumption that firms behave like organisms, that is that they go through a very linear lifespan. These models, which are used to educate students, staff and managers alike, all suggest that growth is both a natural and an absolute stage of any firm. These growth imperatives seem to have been applied to start-up and new firms as well. For example, a generally accepted definition of rapid-growth firms is firms having annual sales growth rates of at least 20 per cent or more for five consecutive years (Fisher and Reuber, 2003). While that is certainly an imperative, it is unclear if this definition is based on empirical evidence with respect to whether such growth actually exists among small, privately held start-up firms as opposed to what is more likely to be found among more established, publicly traded firms. The studies by Autio (2005, 2007) certainly raise some serious doubts about this assumption of high-growth new firms.

It is also unclear what successful business performance really is and how it is measured by researchers (March and Sutton, 1997; Richard et al., 2009). The uncertainty is amplified by the fact that the same variable is often used to measure growth and firm performance (Birley and Westhead, 1990; Kiviluoto et al., 2009). Yet growth and performance are two distinct concepts, where the latter refers to financial measures, such as profitability (Brännback et al., 2009). However, research on the relationship between firm growth and profitability remains inconclusive. Research results range from strong, positive effects, to weak, negative effects, to no relationship at all (Shuman and Seeger, 1986; Capon et al., 1990; Hart, 1992; Gartner, 1997; Baum and Wally, 2003; Markman and Gartner, 2002; Davidsson et al., 2009). Sustained high growth is extremely rare, if non-existent, not the least due to the managerial pressure it creates. Already almost three decades ago Churchill and Lewis (1983), although building the article on a stages theory, gave very practical advice about how small firm growth should be managed and what the major stumbling blocks are. In an article two decades later Churchill and Mullins (2001) suggested that the maximum self-financed growth rate of a firm is slightly below 20 per cent. In other words, with a growth rate above this, a firm cannot be sustained as self-financed in the long run and will experience liquidity problems. The literature also shows that growth is a collective term for a complex phenomenon requiring different methods of inquiry and theoretical considerations (Davidsson and Wiklund, 2000; Delmar et al., 2003). Moreover, there seems to be considerable variation with respect to the choice of growth indicators, calculation of growth measures, length of measurement periods, and whether objective or subjective measures have been used. These issues thus render comparisons between growth studies difficult, if not impossible (Delmar, 1997; Shepherd and Wiklund, 2009). Finally, variations with respect to choice of profitability measures are also considerable in the literature. At times there is a near absence of discussions on the appropriateness of a given measurement tool. Yet the overwhelming majority of the literature seems to agree that growth is a precursor for profitability.

PREVIOUS RESEARCH

Firm performance has consistently been one of the most important areas within business research. March and Sutton (1997) reviewed 439 articles published in three peer-review management journals between 1993 and 1995, and found that 28 per cent of the articles used performance as their dependent variable. Research focusing on performance has been going on for decades. Despite this, when it comes to determining what this concept actually means or how it is measured, very little consensus exists (Murphy et al., 1996; Kirby, 2005; Richard et al., 2009). When it comes to other disciplines, such as accounting, there seems to be an agreement of what performance is, that is there is a clear distinction between a successful firm and a struggling firm. During the last decade critical analyses have been made in attempts to clarify the complex phenomenon called perform-ance in general business studies (March and Sutton, 1997; Richard et al., 2009). In a study of 213 articles from five management journals, Richard et al. (2009) identified up to 207 different performance measures used. In a similar study, but concentrating on the entrepreneurship literature, Murphy et al. (1996) identified 71 different performance measures in 52 articles. It is as if every researcher has his/her own idea of what firm per-formance is as a measure of firm success. Performance is most commonly seen as being equal to success, but one could argue that the use of 207 different performance measures can hardly all be indicators of a success-ful business practice, especially if looking from a broader view. This is especially the case when it has been found that very little concurrent valid-ity exists between measures (Shepherd and Wiklund, 2009). Murphy et al.

(1996) found in their sample that fewer than half of the inter-correlations between different performance measures were significant, and of those that were, more than 25 per cent were negatively correlated. The studies by Shepherd and Wiklund (2009) and Murphy et al. (1996) suggest that any given study using a certain measure for performance would not have the same results if alternative measures were used. Hence the indicated performance effect depends on the actual measure used in any given study.

The study by Richard et al. (2009) concentrated on performance as a dependent variable in articles from three general management journals. The study by Murphy et al. (1996) concentrated on articles with performance as their dependent variable and purely on small businesses and/or new entrepreneurial ventures. The current study concentrates on five journals: three entrepreneurship and two general business journals. Assessing performance generally is a difficult task, but especially so when assessing a new start-up's performance. For decades entrepreneurship scholars have suggested that there are no generally accepted measures of new venture performance (Brush and Vanderwerf, 1992; McDougall et al., 1994), that there are no commonly used measures of firm success (Hitt et al., 1982), and that there is little consensus on how new ventures should even be evaluated (Bloodgood et al., 1996).

THE STUDY

Therefore we found it necessary to review the literature – once again – in order to understand better how growth, performance and profitability are measured, in what contexts, and what the differences are between the three. This assumes that there are differences. In this study, growth, profitability and performance-related articles are reviewed in five peer-reviewed journals; three are top-tier entrepreneurship journals and two are top-tier general management journals.

Sample Selection

Our sample consists of articles from *Entrepreneurship: Theory & Practice* (ETP), *Journal of Business Venturing* (JBV), *Journal of Small Business Management* (JSBM), *Strategic Management Journal* (SMJ), and the *Academy of Management Journal* (AMJ).

After testing and assessing various methods and sources of sample selection, it was decided to use the 'Publish or Perish' database by Harzing. The selection was made by searching articles with the key words 'growth and profitability' or 'growth and performance'. This resulted in an initial

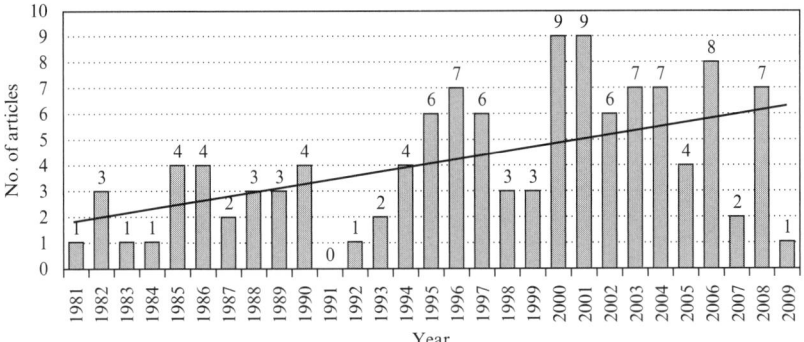

Figure 2.1   Annual distribution of articles (n: 118)

Table 2.1   Number of articles per journal

Journal*	N	%
AMJ	19	16.1
ETP	14	11.9
JBV	38	32.2
JSBM	22	18.6
SMJ	25	21.2
Total	**118**	**100.0**

*Note: * AMJ = Academy of Management Journal, ETP = Entrepreneurship: Theory & Practice, JBV = Journal of Business Venturing, JSBM = Journal of Small Business Management, SMJ = Strategic Management Journal.*

sample of 3032 articles, which were ranked according to their relevance. The ranking system used is a beta version by Google Scholar. Article relevance was finally analysed and determined by two of the authors by reading the title and abstract. The result was that a large number of articles were excluded, leaving a final sample of 118 empirical articles, which would be reviewed for this study.[1]

Figure 2.1 shows the annual distribution of articles in our sample. The trend line shows that the number of articles studying growth and profitability/performance is steadily increasing. Table 2.1 shows the distribution of articles among the different journals.

In the analysis all 118 articles were read, and relevant data was extracted from the articles with respect to the dependent variables, independent variables and control variables, final sample size and firm characteristics, industry type(s), growth measures, performance measures and the growth–performance relationship. Hereafter the data was coded in Microsoft Excel and analysed.

RESULTS

Sample Size

The mean size of the samples used is 572.2 firms. This is most likely distorted by the large variance in the sample sizes. Hence, the median of 186 firms gives a better estimate of the average sample sizes. Interestingly, despite looking at major entrepreneurship journals, only a total of 25 (21.2 per cent) studies are concerned only with small- and medium-sized enterprises (SMEs), and in two studies (1.7 per cent) SMEs are a part of the sample. In only ten studies (8.5 per cent) the sample consists of only private companies, and in an additional six studies (5.1 per cent) the sample consists of both private and public companies. Many studies (43, or 36.4 per cent) are conducted with firms from manufacturing, retail or service industries.

Measuring Performance

One of the research objectives of this study was to determine what performance measures are commonly used. That is, what is actually meant by performance regardless of independent and dependent variables; is it growth, profitability, a combination of these or something completely different? As noted earlier, performance is often regarded as being equal to success and therefore factors that are mentioned as performance measures could be regarded as measures of firm success. Table 2.2 shows the growth measures that were used in our sample.

   Note that the total 'n' is larger than the total sample as some articles used multiple growth measures. A total of 47 articles (39.8 per cent) considered sales growth as a growth measure. In 15 articles (12.7 per cent) the growth measure used was employment growth, and in only two articles (1.7 per cent) was the growth measure used market share. This is surprisingly small as growth in market share is often seen as one of the best measures when assessing a firm's performance in regard to its competition. Thirty-eight of the articles (32.2 per cent) considered growth as a performance measure. A total of 25 of these 38 articles (65.8 per cent) used both growth and profitability measures as a performance measure, while 13 (34.2 per cent) used sales growth as the only performance measure. A common characteristic

Table 2.2   Growth measures

Growth measure	N	% of studies
Sales/revenue	47	39.8
Employment	15	12.7
Market share	2	1.7
Other*	4	3.4
Growth as performance	38	32.2
None/n.a.	18	15.3
Total	**124**	

Note: * Growth in no. of franchisees, growth option value, loss ratio, own determination.

Table 2.3   Performance measures

Performance measures	N	% of articles
Sales growth	72	61.0
Employment growth	21	17.8
Market share growth	8	6.8
Profitability/accounting based*	67	56.8
Other**	4	3.4
Total	**182**	

Notes:
*   Earnings before interest and taxes (EBIT), return on sales (ROS), return on equity
      (ROE), return on investment (ROI), return on assets (ROA), return on capital (ROC).
**   Growth in no. of franchisees, growth option value, loss ratio, own determination.

of these articles was that the different measurements used were all considered as equally good performance measures and the relationship or possible difference between them was rarely acknowledged or discussed. This further highlights the problem of assessing what actually can be considered as performance. Only five articles actually assessed the relationship between measures, and hence they are left out of this criticism.

The performance measures used are shown in Table 2.3. Again, the total 'n' is larger than the total sample as some of the articles use multiple performance measures. The most commonly used performance measure is sales/revenue growth (61 per cent). Almost as common is the use of some profitability or accounting-based measure (56.8 per cent). Employment growth and market share growth are rarer in their usage (17.8 per cent and 6.8 per cent respectively).

Table 2.4   Articles with growth and profitability measures

Measure	N	%
Sales/revenue growth	72	
profitability	33	45.8
Employment growth	21	
profitability	7	33.3
Market share growth	8	
profitability	6	75.0
Total growth measures	**101**	
Total profitability measures	**46**	**45.5**

When comparing the use of growth and profitability measures, it becomes clear that it is much more common to use a growth measure to assess performance as profitability measures only are used in only 45.5 per cent of the articles. Table 2.4 shows the studies using growth measures that also use profitability for assessing performance. In 72 articles where sales/revenue growth is used, less than half (45.8 per cent) also use a profitability measure. In the 21 articles where employment growth is used, only one third (33.3 per cent) also use a profitability measure. In the eight studies where market share growth is used, 75 per cent also use a profitability measure. On average, only 45.5 per cent of the articles that use a growth measure also use a profitability measure. It can also be said that 55 out of 101 growth articles (54.5 per cent), do not look at profitability at all when assessing a firm's performance, but rather assess performance solely through growth.

In fewer than half of the articles, (41.5 per cent), only one performance measure is used. Two measures are used in 29 articles (24.5 per cent), and three measures are used in 16 articles (13.6 per cent). In studies using a single performance measure, the most common performance measure is sales/revenue growth (42.9 per cent). Employment growth is used in 10.2per cent, but market share growth is not used in any article. Hence, growth is used as a single performance measure in more than 53 per cent of the articles. An accounting-based measure of profitability to assess firm performance is used by 38.8 per.cent.

Types of Measures and Time Frames

There is a clear preference for objective measures (71.2 per cent) over subjective measures as well as the use of relative (71.2 per cent) over absolute measures, and a combination of absolute and relative measures (13.6 per cent) is preferred over using only absolute measures. Only one third of

Table 2.5   Dependent variables

Dependent variables			Performance as dependent variable (n: 49)		
Variable	No. of articles	% of articles	Variable	No. of articles	% of articles
Growth	58	49.2 %	Profitability	38	77.6
Performance	49	41.5 %	Sales growth	33	67.3
Profitability	21	17.8 %	Growth as performance	23	46.9
Other	10	8.5	Other growth*	18	36.7
Growth & profitability	10	8.5	Other**	5	10.2
Growth & performance	5	4.2			
Total	**153**		Sales growth & profitability	25	51.0
			Other growth & profitability	3	6.1
			Only profitability	10	20.4
			Only sales growth	4	8.2

Notes:
*   Employment, market share, assets
**   price appreciation, R&D spending, patenting + qualitative determinations.

the articles specified the time frame used in the studies. In these studies, three and five years are the most common measurement periods. Both are used in 14 articles (35.9 per cent). In five articles (12.8 per cent) a one-year measurement period was used.

Dependent Variables

Another goal of this research was to assess the types of dependent and independent variables used. This would allow a better understanding of what kind of factors are most commonly analysed in articles associated with growth, profitability and performance.

Table 2.5 shows the dependent variables used in our sample. Once again the total of 157 is explained by the fact that multiple dependent variables appeared in a number of articles. The three most common dependent variables are growth (49.2 per cent), performance (44.9 per cent) and profitability (17.8 per cent). Articles that use both growth and profitability (8.5 per cent), or growth and performance (4.2 per cent), are not that common,

Table 2.6   Number of dependent variables

No. of variables	No. of articles	% of articles
1	85	72.0
2	21	17.8
3	6	5.1
4	3	2.5
<5	3	2.5
Total	**118**	**100.0**

which is surprising considering the sampling method. Due to the fact that 49 articles use performance as a dependent variable, we decided to look closer at these.

The right-hand side of Table 2.5 shows what is meant by performance in those articles that use performance as a dependent variable. Of those 49 articles, 38 (77.6 per cent) used profitability as a performance measure, while 33 articles (67.3 per cent) used sales growth. Sales growth and profitability together are used in 25 articles (51 per cent), while profitability is used together with another growth measure to assess performance in three articles (6.1 per cent). Even when both growth and profitability are used to assess performance, rarely is a justification given for the particular use of certain variables nor are their differences discussed. Very often the source of the data available explains the performance measures used, rather than what could be regarded as the most suitable measure. Interestingly, performance is assessed based solely on profitability in 10 (20.4 per cent) articles and based solely on sales growth in four articles (8.2 per cent).

Table 2.6 shows the number of dependent variables used. From this table it can be seen that it is most common to use one (72 per cent) or two (17.8 per cent) dependent variables.

Table 2.7 looks more closely at those 85 articles that use a single dependent variable. Of those, 42 articles (49.4 per cent) use performance as a dependent variable and 33 articles use growth dependently (38.8 per cent). In only eight articles (9.4 per cent) is profitability used. This rare use of profitability is quite surprising as one would assume that profitability is a long-term goal of any firm.

Independent Variables

Table 2.8 shows the independent variables used in our sample. There is no single most common independent variable, but instead various variables are used as independent variables. The most common is concerned with

Table 2.7   Single dependent variables

Variable	No. of articles	%
Performance	42	49.4
Growth	33	38.8
Profitability	8	9.4
Other*	2	2.4
Total	**85**	**100.0**

Note: * Strategic change, type of entrepreneur.

Table 2.8   Independent variables

Independent variables	No. of articles	% of articles
Internal resources	27	22.9
Strategy related	26	22.0
Growth/indirect growth	22	18.6
Entrepreneur/management related	21	17.8
Industry related	16	13.6
Planning	12	10.2
External resources	11	9.3
Entrepreneurial orientation	9	7.6
Performance	6	5.1
Product life cycle	5	4.2
Profitability	2	1.7
Corporate social responsibility	2	1.7
Total	**159**	

internal resources, followed by strategy-related variables and growth-related variables. These are used as independent variables in 27 (22.9 per cent), 26 (22 per cent) and 22 (18.6 per cent) articles respectively. There is still a big difference in the use of growth-related variables: 22 articles (18.6 per cent), in comparison to six performance-related articles (5.1 per cent), or two profitability-related articles (1.7 per cent). However, it is noteworthy that often the use of a certain variable in a study comes about by testing a number of different factors, and hence these results should be viewed with care.

Table 2.9 shows the number of independent variables used. The most common approach is to use two variables, which is the case in 35 articles (29.7 per cent). One variable is used in 28 articles (23.7 per cent).

Table 2.9   Number of independent variables

No. of variables	No. of articles	% of articles
1	28	23.7
2	35	29.7
3	23	19.5
4	12	10.2
<5	20	16.9
Total	**118**	**100.0**

Table 2.10   Control variables used

Control variables	N	% of articles
Firm age	113	95.8
Firm size	46	39.0
Industry	32	27.1
Industry growth	7	5.9
Environmental	9	7.6
Capital related	5	4.2
Performance related	8	6.8
Macroeconomic	2	1.7
None/n.a.*	39	33.1
Total	**261**	

Note: * Possible that independent variables are used for control or control is through sample selection.

Interestingly 20 articles (16.9 per cent) use more than five independent variables.

Control Variables

Table 2.10 shows that most studies (95.8 per cent) use firm age as a control variable. Firm size is used in 39 per cent of the studies and industry is controlled for in 27.1 per cent. Macroeconomic control variables are found in only two articles. In approximately one third no control variables are used. It is possible that some control was employed through sample selection or an independent variable may have been used as controls.

Table 2.11 shows the number of control variables used by researchers in the studies within our sample. A single variable is used in 14 articles (11.9

Table 2.11   Number of control variables

No. of control variables	No. of articles	% of articles
0*	39	33.1
1	14	11.9
2	19	16.1
3	14	11.9
4	15	12.7
5	10	8.5
<6	7	5.9
Total	**118**	**100.0**

Note: * Possible that independent variables are used for control or through selection of sample.

per cent), two variables in 19 articles (16.1 per cent) and three in 14 articles (11.9 per cent). On average, two control variables are used.

DISCUSSION

Measuring firm success, performance and growth is clearly a complex task and seems to be the source of growing frustration among researchers. Twenty years ago Pearson et al. (1990) argued that inappropriate performance measures impede the assessment of firm success. This argument is still true today in the study of entrepreneurial firms. Therefore careful consideration should be made by researchers before choosing data sources and research methodology as to why a certain method, measure, or data set has been used rather than another method (Davidsson and Wiklund, 2000; Delmar, 1997; Shepherd and Wiklund, 2009). 'Unlike our independent variables . . . we do not justify why we are using particular dependent variables and why they are the most appropriate dependent variables rather than the most conveniently available in COMPUSTAT' (Richard et al., 2009, p. 26). Delmar (1997) and Davidsson and Wiklund (2000) have shown that there are considerable methodological considerations and inconclusive empirical results with respect to measuring growth, profitability and performance. Interestingly, while the multi-dimensionality of performance has been recognized in accounting and finance, Richard et al. (2009) argue that this has only reached the theoretical level of discussion in the management literature. Perhaps even more disturbing is that within entrepreneurship research, firm performance seems to be an unresolved problem with inconclusive research results. This could be the result of reliance on certain databases. For example the widespread use of convenience samples of publicly traded firms appears to have created a surprising but real research gap in the study of private firms. Studies on growth, profitability and performance in privately held SMEs are extremely rare. In fact it could be argued that there is a near complete lack of empirical studies on these firms, and that is stunning given that 60 per cent of the articles in our sample were published in entrepreneurship journals. In our study a total of 25 (21.2 per cent) studies are only concerned with small- and medium-sized enterprises, and in an additional two studies (1.7 per cent) SMEs are part of the sample, and in only ten studies (8.5 per cent) did the sample consist of private companies. This may well be the result of researchers viewing the subject through the lens of theories based on large firms and assuming they must fit new firms and smaller firms (Brännback and Carsrud, 2009).

There has been a tendency to rely on the most easily available measures, rather than using those best suited for the specific firms in the specific industry that is being studied. The use of certain databases automatically creates a bias towards studying certain firms with those performance measures that are available through that database. This may lead to a researcher relying blindly on those measures available, without considering the fact that very little concurrent validity exists between different indicators (Shepherd and Wiklund, 2009; Brännback and Carsrud, 2009). In a study of more than 3000 global firms in 38 industries, Devinney et al. (2010) showed that the pattern of correlations between different performance measures is such that a minimum of three dimensions is necessary just to characterize the fundamental aspects of firm performance.

The results of our study and previous studies concur strongly. Two-thirds of the studies only use one or two performance measures (Richard et al., 2009; Murphy et al., 1996) and nearly half use only one performance measure. In over half the studies this measure is sales growth, which corresponds with the findings of Ensley et al. (2002); Shepherd and Wiklund, (2009), and Davidsson et al. (2009). Performance is assessed solely based on profitability in only one fifth of the articles. The entrepreneurship literature also argues that it is extremely difficult to measure new venture performance, to a large extent because it can take years for a firm to become profitable (Bantel, 1998). The scarce use of profitability measures may depend on financial data not always being easily available or on the fact that traditional profitability measures, such as ROI, ROA and ROS, are not seen to be appropriate for young firms (Feeser and Willard, 1990). However, there are studies where profitability measures are seen as the most suitable for small firms, even when other measures are available (Begley, 1995). Likewise relative change in turnover is the key growth indicator of rapid growth firms (Fischer and Reuber, 2003). While almost one third of the studies use subjective performance measures, these studies are rarely validated with objective measures, making the results worth questioning (Shepherd and Wiklund, 2009). Due to the low concurrent validity between different performance measures, there is definitely a need for entrepreneurship scholars, and practitioners alike, to read more accounting and finance journals to better understand the relationship between different measures and how different changes within the firm impact these indicators. For example, firms in high-tech industries most commonly raise external funding. If this funding is in the form of a government grant, it will impact the income statement and indicate an increase in revenues – without increase in actual sales. To be blunt – no new customers! If it is an external debt it will impact the balance sheet. Hence, depending on the type of funding, it will make the same firm look very different in terms of performance. Therefore, some careful considerations with respect to accounting and financial statements are necessary when determining a firm's performance.

As said throughout this chapter, firm performance is a complex concept. Performance can be conceptualized as only growth, or only profitability, or as a combination of these two. It can also be conceptualized as a firm's success or effectiveness. Only a handful of articles in our sample gave clear justification for the use of the particular performance measures they used. For example, one study made a categorization of performance measures as a function of financial, product and market-related measures. Richard et al. (2009) used a similar approach, and discussed various measures as financial, market and shareholder returns. This type of approach takes into consideration the stakeholder view, and considers to whom the performance measure is actually directed, and what certain measures mean to certain groups of stakeholders. Especially when studying privately-held SMEs, this becomes a very relevant issue to take into consideration. For example, performance for the lifestyle entrepreneur, performance for the growth-oriented technology entrepreneur, performance for the venture capitalist or performance for the governmental policy-maker will most certainly be very different (Brännback and Carsrud, 2009).

Based on the findings from this study it can be argued that growth and performance *are the same*. This would reflect the reality that most studies that talk about performance in fact actually refer to growth; more specifically, sales growth. Surprisingly often, this is the only measure used when assessing a firm's performance. However, from a broader perspective, the answer is *no, they are not the same*. Performance is most commonly seen as firm success, and assessing a firm's success solely based on growth, would definitely only tell us a small part of the story. It would not be the best assessment of a successful firm, at least not in the long run (Brännback et al., 2009; Davidsson et al., 2009; Shepherd and Wiklund 2009).

Further Research

This study sheds light on questions about growth and performance and will serve as a basis for further research. Clearly there is very little consensus in the use of the term 'performance' and what the concept means. Therefore operational definitions of variables are needed. As our review also showed, performance seems to be in the eyes of the beholder. A performance measure at any single given point might be regarded as a good measure of success, but may not be when looking at the business for a longer period of time. When assessing performance, researchers should try to view this complex phenomenon and its context through a broader perspective. For example, by offering proper justification of the use of a certain method over alternative methods, by using industry-specific factors, by using longer time frames of measurements, by questioning the source of data, by recognizing that successful performance is different for different stakeholders, and especially how the use of an alternative methods could affect the outcome of the study.

As most research focuses on publicly traded and larger companies, there is a clear research gap in focusing on privately held SMEs. What is the most appropriate measure for new venture performance still remains unanswered. A lot of research still continues *talking the talk* and not *walking the walk by* relying on easily obtained and often unverifiable self-reports of sales growth. How relevant this performance measure is among start-ups still remains unanswered.

Finally, the question of the most suitable method for analysing start-ups and small firms is raised. A pure quantitative analysis of the firms may give a somewhat distorted view on this extremely heterogeneous population of high-performing firms. Perhaps it would be necessary to view the firm and the entrepreneur as separate entities and take a more inductive approach when explaining the behaviour of these firms. Maybe after these many years of inconclusive results it is time to go back to basics.

NOTE

1.   Please contact the first author for a complete list of articles.

REFERENCES

Aldrich, H.E. (1999), *Organizations Evolving*, London: Sage Publications.
Autio, E. (2005), 'GEM 2005 High-expectation entrepreneurship: summary report', London: GERA.
Autio, E. (2007), 'GEM 2007 global report on high-growth entrepreneurship', London: GERA.
Bantel, K.A. (1998), 'Technology-based, adolescent firm configurations: strategy identification, context, and performance', *Journal of Business Venturing*, **13**(3), 205–30.
Baum, J.R. and S. Wally (2003), 'Strategic decision speed and firm performance', *Strategic Management Journal*, **24**, 1107–29.
Begley, T.M. (1995), 'Using founder status, age of firm, and company growth rate as the basis for distinguishing entrepreneurs from managers of smaller businesses', *Journal of Business Venturing*, **10**(3), 249–63.
Birch, D. (1987), *Job Creation in America: How our Smallest Companies put the Most People to Work*, New York: Free Press.
Birley, S. and P. Westhead (1990), 'Growth and performance contrasts between "types" of small firms', *Strategic Management Journal*, **11**, 535–57.
Bloodgood, J.M., H.J. Sapienza and J.G. Almeida (1996), 'The internationalization of new high-potential US ventures: antecedents and outcomes', *Entrepreneurship Theory and Practice*, **20**(4), 61–76.
Brännback, M. and A. Carsrud (2009), 'Cognitive maps in entrepreneurship: researching sense making and action', in A. Carsrud and M. Brännback (eds), *Understanding the Entrepreneurial Mind: Opening the Black Box*, New York: Springer, pp.75–96.
Brännback, M., A. Carsrud, M. Renko, R. Östermark, J. Aaltonen, and N. Kiviluoto (2009), 'Growth and profitability in small privately held biotech firms: preliminary findings', *New Biotechnology*, **25**(5), 369–76.
Brush, C.G. and P.A. Vanderwerf (1992), 'A comparison of methods and sources for obtaining estimates of new venture performance', *Journal of Business Venturing*, **7**(2), 157–70.
Capon, N., J.U. Farley and S. Hoenig (1990), 'Determinants of financial performance: a meta-analysis', *Management Science*, **30**(10), 1143–59.
Christensen, C.M. and M.E. Raynor (2003), *The Innovator's Solution, Creating and Sustaining Successful Growth*, Boston, MA: Harvard Business School Press.
Churchill, N.C. and V.L. Lewis (1983), 'The five stages of small business growth', *Harvard Business Review*, **61**(3), 30–50.
Churchill, N.C. and J.W. Mullins (2001), 'How fast can your company afford to grow?', *Harvard Business Review*, **79**(5), 135–43.
Davidsson, P. and J. Wiklund (2000), 'Conceptual and empirical challenges in the study of firm growth', in D. Sexton and H. Landström (eds), *The Blackwell Handbook of Entrepreneurship*, Bath: Blackwell Business, pp.26–44.
Davidsson, P., F. Delmar and J. Wiklund (2002), Entrepreneurship as growth; growth as entrepreneurship', in M.A. Hitt, R.D. Ireland, S.M. Camp and D.L. Sexton (eds), *Strategic Entrepreneurship: Creating a New Mindset*, Oxford: Blackwell Publishing, pp.328–42.
Davidsson, P., P. Steffens and J. Fitzsimmons (2009), 'Growing profitable or

growing from profits: putting the horse in front of the cart?', *Journal of Business Venturing*, **24**(4), 388–406.

Delmar, F. (1997), 'Measuring growth: methodological considerations and empirical results', in R. Donckels and A. Miettinen (eds), *Entrepreneurship and SME Research: On its Way to the Next Millennium*, London: Ashgate Publishing, pp. 190–216.

Delmar, F., P. Davidsson and W. Gartner (2003), 'Arriving at the high-growth firm', *Journal of Business Venturing*, **18**, 189–216.

Dess, G.G., G.T. Lumpkin and J.G. Covin (1997), 'Entrepreneurial strategy making and firm performance: tests of contingency and configurational models', *Strategic Management Journal*, **18**, 677–95.

Devinney, T.M., G.S. Yip and G. Johnson (2010), 'Using frontier analysis to evaluate company performance', *British Journal of Management*, **21**(4), 921–38.

Ensley, M.D., A.W. Pearson and A.C. Amason (2002), 'Understanding the dynamics of new venture top management teams: cohesion, conflict, and new venture performance', *Journal of Business Venturing*, **17**(4), 365–86.

Feeser, H.R. and G.E. Willard (1990), 'Founding strategy and performance: a comparison of high- and low-growth high-tech firms', *Strategic Management Journal*, **11**(2), 87–98.

Fischer, E. and A.R. Reuber (2003), 'Support for rapid-growth firms: a comparison of the views of founders, government policymakers, and private sector resource providers', *Journal of Small Business Management*, **41**(4), 346–65.

Gartner, W.B. (1988), '"Who is an entrepreneur?" is the wrong question', *American Journal of Small Business*, **12**, 11–31.

Gartner, W.B. (1997), 'When growth is the problem, not the solution', *Journal of Management Inquiry*, **6**(1), 62–8.

Hart, S.L. (1992), 'An integrative framework for strategy-making processes', *Academy of Management Review*, **17**, 327–51.

Hitt, M., R. Ireland and K. Palia (1982), 'Industrial firms' grand strategy and functional importance: moderating effects of technology and uncertainty', *Academy of Management Journal*, **25**(2), 265–98.

Kirby, J. (2005), 'Toward a theory of high performance', *Harvard Business Review*, **83**(7), 30–39.

Kirchhoff, B. (1994), *Entrepreneurship and Dynamic Capitalism: The Economics of Business Firm Foundation and Growth*, Westport, CT: Praeger.

Kiviluoto, N., M. Brännback and A. Carsrud (2009), 'Measuring entrepreneurial growth and performance in biotechnology business: a literature review and research agenda', paper presented at NFF 2009 Conference.

Levie, J. and B.B. Lichtenstein (2010), 'A terminal assessment of stages theory: introducing a dynamic states approach to entrepreneurship', *Entrepreneurship Theory and Practice*, **34**(2), 317–50.

Low, M.B. and I.C. MacMillan (1988), 'Entrepreneurship: past research and future challenges', *Journal of Management*, **14**(2), 139–61.

McDougall, P.P., J.G. Covin, R.B. Robinson Jr and L. Herron (1994), 'The effects of industry growth and strategic breadth on new venture performance and strategy content', *Strategic Management Journal*, **15**, 537–54.

March, J.G. and R.I. Sutton (1997), 'Organizational performance as a dependent variable', *Organization Science*, **8**(6), 698–706.

Markman, G.D. and W.B. Gartner (2002), 'Is extraordinary growth profitable?

A study of Inc. 500 high growth companies', *Entrepreneurship Theory and Practice*, **27**(1), 65–75.

Murphy, G.B., J.W. Trailer and R.C. Hill (1996), 'Measuring performance in entrepreneurship research', *Journal of Business Research*, **36**(1), 15–23.

Pearson, J.N., J.S. Bracker and R.E. White (1990), 'Operations management activities of small, high growth electronics firms', *Journal of Small Business Management*, **28**(1), 21–9.

Reynolds, P.D. and S.B. White (1997), *The Entrepreneurial Process: Economic Growth, Men, Women, and Minorities*, Westport, CT: Quorum Books.

Richard, P.J., T.T. Devinney, G.S. Yip and G. Johnson (2009), 'Measuring organizational performance: towards methodological best practice', *Journal of Management*, **35**(3), 718–804.

Schumpeter, J.A. (1934), *The Theory of Economic Development*, Cambridge, MA: Harvard University Press.

Shane, S. (2003), *A General Theory of Entrepreneurship*, Cheltenham, UK and Northampton, MA, USA: Edward Elgar publishing.

Shane, S. and S. Venkataraman (2000), 'The promise of entrepreneurship as a field of research', *Academy of Management Review*, **25**, 217–26.

Shepherd, D. and J. Wiklund (2009), 'Are we comparing apples with apples or apples with oranges? Appropriateness of knowledge accumulation across growth studies', *Entrepreneurship Theory and Practice*, **33**(1): 105–23.

Shuman, J.C. and J.A. Seeger (1986), 'The theory and practice of strategic management in smaller rapid growth firms', *American Journal of Small Business*, **11**, 7–18.

Stevenson, H.H. and J.C. Jarillo (1990), 'A paradigm of entrepreneurship: entrepreneurial management', *Strategic Management Journal*, **11**, 17–27.

Storey, D.J. (1994), 'New firm growth and bank financing', *Small Business Economics*, **6**, 139–50.

3. Developing and testing a typology of growth strategies of entrepreneurial IT service firms

Olivier Witmeur and Alain Fayolle[1]

INTRODUCTION

Since the growth of entrepreneurial ventures is critical for job creation, but remains the exception rather than the rule, understanding the processes that drive it is an important issue for both academics and practitioners. Research on the growth of entrepreneurial ventures has proliferated over the last two decades. Literature review papers (e.g. O'Farrell and Hitchens, 1988; Davidsson et al., 2005; Gilbert et al., 2006) underline that most of the individual variables impacting growth have been investigated and have adopted multiple theoretical approaches. Unfortunately, although there has been major improvement, the work performed so far has generated conflicting results, lacked integration, paid insufficient attention to the connection with theory and should have been more longitudinal (e.g. Davidsson et al., 2005; Davidsson et al., 2006; Garnsey et al., 2006). Furthermore, it is now recognized that growth is a complex phenomenon and it can take very different forms on rather different time frames. As a consequence, it remains difficult to explain heterogeneous growth patterns that have been observed empirically (Delmar et al., 2003; Biga et al., 2007). In other words, entrepreneurship scholars acknowledge that growth patterns of new ventures are not idiosyncratic and recognize that further research is needed to increase our understanding of its how and why. To deal with the aforementioned concerns, Dess et al. (1997), Bantel (1998), Heirman and Clarysse (2004), Wiklund and Shepherd (2005) and Harms et al. (2009) advocate a configurational approach. This is attractive because it provides us with an integrated framework for strategy and organization theories (e.g. Miller, 1986; Snow et al., 2005) and offers both static and dynamic sides, that is, the identification of configurations and the dynamic of configuration changes.

The objective of the chapter is to demonstrate that building a typology of strategic configurations increases our understanding of growth phenomena and opens new avenues for further research. Using an integrated and dynamic perspective, we develop a typology of strategic ideal types and then test it with longitudinal case studies. This is attractive since 'Typologies are based on a unique form of theory building that is intuitively appealing and holds considerable promise for helping management researchers to understand complex, holistic phenomenon' (Doty and Glick, 1994, p. 248). Because of the holistic nature of such exploratory research work, we have restricted our investigations to a specific and reduced area. We have decided to focus on Entrepreneurial IT Services Firms (EISFs) with business-to-business activities because they represent an interesting population for two reasons. First of all, EISFs face three traditional growth options that are not mutually exclusive (Ansoff, 1965 [1988]; Roberts, 2003): getting more customers on the same market with the same provision of services (or deepening); extending to new territories (or internationalization); and/or developing a new service offering (or diversification). Secondly, their strategic challenge is augmented by a possible evolution from a service- to a software-business model. As a matter of fact, adding a product offering to the initial service offering often sounds like an attractive growth option to EISFs (Kaye, 1998; Nambisan, 2001). Kaye (1998) highlighted that 'In many situations, your clients will pay you to develop new technology for them. This is not only exciting and fun; the new technical capabilities you develop will lead to new business opportunities' (p. 275).

The structure of this chapter is as follows. In the second section, we develop a typology of strategic configurations for EISFs. The outcome consists of a detailed description of seven ideal types, including three that are fully specific to EISFs. In the third section, we introduce four retrospective longitudinal case studies that enable us to observe 15 strategic configurations. The fourth section is then devoted to the analysis of the findings according to a systematic numerical coding technique that allows for the comparison of ideal types and configurations. In the last section, we discuss the findings and underline the main limitations. We conclude with the contribution to the growth literature and the main implications.

TYPOLOGY

In this section, we first review the literature on configuration and typology studies in the fields of both management and entrepreneurship. We then explain how we have built a typology of strategic configurations for EISFs and describe it in more detail.

Configurations, Typologies and Entrepreneurship

Configuration studies became popular during the late 1970s with the prominent works of Mintzberg (1978) or Miller and Friesen (1984b), for example. The main objective was to isolate coherent, commonly occurring clusters of attributes related to strategy, organizational structure and environment, in order to understand firm performance. The guiding principle in this type of approach is the existence of a minimum fit or coherence levels between the attributes and restricting the scope of analysis to a limited number of coherent configurations, also called gestalts, archetypes or ideal-types, rather than reviewing all possibilities (Miller, 1981; Meyer et al., 1993). From that point of view, a configuration approach differs from a traditional contingency approach. Although both approaches focus on the fit between elements, contingency theory looks for one unidirectional and linear law to explain incremental changes, while configuration adopts a more holistic system view that is reciprocal and non-linear (Meyer et al., 1993). Also, due to the coherence between the elements of a configuration, 'the presence of some attributes can lead to the reliable prediction of the others' (Miller and Mintzberg, 1983, p. 57). Another important principle of the configuration approach is that configurations are supposed to be stable over time and can only be modified during periods of dramatic change, sometimes also called 'revolutions' or 'second-order changes' (Levy, 1986). This is only a logical consequence of the coherence principle which implies that change in one element automatically entails change in the others.

Research on configurations has been closely associated with the development of taxonomies and typologies (Ketchen et al., 1993; Miller, 1996). More specifically, Ketchen et al. (1993) demonstrated that typologies explain performance better than taxonomies. Nevertheless, many so-called typologies have been criticized because they mainly consist of sloppy categorization analyses (Bacharach, 1989). Doty and Glick (1994) suggested that this is partly because of semantic confusion between notions such as classification schemes, taxonomies and typologies. While the first two are pure classification systems, typologies refer to 'conceptually derived interrelated sets of ideal types' (p. 232). Accordingly, typologies represent a valuable way to develop complex theories and, for the most part, these are middle-range theories. But this is valid only if researchers pay attention to four central concerns that must be addressed by any theoretical proposition: (1) clear identification of the constructs; (2) explanation of the relationship between the constructs; (3) falsifiability; and (4) definition of the validity domain (Bacharach, 1989; Whetten, 1989; Doty and Glick, 1994).

Existing research work in entrepreneurship validates the relevance of the configurational approach. First of all, Miller (1983), Dess et al. (1997) and Wiklund and Shepherd (2005) have empirically confirmed that the configuration approach offers better explanations for performance outcomes than traditional one-variable-at-a-time and contingency approaches. Secondly, Vohora et al. (2004) and Garnsey et al. (2006) have highlighted that a limited number of development thresholds and crises exist. Thirdly, there are important connections between research on lifecycle or staged models and configurations (Miller and Friesen, 1984b; Hanks et al. 1993). As Miller and Friesen (1984a) pointed out: 'there is something of a "gestalt" or configural nature to the phases of the lifecycle' (p. 1176). However, entrepreneurship research has paid little attention to the identification of post-start-up configurations. Furthermore, the few existing papers (e.g. Bantel, 1998; Heirman and Clarysse, 2004) refer to empirically inducted taxonomies, not theory deduced typologies.

Development of the Typology

In this subsection, we propose to deduce ideal types of 'strategic configurations' from the literature which are associated with distinctive growth strategies. Each ideal type is described with uni-dimensional constructs frequently used in both academic and professional literature.

Over time, academics and practitioners have developed multiple contingency and/or configurational frameworks to analyse the entrepreneurial process (e.g. Sahlman, 1996; Chrisman et al., 1999; Timmons, 1999; Davidsson and Klofsten, 2003). In aggregate terms, they combine constructs such as (1) the entrepreneurs; (2) the opportunity (or the activities); (3) the organizational structure; (4) the resources; (5) the environment; and (6) the strategy. They also highlight that the role of the entrepreneur is either to develop a strategy that creates and maintains the fit between these constructs or to change strategy when the fit is not reached. From a theoretical perspective, multiple approaches can be used to explain the relations between these constructs: the traits approach (e.g. Davidsson, 1989; Gundry and Welsch, 2001 and Delmar and Wiklund, 2003); the life-cycle and staged models (e.g. Churchill and Lewis, 1983; Kazanjian and Drazin, 1990; Hanks et al., 1993); the strategic management perspective (e.g. Miles and Snow, 1978; Porter, 1985; Lumkin and Dess, 1996; Ireland et al., 2003); the ecology of population (Hannan and Freeman, 1977); and the resources-based/dynamic capabilities approach (e.g. Brush et al., 2001 and Zahra et al., 2006).

Building a typology of strategic configurations for EISFs implies combining complementary perspectives. Furthermore, in order to understand a decision that can be made on whether or not to adopt a service- or

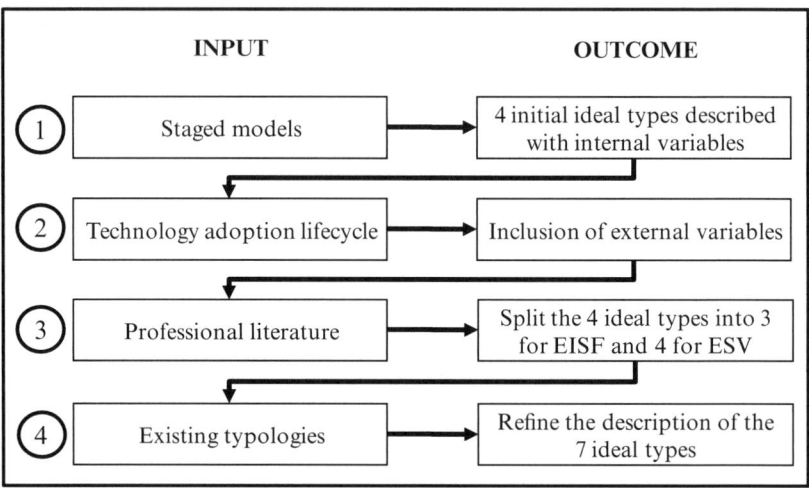

Figure 3.1   The building of the typology

software-business model requires that we focus not only on EISFs, but also on entrepreneurial software ventures (ESVs). In this context, we have adopted a four-step method to develop our typology. It is summarized in Figure 3.1 and described in more detail in the remainder of this subsection.

First of all, we started building the typology with a description of individual growth stages suggested in staged models specific to hi-tech ventures (e.g. Kazanjian and Drazin, 1990; Hanks et al., 1993). This choice is logical if we take into consideration the multiple shared characteristics and empirical results between generic stages of growth and configurations (e.g. Miller and Friesen, 1984a). As a matter of fact, with the notable exception of environmental variables that are often omitted in staged models, they both use the same kind of constructs (i.e. the role of the entrepreneur, the strategic focus, the resources mix and the organizational structure), presume the existence of a limited set of discrete states (called 'stages' or 'configurations') and highlight the importance of disruptive changes from one state to another. Hanks et al. (1993) mentioned that 'we have chosen to define a life-cycle stage as a unique configuration of variables related to organization, context and structure' (p. 7). We then used four presumed successive ideal types described with the internal characteristics of the hi-tech ventures (i.e. the role of the entrepreneur, the nature of activities, the organizational structure and the resources at stake) at the 'seed', 'start-up', 'early growth' and 'continued growth' stages.

At the second step, we introduced the core ideas of the technology adoption cycle (e.g. Rosen et al., 1998; Moore, 1999). Here, we have enriched the description of the four successive idea types (from step 1) with insights related to market conditions and evolving customer profiles. An additional conceptual argument for this step is the rich literature that focuses on the fit between strategy and overall environmental conditions. As Zammuto (1988) stated, 'it is possible to apply the logic of the ecological approach to better understand constraints on strategic choice' (p. 112). For instance, focused on new software ventures, Zahra and Bogner (1999) highlighted the fact that environmental moderators impacted multiple dimensions of technological strategy such as rhythm of introduction of new products, intensity of product upgrade, level of R&D spending, use of external technology sources and the use of copyrights. Overall, this second step has allowed us to introduce three environmental variables: the type of customers served by the firm, the pattern of condition changes and the competition intensity.

At the third step, we compared the best practices that have been identified in practical literature on the management of IT consulting and professional services firms (Kaye, 1998; Biswas and Twitchell, 2002) and pure software firms (McHugh, 1999; Hoch et al., 2000). The comparison between services and software practices highlights significant differences between EISFs and ESVs (Nambisan, 2001). These mainly refer (1) to the lower impact of the environment for EISFs, especially at early and later stages; (2) to the fact that ESVs need more managerial and financial resources during their early development; (3) to the priority given to vertical organizational structures in EISFs (i.e. linked with career path and project-based organization), while ESVs pay more attention to horizontal specialization (i.e. separation between development, marketing and support functions); and (4) to the absence of R&D activities in EISFs, while these are mission critical in the early stages of ESVs. This comparison has also clarified the type of growth strategy adopted by EISFs and ESVs over time, that is, earlier deepening and practice diversification strategies in EISFs, earlier internationalization strategy in ESVs. As a result, and taking into account the fact that the initial seed stage did not appear to be relevant for EISFs, since they get revenues from the start, it was then possible to make a clear distinction between the two types of firms and propose seven configurations. Three presumed chronologically successive ideal types refer to EISFs and are code named 'S1/the expert', 'S2/the local services champion' and 'S3/the diversified services firm'. Four presumed chronologically successive ideal types refer to ESV and are code named 'P0/the software lab', 'P1/the software workshop', 'P2/the software specialist' and 'P3/the software reference'.

At the fourth and final step, we compared our seven types with the

Table 3.1   Comparison of typologies

	Lifecycle models	Mintzberg (1978)	Miles and Snow (1978) and Zammuto (1988)	Growth strategy adapted from Roberts (2003)
S1	Start-up	Simple structure	Defender or entrepreneur	Deepening or no growth
S2	Early growth	Between simple structure and professional bureaucracy	Defender or analyser	Deepening
S3	Continued growth	Between professional bureaucracy and adhocracy	Analyser	Geographic and/or offering diversification
P0	Seed	Simple structure	Prospector or entrepreneur	No growth
P1	Start-up	Simple structure	Prospector or entrepreneur	Deepening
P2	Early growth	Between simple structure and adhocracy	Prospector	Deepening + early geographic diversification
P3	Continued growth	Towards adhocracy	Prospector or analyser	Geographic diversification and early offering diversification

organizational ideal types taken from Mintzberg (1978), the strategic ideal types from Miles and Snow (1978), as refined by Zammuto (1988) and generic strategies derived from Roberts (2003 based on Ansoff, 1965[1988]. This helps refine the description of each ideal type and clarifies connections with established typologies. Table 3.1 summarizes a comparison of these typological research works. For the sake of clarity, it also includes a comparison with lifecycle models.

The Proposed Typology

When combined, the four steps provide a full description of the seven ideal types with a set of 23 items. We have described each of them in a few lines here, while Table 3.2 describes them in greater detail. It is interesting to highlight that while the literature frequently suggests mixed service- and software-business models, there is no description of such hybrid situations. As a consequence, they are not included in the typology.

Table 3.2 Ideal types for EISFs and ESVs

Dimensions	Items	Typical variables	S1 Expert service	S2 Local service champion	S3 Diversified service firm	P0 Software Lab	P1 Software Work-shop	P2 Software specialist	P3 Software reference
Entrepre-neurial team	Importance of management experience	Educational and business background (strategy, marketing, finances, HR . . .), number of years of experience in management positions	Low	Low	Medium	Low	Medium	Medium	High
	Importance of technical experience	Educational and technical background, number of years of experience in technological position	High	Medium	Low	High	High	Medium	Low
	Importance of willingness to grow	Positive attitude towards growth, growth as one specific objective	None	Medium	Medium	Medium	High	High	High

Table 3.2 (continued)

Dimensions	Items	Typical variables	S1 Expert service	S2 Local service champion	S3 Diversified service firm	P0 Software Lab	P1 Software Work-shop	P2 Software specialist	P3 Software reference
Activities	Importance of R&D	Relative size of the team and/or budget dedicated to R&D	None	None	Low	High	High	Medium	Medium
	Importance of service delivery	Relative size of the team dedicated to service delivery	High	High	High	None	Low	Low	Medium
	Relevance of indirect sales	Relative size of team and/or budget dedicated to indirect sales, number and types of partnerships, use of indirect marketing techniques	None	None	Low	None	Low	Medium	High
	Relevance of direct sales	Relative size of team and/or budget dedicated to direct sales, use of direct marketing techniques	High	High	High	Low	Medium	Medium	Low
Resources mix	Relevance of self-financing	Fully owned company, importance of bank financing, profitability	High	High	High	None	Low	Medium	Medium

	Relevance of external investor	Presence of business angles, venture capitalist, IPO	None	None	Medium	High	High	High	Medium
	Importance of middle management	Relative number of middle managers	None	Medium	High	None	Low	Medium	Medium
	Importance of senior management	Relative number of senior managers	Low	Medium	High	Low	Medium	High	High
	Importance of IP	Existence of patents, trademarks, copyrights, internal methodologies, non disclosure agreements . . .	None	None	Low	Medium	Medium	High	High
Organizational structure	Level of central decision-making	Locus of control of the entrepreneur, type of decisions taken at senior and middle management levels (delegation)	High	High	Low	High	High	Medium	Low
	Level of formalization	Existence of formal processes (policies, budget . . .), corporate governance structure (Board of Directors, Executive Committee), type of management system	None	Medium	High	None	Low	Medium	Medium

Table 3.2 (continued)

Dimensions	Items	Typical variables	S1 Expert service	S2 Local service champion	S3 Diversified service firm	P0 Software Lab	P1 Software Work-shop	P2 Software specialist	P3 Software reference
	Importance of vertical specialization	Distinction between junior/senior/ manager in each activity	Low	Medium	High	None	None	Low	Low
	Importance of horizontal specialization	Distinction between R&D, production, sales & marketing and back office functions	None	None	Low	Low	Medium	High	High
	Company size	Sales, headcount	Small	Medium	Larger	Very small	Small	Medium	Larger
Environment	Type of customers	Typical profile of the customer in terms of technology adoption, stage of technology adoption	Early adopters	Early majority	Late majority	Inno-vators	Early adopters	Early majority	Late majority
	Pattern of conditions change	Duration of technology lifecycle, importance of switching costs, demand stability, size of growth rate of the industry	Medium	Medium	Slow	Fast	Fast	Medium	Medium

	Description								
Competition intensity	Number of competitors, aggressiveness of the competition, industry concentration, barriers to entry, availability of substitute products	Low	Medium	High	Low	High	Medium	Medium	High
Growth strategy									
Level of depending	Focus on the local market with one single offering	High	High	Medium	High	Medium	Low	Medium	Low
Level of offering diversification	Number of distinctive business lines (number of practices or software offering)	None	Low	High	None	None	None	Low	Medium
Level of internationalization	Number of offices abroad, relative number of people working out of the initial geographical location, relative weight of foreign sales	None	Low	Medium	None	Low	Medium	Medium	High

- (S1) The 'expert' ideal type is a small service firm typically managed by one IT specialist with deep knowledge in a narrow practice. In fact, the specialist focuses on the long-term sustainability of his/her business. He/she possibly works with a few employees, typically fewer than 10, and does not follow any kind of growth strategy. As a consequence, the impact of competition on the firm is limited. In such firms, everything relates to the entrepreneur: his/her technical expertise (the entrepreneur is involved in all assignments) and his/her willingness to control operations with a basic informal and centralized organizational structure. Such expert firms are easily self-financed through regular service assignments to customers looking for a high level of technological expertise.

- (S2) The 'local services champion' ideal type is a more structured, medium-sized service firm. It works mainly at a local level, where it is recognized as one of the few specialized players in its field. Such firms operate according to a simple vertical organization where middle managers start playing a role in service delivery that often involves junior consultants. This allows the entrepreneur to take care of and manage the professionalization of the firm and to initiate early formalized management processes. Decision-making remains rather centralized. Such firms follow a deepening strategy on their local market. They are able to self-finance their growth with the support of banks to meet their working capital requirements. The typical size of such firms is 30–50 people.

- (S3) The 'diversified services firm' ideal type refers to a firm that is larger than the local champion firm because it encompasses multiple business units associated with diversification of their practices and/or internationalization (i.e. multiple local branches). Accordingly, its organizational structure is more complex and combines robust vertical (i.e. clear hierarchy between the consultants) and initial horizontal specialization. In this type of firm, the entrepreneur takes care of the general management of the firm and is no longer involved in front-end operations that are managed by senior managers. Whilst they are growing quickly in favourable market periods, diversified service firms may need the support of external investors. The typical size is more than 100 people. Such firms typically compete with other large professional services firms with specialized practices.

- (P0) The 'software lab' ideal type is a typical seed stage firm, focusing on product development with a very small team of highly qualified technical people. Beyond possible contact with technology obsessed customers, it has virtually no sales activity and finances its significant R&D efforts with equity raised from angel investors or venture capitalists. The organization is purely informal and not structured. As such, this configuration is not sustainable over the long term.

- (P1) The 'software workshop' ideal type is a small firm with limited local sales activities aimed at early adopter customers. Accordingly, it has a small dedicated direct sales force and starts by developing a horizontal organization. Nevertheless, operation remains fully under the control of the entrepreneur. Software workshop firms often operate below the break-even level and require additional external capital. When they do manage to break even, they may stabilize and remain a small local firm typically with under 10 people.

- (P2) The 'software specialist' ideal type is a medium-sized firm with a growing sales force to address the needs of their first international customers and/or develop indirect distribution channels, most of the time with one single product offering with critical intellectual property management needs. Accordingly, its organization is less centralized and becomes more formal with clear horizontal organizational lines, including specialized departments. Overall operations remain under the supervision of the entrepreneur. Since sales and marketing investments may be important in fast-growing market conditions, such a firm may raise additional venture capital. The typical size is 30–50 people.

- (P3) The 'software reference' ideal type refers to a larger firm with diversified sales channels which are mostly indirect when possible. Its objective is to be a leading firm in an established but continually maturing global market segment and to compete with larger international software firms on this segment. With international activities and initial product diversification, their operations are more complex. They require a more formalized management style with robust horizontal organization and have dedicated senior managers in key positions. If it is not investing aggressively in geographical developments, such a firm may be profitable. When this is not yet the case, they may raise additional capital. Going public may be an interesting option in order to facilitate the withdrawal of the initial investors and/or raise additional money.

CASE STUDIES

In this section, we introduce four case studies. We first explain our methodology and then present the empirical material.

Methodology

Four firms were selected from an initial shortlist of ten Belgian EISFs and ESVs with business-to-business activities. For each of these firms, we conducted at least one open-ended interview (for a minimum of one hour) with the founder/manager, and analysed secondary corporate data (for example, annual report, press releases), in order to identify both major events and strategy changes. The final selection of the four cases was based on 'purposeful sampling' (Patton, 2002). This includes using an initial estimate of observable configurations, the coexistence of both service and software business opportunities in order to analyse the tension between these two business models, the availability of multiple sources of evidence and the overall heterogeneity of the development patterns in order to obtain maximum variation inside the sample (Neergaard, 2007). In addition, while our focus is on EISFs with three such firms inside the sample, we have also included one pure ESV in the final case selection in order to test the entire set of ideal types (Doty and Glick, 1994) and further analyse hybrid cases. Additionally, the selected cases can also be considered as 'typical' cases (Yin, 2003).

Beyond the initial data collection and preliminary interviews performed prior to the final case selection, the case study protocol follows the guidelines and recommendations from Patton (2002) and Yin (2003). This includes six distinct steps that allowed for a replication logic from case to case. First of all, we conducted two 60- to 120-minute semi-structured interviews with (one of) the founder(s)/manager(s) of the company in order to recreate a chronological overview. People were not informed about the typology at the beginning of the process, but the second interview included questions about each item used to describe ideal types. In the second step, we organized an extensive collection of formal corporate documents (e.g. financial reports, business plans and board minutes). In the third step, we triangulated the data from interviews with the documents and, where possible, held one additional interview with an external observer of the company (i.e. investor or independent director). Table 3.3 summarizes the data collected for each case.

In the fourth step, we reorganized the dataset into a time-ordered matrix (Miles and Huberman, 1994), including all items used to describe the ideal types. The fifth step entailed using this matrix to identify possible configurations. In the sixth step, we carried out at least one respondent validation interview. This final step also proved to be an interesting way to perform intra-case analyses. It included an assessment of the configurations, a comparison between the configurations and proposed ideal types with a systematic match/mismatch analysis of every dimension used in Table 3.2 and a discussion about the major fits and gaps.

Table 3.3   Data sources

	All4it	CODE	Callatay & Wouters	Mobile Token
Interviews with entrepreneurs	1 with one founder 1 with one founder for validation	1 with two founders 1 with CFO 2 for validation (one with each of the founders)	2 with one founder 1 with the same founder for validation	1 with one founder 1 with one founder for validation
Interviews with external observers	1 independent director	1 banker	–	2 independent directors
Business plan	2007	1999 + 2001	1997	2002 + 2006
Financial statement and headcount details	Yes	Yes	Yes	Yes
Official annual report with management comments	Not available	2003–2005	2002–2007	Not available
Access to Board of Directors' minutes	No	Yes	No	Yes
Number of industry research available	1	5	2	1
Additional sources	1 R&D grant application file	2 R&D grant application files	Multiple press releases	2 R&D grant application files

Summary of the Case Studies

Overall, the four cases describe the evolution of four companies and allow for an analysis of 15 configurations. The first one is All4it, an EISF that specializes in data management. From 1997 to 2008, it focused on services (i.e. three configurations coded from A1 to A3) but decided to spin off a software product development identified in 2007 (i.e. one configuration coded F1). The second company is Callatay & Wouters, an EISF that specializes in banking systems. From 1987 to 2007, the company gradually shifted its business model and eventually became an ESV with international business (i.e. five configurations coded from W1 to W5). The third company is CODE, an EISF that focused on human resources management systems. From 1994 to 2003, it tried to develop a software practice but went back to consulting before being sold to a competitor in 2006 (i.e. three configurations coded from C1 to C3). The fourth company is Mobile Token, an ESV created in 2002 that specializes in mobile internet solutions. It combined software development and service activities for a few years before deciding to focus solely on its software business (i.e. three configurations coded from M1 to M3). The cases are chronologically summarized in Table 3.4, in which each line corresponds to one observed configuration.

FINDINGS

In this section, we compare the theoretically-deduced ideal types (Table 3.2) and the observed configurations (Table 3.4). To do so, we developed a systematic coding and matching process. First, all ideal types and configurations are coded with the same technique to become comparable. Then, we compare ideal types with each other and do the same with configurations. Finally, we compare ideal types with configurations. This process is explained in greater detail in the remainder of this subsection.

In order to create comparable datasets, all ideal types and configurations were numerically coded according to a 4-level scale summarized in Table 3.5. We highlight that this coding technique is not an attempt to quantify a qualitative dataset. In our view, it is only a way to organize and generalize a rigorous comparison between ideal types and configurations or, in other words, a way to organize 'cross-case displays' (Miles and Huberman, 1994).

Table 3.6 presents the outcome of this exercise according to the seven ideal types and 15 configurations. It includes the duration of each observed configuration which vary from two to ten years with an average of 4.6 years (the calculation does not include configurations that were still observable at the end of the study period).

The codified[2] dataset made it possible to perform systematic matching measurements through the calculation of absolute differences (Doty and Glick, 1994) between two items (e.g. if one item scores 1 in one configuration and 3 in another, the result of the matching is 2, the absolute value of the difference between 1 and 3). The comparisons between ideal types and configurations were then organized according to a three-step process. First of all, we compared the theoretically-deduced ideal types with each other in order to measure how much they really differ. This was also a way to verify that the coding technique was consistent with the disruptive

Table 3.4   Summary of the case studies

Ref	Description
All4it	
A1	All4it was created in 1997 by Xavier Ghyssens (XGH), who has a master's degree in physics, when he was 25. From 1997 to 2002, the company was mainly a legal vehicle for his services as a freelance consultant specialized in data quality and business intelligence (BI). By 2002, XGH started recruiting consultants who performed assignments in the BI field. He also broadened the activities to the pharmaceutical sector where data quality is critical. From 2002 to the end 2003, the company grew from 1 to 10 people with operations in Belgium and a limited number of projects in France. The organization was purely informal.
A2	By the beginning of 2004, XGH opened the capital of All4it to a senior partner who obtained 30% of the shares. The new partner headed sales and marketing and helped to extend the scope of activities to system outsourcing. From 2004 to 2006, the company grew from 10 to 70 people with significant development of operations in France. At that time, All4it had no clear organizational structure except practice groups for consultants, headed by one dedicated manager and one sales team. The fast growth was significantly supported by the rapid development of BI and the increasing demand from pharma. Up to 2006, All4it was profitable and fully self-financed without external investors or banks. However, because of the increase in working capital requirement, cash was tight. This tension generated conflicts between the shareholders. Furthermore, by the end of 2005, the pharma consultants started developing an electronic data capture software product, mainly aimed to distinguish the firm from their competitors. This investment was mainly financed with an R&D grant from the local government.
A3	2007 was a turning point for All4it. Increasing tensions between shareholders led to the departure of the senior partner and the need to reorganize the company. XGH bought back all of the shares and recruited one interim manager who set up a new organizational structure and introduced a set of internal processes. The BI and pharma consulting practices were reorganized in each country as independent business units with dedicated managers and a sales force. The back-office functions were shared inside the company. All key people in the management bought shares of the company. In 2007, All4it grew to 100 employees and was financially supported by a bank. All4IT plans to recruit an HR manager and a CFO in 2008.
F1	Also, by the end of 2007, All4it had decided to spin off the software project into a separate company named Flexcipio. All4it was the main shareholder of the spin-off and decided to finance it through venture capital investors. Two key people received shares in the new venture, while XGH continued managing the project. Flexcipio planned to be able to break even by 2009, with sales organized through distributors.

Table 3.4   (continued)

Ref	Description
Callatay & Wouters (C-W)	

Ref	Description
W1	C-W was created in 1983 by Didier de Callatay (DDC) and Godefroid de Wouters (GDW), two engineers with up to 5 years' business experience. The company was an IT service provider that focused on banks. From 1983 to 1987, the company had no formal organization and grew from 2 to 10 people through operations in Belgium.
W2	By 1988, C-W adopted a more structured organization with the arrival of new project managers. Over 3 years, the company moved from 10 to 35 people with operations centred on service delivery to Belgian banks. One important project in 1989 included the development of management software that appeared to answer the needs of multiple customers. Software development efforts were financed by customers.
W3	By 1991, C-W opened one branch in Luxembourg. It also created its own pure R&D team by the beginning of 1993. From 1993 to 1995, multiple projects allowed C-W to refine its software offering so that, by 1995, the company was in position to market its first software known as Thaler. From 1995 to 1997, C-W continued growing its consulting practice and managed to close repetitive sales on its own software solution thanks to major marketing expenses. C-W grew to 85 people by the end of 1997.
W4	In 1998, venture capitalists invested in C-W to further extend its international operations. From 1998 to 2006, the company opened branches in multiple countries, continued increasing its investment in R&D, extended its software offering and negotiated partnerships with international consultants who were able to install C-W software solutions. As a result of this strategy, the company grew to 400 people in seven countries and managed to have 30% of software revenues. In the meantime, by 2000, GDW decided to stop his day-to-day involvement in the management of the company to focus on strategy.
W5	By 2007, DDC resigned as CEO and appointed his successor from amongst the existing management team. Also in 2007, C-W managed to close a strategic partnership with SAP to further support its international growth. DDC and GDW kept working at C-W board level in order to refine strategy and support business development. By the middle of 2008, C-W had 520 employees and was active in 15 countries.

Ref	Description
COnsulting & DEvelopment (CODE)	

Ref	Description
C1	CODE was incorporated in 1997 by four computer engineers with brief consultant experience as employees and a minimal initial capital. CODE initially focused on delivering services associated to the human resources module of SAP (SAP-HR), a leading ERP product. Nevertheless, the

Table 3.4   (continued)

Ref	Description
COnsulting & DEvelopment (CODE)	

	purpose of CODE was not only to deliver services, but also to capitalize on identified market needs to develop add-on software solutions to complement SAP-HR. From 1997 to 1999, the provision of services was a cash-cow activity. Since the ERP market was hot at that time, CODE grew from 4 to 16 people (100% growth every year) and generated enough cash to cover the costs of the R&D (mostly included in service projects) and marketing of its first software products, while closing with a small profit. While CODE closed its first sales in France, Spain, Switzerland, UK and USA by 1999, the activities were based in Belgium with no formal structure. At that time, the only financing issue was an increase in working capital requirement, but this was covered by the banks.
C2	By 2000, CODE opened branches with local sales & consulting teams in France and USA. A CFO joined and became a fifth partner. CODE adopted a formal structure and appointed one founding member as CEO. CODE grew again 100% up to 32 people and was still able to break even. Sales included 70% from services and 30% from software licenses. By 2001, CODE increased its investment in R&D and opened one branch in Spain. By the end of 2001, CODE had 60 people. Each local team had dedicated management, sales teams and consulting staff. There was also one central R&D team and one corporate management team. Sales grew again 100% with licences accounting for 40% of it. Banks continued to cover every increase in working capital requirement and local research grants financed most of the development expenditure. By 2002, ERP market conditions changed significantly. Sales stagnated and licence sales dramatically decreased. Since the company continued investing in R&D, it showed significant losses that put CODE at high risk. The financial crisis generated trouble inside CODE, and the banks threatened to withdraw their support due to the credit squeeze.
C3	By 2003 and 2004, sales had stabilized with more and more services sales and decreasing licences sales. The headcount was reduced by 20% through cutbacks to the R&D and administration team. In this way, CODE was able to reduce its losses, but the financial position remained tricky. By the end of 2004, in order to reduce costs and risks in a more significant way, CODE decided to appoint a new CEO. The initial CEO agreed to leave and was replaced by another founder who refocused CODE on the services business and on the European markets. By 2005 and 2006, CODE was successful with its service business without extending its geographical scope. Sales and headcount grew by about 15% up to 70 employees and the company was back in the black. The software activities remained marginal, i.e. mainly limited to small opportunistic licences sales and maintenance tasks. By 2007, CODE was sold to its major local competitor.

Table 3.4   (continued)

Ref	Description
Mobile Token (MT)	
M1	MT was created in 2002 by Lionel Anciaux (LAN), a computer engineer with nine years' business experience, and M-Invest, a Belgian venture capital fund specialized in mobile internet services. LAN was also initially associated with one minority part-time partner who resigned by the middle of 2003. The initial plan was to develop applications dedicated to banks. However, MT quickly changed its plan and focused on field marketing. In 2002–03, the company mainly performed R&D and pre-sales activities with two employees.
M2	From 2003 to 2006, MT grew from 3 to 16 people with 13 developers, 2 sales staff and LAN. It also obtained a local R&D grant to support the development of its field marketing product. At the same time, in order to keep cash under control, the company proposed to the majority of its initial customers a project-based collaboration with significantly customized work (i.e. services offering). The organization was informal with most of the IT profiles performing both R&D and consulting. By 2006, M-invest got into trouble and proposed to LAN to buy back their shares at a significant discount. LAN accepted and offered two key people inside the company the possibility of buying part of the shares. Together, they realized that MT needed more cash to further develop its software offering and managed to get support from another investor early in 2007. In the meantime, MT was dealing with an increasing number of projects, each of them with quite different requirements. Because of this diversity, MT found it difficult to deliver and faced internal organizational issues. However, a positive learning from this experience was to identify another product opportunity for companies working with large numbers of off-site technicians, a much larger market than the initial field marketing sector. By the end of 2007, MT had 20 people.
M3	By the end of 2007, MT managed to resolve its organizational problems and decided to refocus its R&D effort on the field technicians business. The company recruited a marketing manager to develop an aggressive plan in order to market the new product through an international network of resellers. MT also decided to continue selling its field marketing solution on a local basis with a limited internal sales force and considered this activity as a cash-cow. By the beginning of 2008, MT was reorganized to support this mix of activities.

change assumption of the configurational approach and an opportunity to establish benchmarks for the next matching exercises. Table 3.7 presents the result of the calculation.

Table 3.7 also highlights the fact that couples of each ideal type in the presumed chronological sequence (e.g. P0–P1, P1–P2, S1–S2) significantly

Table 3.5   Scoring gridline

Score	Importance/ relevance/level of	Pattern	Type of customers	Size
0	None		Innovators	Very small
1	Low	Slow	Early adopters	Small
2	Medium	Medium	Early majority	Medium
3	High	Fast	Late majority	Larger

differ, meaning there are differences in more than 50 per cent of the 23 items used to describe the ideal types. This result fits with the idea that moves from one ideal type to the next involve changes in every major dimension and must then be analysed as 'second order' changes (Levy, 1986). Another interesting fact is that the differences increase when we compare ideal types which relate to different activity orientations (e.g. P1–S1, P2–S2). This is consistent with the idea that product and service configurations, even when they relate to presumed equivalent maturity/size stages, are very different from each other. Thus, a unique lifecycle approach as suggested by traditional lifecycle or staged models, is not refined sufficiently enough to deal with the heterogeneity of these business models and associated growth strategies. An additional insight comes from the fact that all lines in Table 3.7 contain non-zero values. This validates the choice of the 23 items, even if the ones associated with entrepreneurs and activities vary less than the others. Finally, the differences between ideal types also increase when we compare presumed chronological-distant stages within one homogeneous activity orientation (e.g. S1–S3, P0–P3). This suggests that jumping/missing one stage in the presumed sequence requires more changes and will thus be more difficult to manage.

The second step was to compare the successive configurations adopted by each firm. Table 3.8 presents the result of this calculation revealing that successive configurations also differ significantly from each other (e.g. A1–A2, A2–A3, C1–C2) and that the same magnitude of change occurs as with changes from ideal type to another in the first part of Table 3.7. It is also important to observe that no line includes only zero values. This offers strong support for a configurational approach (including changes at every level to reach coherence) and the associated second-order change approach. Indeed, this also assesses the relevance of our selection of items to describe configurations. As a matter of fact, both theoretical ideal types and empirical configurations can be described discriminately with the same set of items.

The third step is, of course, to compare the 15 configurations with the

Table 3.6 Codification of the ideal types and observed configurations

		Ideal types														Observed configurations							
		S1	S2	S3	P0	P1	P2	P3	A1	A2	A3	C1	C2	C3	F1	M1	M2	M3	W1	W2	W3	W4	W5
Entrepreneurial team	Importance of management experience	1	1	2	1	2	2	3	0	1	2	1	2	3	2	1	1	2	1	2	3	3	3
	Importance of technical experience	3	2	1	3	3	2	1	2	2	2	3	2	1	2	2	2	2	3	3	3	2	1
	Importance of willingness to grow	0	2	2	2	3	3	3	1	3	3	3	3	2	3	3	2	3	2	2	3	3	3
Activities	Importance of R&D	0	0	1	3	3	2	2	0	0	0	2	3	1	3	2	2	2	0	0	2	3	3
	Importance of service delivery	3	3	3	0	1	1	2	3	3	3	3	3	3	1	1	3	1	2	3	3	3	2
	Relevance of indirect sales	0	0	1	0	1	2	3	1	1	1	0	2	1	1	0	1	2	0	0	0	1	2
	Relevance of direct sales	3	3	3	1	2	2	1	2	2	3	3	2	3	2	2	3	2	2	2	3	3	2
Resources mix	Relevance of self-financing	3	3	3	0	1	2	2	3	2	3	3	2	3	0	0	2	1	3	3	1	2	3
	Relevance of external investor	0	0	2	3	3	3	2	0	0	1	0	2	0	3	3	1	3	0	0	3	2	1
	Importance of middle management	0	2	3	0	1	2	2	0	1	2	0	2	3	0	1	1	2	0	0	1	2	3

	Importance of senior management	1	2	3	1	2	3	3	0	2	3	1	3	2	2	1	2	3	1	2	2	3	3
	Importance of IP	0	0	1	2	2	3	3	0	0	1	2	2	1	2	2	1	2	0	0	2	3	3
Organizational structure	Level of central decision-making	3	3	1	3	3	2	1	3	3	2	3	2	2	3	3	3	2	3	3	3	2	2
	Level of formalization	0	2	3	0	1	2	2	0	1	2	0	2	3	1	1	1	2	0	1	2	2	3
	Importance of vertical specialization	1	2	3	0	0	1	1	0	1	2	1	2	3	0	0	1	1	0	1	3	2	2
	Importance of horizontal specialization	0	0	1	1	2	3	3	0	0	1	1	2	1	2	1	0	2	0	0	1	2	3
	Company size	1	2	3	0	1	2	3	1	2	3	1	3	3	1	0	1	2	0	1	2	3	3
Environment	Type of customers	1	2	3	0	1	2	3	1	2	3	1	1	2	0	0	1	1	2	2	1	2	3
	Pattern of conditions change	2	2	1	3	3	2	2	3	2	1	2	3	1	2	3	3	2	2	2	3	3	2
	Competition intensity	1	2	3	1	2	2	3	1	2	3	2	2	3	1	1	2	2	1	2	2	3	2
Growth strategy	Level of deepening	3	3	2	3	3	2	1	1	2	2	2	1	3	2	2	2	1	2	3	2	2	1
	Level of offering diversification	0	1	3	0	0	1	2	0	1	2	2	3	1	0	0	1	2	0	1	2	2	1
	Level of internationalization	0	1	2	0	1	2	3	0	1	2	1	3	2	0	0	0	1	0	0	1	2	3
Duration (years)									7	3	?	3	3	4	?	2	4	?	5	4	6	10	?

Table 3.7 Differences from one ideal type to another

	From one ideal type to another													
	P0– P1	P1– P2	P2– P3	S1– S2	S2– S3	P0– S1	P1– S1	P1– S2	P2– S2	P2– S3	P3– S3	S1– S3	P0– P2	P0– P3
Management experience	1	0	1	0	1	0	1	1	1	0	1	1	1	2
Technical experience	0	1	1	1	1	0	0	1	0	1	0	2	1	2
Willingness to grow	1	0	2	2	0	2	3	1	1	1	1	2	1	1
R&D	0	0	0	0	1	3	3	3	2	2	1	1	1	1
Service delivery	1	0	1	0	0	3	2	2	2	2	1	0	1	2
Indirect sales	1	1	1	0	1	0	1	1	2	1	2	1	2	3
Direct sales	1	0	0	0	0	2	1	1	2	1	2	0	1	0
Self-financing	1	1	0	0	0	3	2	2	1	1	1	0	2	2
External investor	0	0	1	2	2	3	3	3	3	1	0	2	0	1
Middle management	1	0	0	2	1	0	1	1	0	1	1	3	2	2
Senior management	1	0	0	1	1	0	1	0	1	0	0	2	2	2
IP	0	1	0	0	1	2	2	2	3	2	2	1	1	1

	14	17	13	14	22	23	28	27	25	24	21	36	31	42
Central decision-making	0	1	1	0	2	0	0	0	1	1	0	2	1	2
Formalization	1	1	0	2	1	0	1	1	0	1	1	3	2	2
Vertical specialization	0	1	0	1	1	1	1	2	1	2	2	2	1	1
Horizontal specialization	1	1	0	0	1	1	2	2	3	2	2	1	2	2
Company size	1	1	1	1	1	1	0	1	0	1	0	2	2	3
Type of customers	1	1	1	1	1	1	1	1	1	1	0	2	2	3
Conditions change	0	1	0	0	1	1	1	1	0	1	1	1	1	1
Competition intensity	1	0	1	1	1	0	1	0	0	1	0	2	1	2
Deepening	0	1	0	0	1	0	0	0	1	0	1	1	1	2
Offering diversification	0	1	1	1	2	0	0	1	0	2	1	3	1	2
Internationalization	1	1	1	1	1	0	1	0	1	0	1	2	2	3
TOTAL	**14**	**17**	**13**	**14**	**22**	**23**	**28**	**27**	**25**	**24**	**21**	**36**	**31**	**42**
Average		16.0						24.7					36.3	

Table 3.8   Difference between successive configurations

	A1– A2	A2– A3	C1– C2	C2– C3	M1– M2	M2– M3	W1– W2	W2– W3	W3– W4	W4– W5
					From one configuration to another					
Management experience	1	1	1	1	0	1	1	1	0	0
Technical experience	0	0	1	1	0	0	0	0	1	1
Willingness to grow	2	0	0	1	1	1	0	1	0	0
R&D	0	0	1	2	0	0	0	2	1	0
Service delivery	0	0	0	0	2	2	1	0	0	1
Indirect sales	0	0	2	1	1	1	0	0	1	1
Direct sales	0	1	1	1	1	1	0	1	0	1
Self-financing	1	1	1	1	2	1	0	2	1	1
External investor	0	1	2	2	2	2	0	3	1	1
Middle management	1	1	2	1	0	1	0	1	1	1
Senior management	2	1	2	1	1	1	1	0	1	0
IP	0	1	0	1	1	1	0	2	1	0
Central decision-making	0	1	1	0	0	1	0	0	1	0
Formalization	1	1	2	1	0	1	1	1	0	1
Vertical specialization	1	1	1	1	1	0	1	2	1	0
Horizontal specialization	0	1	1	1	1	2	0	1	1	1
Company size	1	1	2	0	1	1	1	1	1	0
Type of customers	1	1	0	1	1	0	0	1	1	1
Conditions change	1	1	1	2	0	1	0	1	0	1
Competition intensity	1	1	0	1	1	0	1	0	1	1
Deepening	1	0	1	2	0	1	1	1	0	1
Offering diversification	1	1	1	2	1	1	1	1	0	1
Internationalization	1	1	2	1	0	1	0	1	1	1
TOTAL	**16**	**17**	**25**	**25**	**17**	**21**	**9**	**23**	**15**	**15**
Average					18.3					

seven ideal types. Table 3.9 summarizes this calculation (only the total differences are shown).

In order to highlight matches and patterns in configuration changes (or trajectories), we have decided to stylize each result. To do so, we have marked the differences (i.e. the rounded half of the average difference between two ideal types in the first part of Table 3.6) that were under 9 with *** (strong match), those that were in the rage of 9 and 12 with ** (medium match) and those that ranged from 13 to 16 with * (low match). All other differences (no match) are not displayed. Table 3.10 presents the results.

Table 3.10 shows four strong matches (A2, M1, M3 and W1), six average matches (A1, A3, C3, F1, W2 and W5) and five low matches (C1, C2, M2, W3 and W4). These observations give rise to five comments.

Table 3.9 *Difference between ideal types (rows) and configuration (columns)*

	A1	A2	A3	C1	C2	C3	F1	M1	M2	M3	W1	W2	W3	W4	W5
P0	25	31	42	22	35	42	12	8	23	28	19	26	25	36	43
P1	27	21	30	20	21	32	8	12	17	14	25	22	15	22	29
P2	36	20	19	25	14	25	19	23	22	7	32	27	20	13	14
P3	43	29	20	32	15	26	32	36	31	16	41	36	27	14	11
S1	10	16	29	13	38	29	27	25	16	35	8	9	28	37	42
S2	20	8	15	17	26	15	31	29	14	25	16	9	20	23	28
S3	38	26	9	29	20	9	37	39	26	25	36	29	24	17	20

Table 3.10 *Identifying matching and change patterns*

	A1	A2	A3	C1	C2	C3	F1	M1	M2	M3	W1	W2	W3	W4	W5
P0							**	***							
P1							***	**	*			*			
P2				*						***				*	*
P3				*					*					*	**
S1	**	*		*				*		***	**				
S2		***	*		*			*		*	**				
S3		**			**										

First, all configurations that were observed match with one ideal type. This confirms that a typological approach to growth strategy is possible (i.e. strategy changes are not idiosyncratic) and that the proposed typology makes sense since it fits with actual configurations. In other words, the proposed ideal types seem to be relevant even though further quantitative work is necessary to ensure that there are no additional ideal types that we may have missed. Secondly, most of the successive matches for each firm correspond to a presumed chronological sequence, that is, a typical service pattern with S1–S2–S3 or a typical product pattern with P0–P1–P2–P3. This is very clear in the evolution of All4it which follows a pure service pattern, in the beginning of the evolution of Callatay & Wouters that also follows a service pattern and in its later evolution that fits with a product pattern. Thirdly, a very interesting point is that the 'low match' cases correspond with instances where firms were changing from service to product pattern (C1, C2, W3 and W4) or the other way around (M2). This suggests that a move from one pattern to another requires going through some kind of hybrid configuration. Unfortunately, since these hybrid configurations do not share regularities, it is not possible to describe them in greater detail at this stage of the research. Nevertheless, the fact that the three companies adopted the next configuration in line with those of the typology suggests that hybrid configurations are temporary in nature. Fourthly, the fact that CODE failed in its attempts to move from a service to pure product business models and that Mobile Token went back to its product business model, confirms the idea that changing business model is a complicated endeavour due to the need for very significant changes at multiple levels. This can be seen in Table 3.8 where the total difference of moves C1–C2, C2–C3, M2–M3 and W2–W3 are above average. This suggests some kind of heredity effect that makes it very difficult for drastic business model changes to succeed. A more detailed analysis of Table 3.8 reveals that major differences frequently occurred at the resources level. This relates to one of the core ideas of the resource-based view which states that companies differ because of variations in their resources endowments that originally created a competitive advantage. It is then possible to propose that transitions fail due to significant changes in resources that drastically modify the very nature of the company and put it in a rather difficult situation. In other words, this suggests that these companies had internal difficulties in trying to manage so many changes and preferred to return to what they had initially mastered. Finally, the four companies may have adopted rather clear trajectories; pure service pattern for All4it; aborted transition from service to product for CODE; aborted transition from product to service for Mobile Token; and successful transition from service to product for Callatay & Wouters. Figure 3.2 simplified and stylized these evolutions. Ideal types are designated by circles, actual configurations by boxes and the distances between items refer to the matching score (absolute differences calculated in Table 3.9).

Taken together, the findings in this subsection support the idea that configurations adopted by EISFs clearly differ from those of ESVs. They also confirm the relevance of the configuration typology proposed in Table 3.2 that enables us to predict how the elements evolve when firms change their growth strategies.

DISCUSSION

In light of our research methodology and results, this section contains a discussion about the relevance of our configuration approach, the theoretical quality of the proposed typology, the dynamics of configuration changes and the limitations of this research.

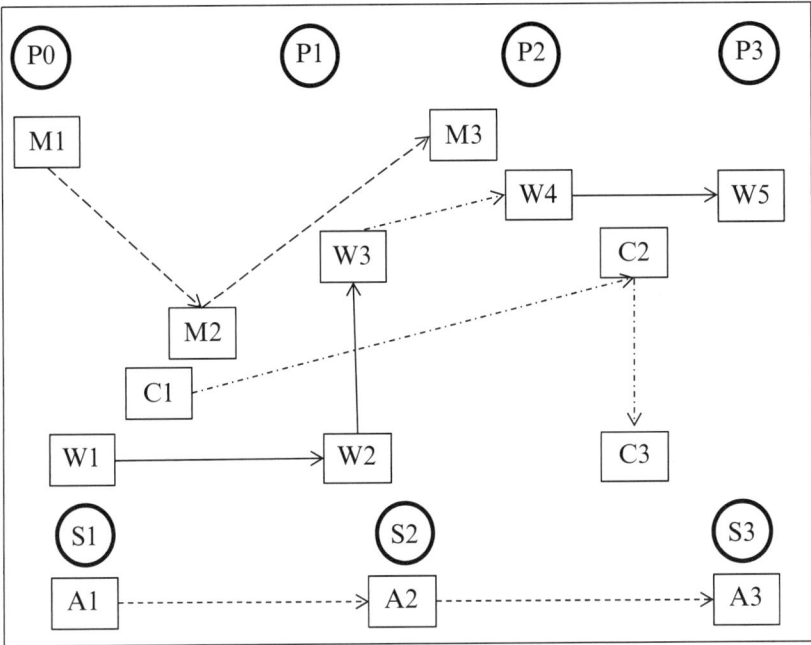

Figure 3.2   Stylized growth patterns of four firms

Relevance of the Configuration Approach

Miller (1996) deplored that 'what is often missing in configuration literature is the search for configuration itself' (p. 505). We believe that this chapter echoes his call and offers proponents of the configuration approach with additional arguments. As a matter of fact, from a theoretical point of view, this research is a validation of the configuration approach in entrepreneurial settings, particularly when dealing with mid- or long-term issues (see the section about limitations). Our argument is three-fold and follows the most important features that have been highlighted by configuration theorists. First of all, we are able to derive distinctive ideal types from literature and match them with observed configurations. This confirms that 'there are ties that unite strategy and structure; that given a particular strategy there are only a limited number of suitable structure and vice versa' (Miller, 1986, p. 234). Second, the observed configurations tend to be stable over time (see last line of Table 3.6). Third, observed changes in configuration involved second-order types of change, that is, changes in many (if not all) of the dimensions used to describe it. The combination of these two last comments clearly points to the relentless debate between proponents of configuration versus a contingency approach and suggests that the first one is more relevant to study the strategies adopted by entrepreneurial ventures, at least in the case of long-term changes.

Is the Proposed Typology a Theoretical Contribution?

Since this chapter is about proposing a typology, we believe it is useful to discuss the extent that the proposed typology matches or does not match the criteria of a 'middle range' theoretical contribution (Whetten, 1989). First of all, we believe that in terms of identifying constructs, both the ideal types and the variables used to describe them are clearly articulated and connected with existing research. Of course, descriptions could be refined, but that is not the main purpose of this chapter. Secondly, to explain the relationship between the constructs, we again rely on existing research and, of course, on the concept of fit. Fit is quite clearly associated here with a gestalt logic and is 'criterion-free and minimally precise' (Venkatraman, 1989, p.432). We recognize that it is possible to develop this argument further, but this goes beyond the objectives of this exploratory research. Thirdly, our sampling strategy was important to assess the specific nature of the typology. This was one of the very motivations for the inclusion of the Mobile Token case (i.e. an ESV) which did not adopt the configurations that were expected for an EISF. This case clearly confirms that our typology is falsifiable. Finally, the definition of the validity domain needs further explanation since it has not been addressed so far. Basically, in our view, the validity domain of the typology is associated with the entrepreneurial nature of the business. Of course, this raises a major definition issue that points to endless debates between entrepreneurship scholars. We will not engage in this debate, but will only mention that we rely on the definition suggested by Bruyat and Julien (2001) and Fayolle (2007), which is based on a constant dialogic interaction between entrepreneurs and the characteristics of their projects. Overall, we then believe that, considering the exploratory dimension of this chapter, the proposed typology is valid since it meets the main characteristics of theoretical contribution, even though there are avenues open for further refinements.

Analysing Configuration Changes

When it comes to analysing changes, Van de Ven and Engleman (2004) recommend a process- or event-driven approach. Indeed, it represents a relevant framework to understanding change, particularly configuration change. As a matter of fact, a configuration change is one type of event that can be analysed as a complex multi-motor process. Additionally, the possibility of linking major research streams that focus on growth with process types, further complements the configuration approach (Van de Ven and Poole, 1995 and Witmeur, 2007). Miller (1987) proposed that configuration adoption is driven by four successive 'imperatives', that is, 'those of environment (including technology), organization structure, leadership and strategy' (p. 686). These imperatives can be compared with the four types of 'process theories' or 'motors' to analyse organizational change, that is, respectively evolution, lifecycle, dialectic, and teleology, suggested by Van de Ven and Poole (1995). However, research available on the links between configuration adoption and its related processes is very limited. Taking this into consideration, we do not believe it is possible at this stage to propose the generic growth patterns and to explain their dynamics. Nevertheless, the aforementioned suggestions and the literature mentioned earlier in this chapter enable us to suggest five processes that may drive configuration changes. First of all, the traits approach refers to a dialectical process relating to the willingness to grow or stay stable. Secondly and thirdly, the ecology of population and the technology adoption cycle refer to two evolutionary processes related to 'market acceptance' and 'investor acceptance' (Heirman and Clarysse, 2005). Fourthly, organizational changes and the need for professionalization refer to a staged organizational structuring process. Last but not least, both the strategic management perspective and the resource-based view refer to a teleological process where resources acquisition and transformation (Lichtenstein and Brush, 2001) as well as comparison between expected and actual performance (Gersick, 1994), play central roles.

A closer analysis of the case suggests four propositions. First of all, 'willingness to grow' is more often associated with moves towards product configurations. Secondly, service configurations are driven by 'market acceptance', while early product configuration needs 'investor acceptance' because of the existence of a prototyping stage before reaching the market. Thirdly, organizational structuring does not appear to be relevant in the beginning for both service and product configurations, but instead is critical during later stages. Fourthly, although strategic planning is only relevant in later stages for firms adopting service configurations, it is more constantly important in product configurations. Overall, a 'willingness to grow' and 'market acceptance' seem to be the most important processes. Indeed, organizational structuring and strategic planning seem to follow them, while 'investor acceptance' seems to be important only when products are not yet ready for market entry, or when growth (linked to strategic intent) requires more resources than those generated by operations.

Limitations of the Research

Because of its exploratory and case-based nature, this research suffers from clear limitations. First of all, there is no definitive best research practice to develop typologies (Miller, 1996). The way we have developed ours (i.e. the steps, the selection of items, their rating and the coding of the dataset) is debatable since it is directly subject to interpretation by the researcher. Secondly, despite the cautious case protocol, we have not been able to completely avoid classical issues associated with case studies such as reinterpretation, partial remembering, limited existence of external or written evidences and, once again, the personal biases of the researcher. Thirdly, and along the same lines, while the validity of qualitative research rests on the concept of theoretical saturation, we cannot definitively claim this with four cases and 15 configurations. Fourthly, retroactive research over multiple years is not sufficiently refined to detect small incremental changes, thus we may have overlooked small adaptive decisions and events. This means that our findings are relevant to test the existence of second-order changes, but cannot be used to refute the importance of adaptive or first-order changes. In other words, while configuration appears to be stable on a mid-term horizon, our research does not eliminate the possibility of smaller adaptive and/or incremental changes over shorter-term periods. Fifth, this research does not even try to crack the code for any of the black boxes associated with problems such as the way business people perceive their environment, analyse fit or coherence between elements, and evaluate performance. Sixth, the selected cases are only about internal growth strategies. As a consequence, mergers and acquisitions have not been analysed. Finally, we paid no attention to growth measurement issues.

CONCLUSION

The primary purpose of this chapter was to propose an integrated framework for the analysis of growth strategies of young entrepreneurial firms and the way these strategies change over time. The typology that we have developed and applied to the case studies, reinforces the idea that a configurational approach is relevant in order to analyse growth strategy adoption in entrepreneurial settings. An additional contribution is the insight that a set of predefined processes may help to provide a better understanding of configuration changes.

As a matter of fact, on a theoretical level, ideal types were possible to define while, on an empirical level, configurations were isolated. One of the contributions of this chapter is to propose a systematic approach to compare them or, in other words, to test the typology. The fact that the observed configurations were quite similar to hypothesized ideal types confirms that the approach 'makes it possible for us to order our world of organizations in a rich and holistic way' (Miller, 1986, p. 235). Thus this chapter offers researchers a kind of middle-range theory that delivers clear insights into the conditions and implications of growth strategies which are available to entrepreneurial ventures.

On a practical level, this research has interesting implications for practitioners since it contributes to a better understanding of growth strategies adopted by EISFs. The typology indicates, and the cases confirm, that beyond the entrepreneur's profile and willingness to grow, the adoption of strategies such as deepening, practice diversification and internationalization, must be associated with different sets of activities, market conditions, resources endowment and organizational challenges. The research also suggests the driving forces that generate changes in these elements. More specifically, even if diversification to software is often highly desirable, the very different nature of service- versus product-based configurations explains why business model shift must be analysed carefully and is so difficult to carry out successfully.

Anderson and Atkins (2002) pointed out: 'the process of configuration and reconfiguration is likely to be the quintessence of successful small-firm planning' (p. A1). This chapter could be the starting point for the development of a practical tool to assist entrepreneurs during this endeavour. As a matter of fact, the description of ideal types and the possibility of comparing them with actual configurations, suggests the development of a diagnostic toolkit where differences can be analysed and contextualized. In such a tool, positive differences may point towards future configurations that are elaborated further, while negative differences may point towards specific aspects that may require additional attention from the management. On a more general level, this research highlights the fact that growing a business is about managing dynamic fit with multiple elements and processes. We believe that understanding the issues associated with each ideal type and monitoring the five processes analysed in this chapter will help managers to focus their attention.

We hope that our work will be echoed by other researchers. Due to its exploratory nature, multiple avenues for future research are suggested. The first avenue is to replicate this project across other types of new ventures. While the extension to an ESV is the most natural step, moving to other industries is possible with the same kind of research design. A second important endeavour is to address the limitations mentioned at the beginning of this section. With regard to typologies, this means testing alternative ways to develop and/or formulate them. We believe that grounded theory protocols are probably an interesting way to do so (Eisenhardt, 1989). On a case study level, this implies more in-depth and real-time case research. Ideally, this also points to a quantitative approach in the future. Along the same lines, a third avenue is to use the insights from the case studies to further refine the typologies (e.g. the selection of the elements, the definition of the ideal types and the associated explanations) and to understand the processes or *imperatives* that drive configuration changes (Miller, 1987). A fourth avenue that could also be interesting is to take a more detailed look at correlations between strategic configuration and growth or performance measurement in general.

Finally, this research can also be considered as a step towards a more comprehensive and dynamic framework which combines configuration and process approaches in order to understand growth strategy changes in entrepreneurial firms. Although the research currently available does not offer many insights into how to perform this integration, our results support the ideas that configuration changes are driven by multiple processes, that the influence of these processes changes over time and that this influence is not idiosyncratic since regularities appear. Of course, at this stage, the findings are very preliminary but they do echo work provided by Mintzberg (1983) and Miller (1987) who both suggested typical transitions from one configuration to another. Van de Ven and Engleman (2004) suggested that researchers 'must isolate meaningful elements that lead to the outcome and then derive a narrative process story that ties these elements into a coherent whole' (p. 356). We believe that this exploratory research is an early attempt at taking up this challenge.

NOTES

1. Special thanks are expressed to the Bernheim Fondation for its support to entrepreneurship at the Solvay Brussels School of Economics and Management. We also thank RENT XXIII participants and two anonymous reviewers for suggestions on an earlier version of this chapter.
2. The coding is inevitably somewhat arbitrary, but we have performed sensibility analysis tests that reveal that a modest bias does not change any of the conclusions.

REFERENCES

Anderson, A.R. and M.H. Atkins (2002), 'Configuration and reconfiguration: planning for uncertainty?', *International Journal of Entrepreneurship and Innovation Management*, **2**(4), 406–23.

Ansoff, I. (1965 [1988], *Corporate Strategy*, revised edition (first published in 1965, McGraw-Hill, USA), London: Penguin Books.

Bacharach, S.B. (1989), 'Organizational theories: some criteria for evaluation', *Academy of Management Review*, **14**(4), 496–515.

Bantel, K.A. (1998), 'Technology-based "adolescent" firm configurations: strategy identification, context, and performance', *Journal of Business Venturing*, **13**, 205–30.

Biga, Diambeidou M., B. Gailly and M. Verleysen (2007), 'Une taxonomie des trajectoires de croissance initiales des jeunes entreprises', 5ème Congrès de l'Académie de l'Entrepreneuriat, Sherbrooke, Canada.

Biswas, S. and D. Twitchell (2002), *Management Consulting,* New York: John Wiley.

Brush, C.G., P.G. Greene and M.M. Hart (2001), 'From initial idea to unique advantage: the entrepreneurial challenge of constructing a resource base', *Academy of Management Executive*, **15**(1), 64–78.

Bruyat, C. and P.-A. Julien (2001), 'Defining the field of research in entrepreneurship', *Journal of Business Venturing*, **16**(2), 165–80.

Chrisman, J.J., A. Bauerschmidt and C.W. Hofer (1999), 'The determinants of new venture performance', *Entrepreneurship Theory and Practice*, **23**(1), 5–29.

Churchill, N.C. and V.L. Lewis (1983), 'The five stages of small business growth', *Harvard Business Review*, May–June.

Davidsson, P. (1989), 'Entrepreneurship and after? A study of growth willingness in small firms', *Journal of Business Venturing*, **4**, 211–26.

Davidsson, P. and M. Klofsten (2003), 'The business platform: developing an instrument to gauge and to assist the development of young firms', *Journal of Small Business Management*, **41**(1), 1–26.

Davidsson, P., L. Achtenhagen and L. Naldi (2005), 'Research on small firm growth: a review', paper presented at the 35th EISB Conference, Barcelona, Spain, A1–A27.

Davidsson, P., F. Delmar and J. Wiklund (2006), 'Introduction', *Entrepreneurship and the Growth of Firms*, Cheltenham, UK and Northampton, MA, USA: Edward Elgar Publishing, pp. 1–18.

Delmar, F. and J. Wiklund (2003), 'Growth motivation and growth: untangling causal relationship', paper presented at the Academy of Management Conference, August, Seattle, WA.

Delmar, F., P. Davidsson and W.B. Gartner (2003), 'Arriving at the high-growth firm', *Journal of Business Venturing*, **18**, 189–216.

Dess, G.G., G.T. Lumpkin and J.G. Covin (1997), 'Entrepreneurial strategy making and firm performance: tests of contingency and configurational models', *Strategic Management Journal*, **18**(9), 677–95.

Doty, D.H. and W.H. Glick (1994), 'Typologies as a unique form of theory building: toward improved understanding and modeling', *Academy of Management Review*, **19**(2), 203–51.

Eisenhardt, K.M. (1989), 'Building theories from case study research', *Academy of Management Review*, **14**(4), 532–50.

Fayolle, A. (2007), *Entrepreneurship and New Value Creation: The Dynamic of the Entrepreneurial Process*, Cambridge: Cambridge University Press.

Garnsey, E., E. Stam and P. Hefferman (2006), 'New firm growth: exploring processes and paths', *Industry & Innovation*, **13**(1), 1–20.

Gersick, C.J.N. (1994), 'Pacing strategic change: the case of a new venture', *Academy of Management Journal*, **37**(1), 9–45.

Gilbert, B.A., P.P. McDougall and D.B. Audretsch (2006), 'New venture growth: a review and extension', *Journal of Management*, **32**(6), 926–50.

Gundry, L.K. and H.P. Welsch (2001), 'The ambitious entrepreneur: high growth strategies of women-owned enterprises', *Journal of Business Venturing*, **16**, 453–70.

Hanks, H.H., C.J. Watson, E. Jansen and G.N. Chandler (1993), 'Tightening the life-cycle construct: a taxonomic study of growth stage configurations in high-technology organizations', *Entrepreneurship Theory and Practice*, **17**(2), 5–30.

Hannan, M.T. and J. Freeman (1977), 'The population ecology of organizations', *American Journal of Sociology*, **82**(5), 929–64.

Harms, R., S. Kraus and E. Schwarz (2009), 'The suitability of the configuration approach in entrepreneurship research', *Entrepreneurship & Regional Development*, **21**(1), 25–49.

Heirman, A. and B. Clarysse (2004), 'How and why do research-based start-ups differ at founding? A resource-based configurational perspective', *Journal of Technology Transfer*, **29**(3–4), 247–68.

Heirman, A. and B. Clarysse (2005), 'The imprinting effect of initial resources and market strategy on the early growth path of start-ups', paper presented at the Academy of Management Conference, August, Honolulu, HI.

Hoch, D.J., C.R. Roeding, G. Purkert and S.K. Lindner (2000), *Secrets of Software Success*, Boston, MA: Harvard Business School Press.

Ireland, R.D., M.A. Hitt and D.G. Sirmon (2003), 'A model of strategic entrepreneurship: the construct and its dimensions', *Journal of Management*, **29**(6), 963–89.

Kaye, H. (1998), *Inside the Technical Consulting Business*, 3rd edn, New York: John Wiley.

Kazanjian, R.K. and R. Drazin (1990), 'A stage-contingent model of design and growth for technology based new ventures', *Journal of Business Venturing*, **5**, 137–50.

Ketchen, D.J. Jr, J.B. Thomas and C.C. Snow (1993), 'Organizational configurations and performance: a comparison of theoretical approaches', *Academy of Management Journal*, **36**(6), 1278–313.

Levy, A. (1986), 'Second-order planned change: definition and conceptualization', *Organizational Dynamics*, Summer, pp. 5–20.

Lichtenstein, B.M. and C.G. Brush (2001), 'How do "resource bundles" develop and change in new ventures? A dynamic model and longitudinal exploration', *Entrepreneurship Theory and Practice*, **26**(1), 37–58.

Lumkin, G.T. and G.G. Dess (1996), 'Clarifying the entrepreneurial orientation construct and linking it to performance', *Academy of Management Review*, **21**(1), 135–72.

McHugh, P. (1999), *Making it Big in Software*, Tiverton: Rubic Publishing.

Meyer, A.D., A.S. Tsui and C.R. Hinings (1993), 'Configurational approaches to organizational analysis', *Academy of Management Journal*, **36**(6), 1175–95.

Miles, M.B. and A.M. Huberman (1994), *Qualitative Data Analysis*, 2nd edn, Thousand Oaks, CA: Sage.

Miles, R.E. and C.C. Snow (1978), *Organizational Strategy, Structure, and Process*, New York: McGraw-Hill.

Miller, D. (1981), 'Toward a new contingency approach: the search for organizational gestalts', *Journal of Management Studies*, **18**(1), 1–26.

Miller, D. (1983), 'The correlates of entrepreneurship in three types of firms', *Management Science*, **29**(7), 770–91.

Miller, D. (1986), 'Configuration of strategy & structure: towards a synthesis', *Strategic Management Journal*, **7**(3), 233–49.

Miller, D. (1987), 'The genesis of configuration', *Academy of Management Review*, **12**(4), 686–701.

Miller, D. (1996), 'Configurations revisited', *Strategic Management Journal*, **17**(7), 505–12.

Miller, D. and P.H. Friesen (1984a), 'A longitudinal study of the corporate life cycle', *Management Science*, **30**(10), 1161–78.

Miller, D. and P.H. Friesen (1984b), *Organizations, a Quantum View*, Englewood Cliffs, NJ: Prentice Hall.

Miller, D. and H. Mintzberg (1983), 'The case for configuration' in G. Morgan (ed.), *Beyond Method*, Beverly Hills, CA: Sage Publications, pp. 57–73.

Mintzberg, H. (1978), *Structure et Dynamique des Organisations*, Paris: Editions d'Organisation.

Mintzberg, H. (1983), *Power in and around Organizations*, Englewood Cliffs, NJ: Prentice Hall.

Moore, G.A. (1999), *Crossing the Chasm*, 2nd edn, New York: Capstone.

Nambisan, S. (2001), 'Why service businesses are not product businesses', *MIT Sloan Management Review*, **42**(4), 72–80.

Neergaard, H. (2007), 'Sampling in entrepreneurial settings' in H. Neergaard and J.P. Ulhoi (eds), *Handbook of Qualitative Research Methods in Entrepreneurship*, Cheltenham, UK and Northampton, MA USA: Edward Elgar Publishing, pp. 253–78.

O'Farrell, P.N. and D.M.W.N. Hitchens (1988), 'Alternative theories of small-firm growth: a critical review', *Environment and Planning A*, **20**, 1365–83.

Patton, M.Q. (2002), *Qualitative Research and Evaluation Methods*, 3rd edn, Newbury Park, CA: Sage.

Porter, M.E. (1985), *Competitive Advantage*, New York: Free Press.

Roberts, M.J. (2003), 'Managing the growing venture', Boston, MA: Harvard Business School.

Rosen, D.E., J.E. Schroeder and F.F. Purinton (1998), 'Marketing high tech products: lessons in customer focus from the marketplace', *Academy of Marketing Science Review*, **6**, A1–A19.

Sahlman, W.A. (1996), 'Some thoughts on business plans', *The Entrepreneurial Venture*, Boston, MA: Harvard Business School Press.

Snow, C.C., R.E. Miles and G. Miles (2005), 'A configurational approach to the integration of strategy and organization research', *Strategic Organization*, **3**(4), 431–9.

Timmons, J.A. (1999), *New Venture Creation*, 5th edn, Boston, MA: Irwin McGraw-Hill.

Van de Ven, A.H. and R.M. Engleman (2004), 'Event- and outcome-driven explanations of entrepreneurship', *Journal of Business Venturing*, **19**, 343–58.

Van de Ven, A.H. and M.S. Poole (1995), 'Explaining development and change in organizations', *Academy of Management Review*, **20**(3), 510–40.

Venkatraman, N. (1989), 'The concept of fit in strategy research: toward verbal and statistical correspondence', *Academy of Management Review*, **14**(3), 423–44.

Vohora, A., M. Wright and A. Lockett (2004), 'Critical junctures in the development of university high-tech spinout companies', *Research Policy*, **33**, 147–75.

Whetten, D.A. (1989), 'What constitutes a theorethical contribution?', *Academy of Management Review*, **14**(4), 490–95.

Wiklund, J. and D. Shepherd (2005), 'Entrepreneurial orientation and small business performance: a configurational approach', *Journal of Business Venturing*, **20**, 71–91.

Witmeur, O. (2007), 'Growth strategies of entrepreneurial ventures: toward a process and configuration based modeling', paper presented at RENT XXI Conference, Cardiff, UK.

Yin, R.K. (2003), *Case Study Research*, 3rd edn, Thousand Oaks, CA: Sage.

Zahra, S.A. and W.C. Bogner (1999), 'Technology strategy and software new ventures' performance: exploring the moderating effect of the competitive environment', *Journal of Business Venturing*, **15**, 135–73.

Zahra, S.A., H.J. Sapienza and P. Davidsson (2006), 'Entrepreneurship and dynamic capabilities: a review, model and research agenda', *Journal of Management Studies*, **43**(4), 917–55.

Zammuto, R.F. (1988), 'Organizational adaptation: some implications of organizational ecology for strategic choice', *Journal of Management Studies*, **25**(2), 105–20.

4. Understanding the start-up funding process in venture capital-backed and non-venture capital-backed firms

Teresa Hogan and Elaine Hutson

INTRODUCTION

The lack of a well-developed venture capital market has long been viewed as a major barrier to the emergence and development of New Technology-Based Firms (NTBFs) in Europe (European Commission, 1995, 1999, 2001 and ENSR, 2002). The last decade has seen a dramatic increase in venture capital investment in Europe, and in 2005 total fund activity exceeded that of the US for the first time (Oehler et al., 2007). Ireland's venture capital market also expanded rapidly during this period. Over €2 billion was invested between 2000 and 2005, of which €1.2 billion came from local investors (IVCA, 2006). The main beneficiary has been the indigenous information technology (IT) industry, and in particular the software sector, which until recently has had little competition for funds from emerging technology sectors such as healthcare and biotechnology. Even today the investment portfolios of Irish venture capitalists are dominated by IT companies, which attracted 60 per cent of their total investment funds in 2005 (IVCA, 2006). The Irish software sector therefore provides an excellent laboratory for examining the financing of NTBFs.

Despite the expansion of venture capital in recent years, policy-makers remain concerned about the supply of funds to NTBFs (Murray and Dimov, 2007). In Ireland, for example, a major review of enterprise policy at the height of the economic boom concluded that: 'While the financial environment for enterprise has improved considerably over the past decade, there are still market failures in the provision of services to SMEs and in the availability of risk capital for start-up companies' (Enterprise Strategy Group, 2004, p. 15).

The continued concern over funding in part reflects the lack of research on the financing of NTBFs. Most studies of NTBF financing provide a description of financing patterns at different stages in the firm's lifecycle (Roberts, 1991; Moore, 1994). Few studies have tested the relation between the formation patterns of NTBFs and their funding choices. Gartner and Carter (2004) argue that the key to understanding the start-up process lies in explaining how some of these key events are connected. This chapter addresses this gap by examining how key events in the NTBF formation process are linked to their funding. It draws on stage model theory, which has long been the dominant framework for the analysis of the formation and development of NTBFs and of their financing. It also draws on event history analysis which was used to examine the start-up process by Reynolds and Miller (1992) and later by the Consortium (Gartner et al., 2004) in the Panel Study of Entrepreneurial Dynamics (PSED).

Unlike other technology sectors such as electronics and biotechnology, product lead times in software development are relatively short. In addition, software development companies can opt for a 'soft start' strategy (Bullock, 1983; Segal, Quince and Partners, 1985 and Roberts, 1991) by engaging in consulting activities and evolving (or 'hardening') over time to become product companies. Together these characteristics of software development suggest that software entrepreneurs may be less dependent on external sources of funding, in particular venture capital, at start-up than their counterparts in other high technology sectors. We find no significant difference in product lead times between venture capital and non-venture capital-backed software development firms. However, we find that venture capital-backed firms are more likely to access external funding prior to completion of product development when compared with their non-venture capital-backed counterparts. We also find that venture capital-backed firms are more dependent on external financing to fund prototype development, whilst non-venture capital-backed firms engage in consulting activities significantly earlier than their venture capital-backed counterparts and are less dependent on external resources to fund prototype development. The pattern of formation in the non-venture capital-backed cohort is consistent with Bullock's (1983) 'soft start' strategy, indicating that revenues from consulting activities provide an alternative to external funding in this sector.

The remainder of the chapter is structured as follows. The next section highlights the importance of the software sector as a source of NTBFs in Europe. This is followed by an overview of the literature on NTBFs. It links literature on NTBF financing and the formation process of NTBFs to develop testable hypotheses on the start-up funding of venture capital-backed and non-venture capital-backed software product start-ups. In the next section, the survey methodology is discussed and summary characteristics of the sample are presented. The findings are discussed in the next section and the final section summarizes and concludes.

THE IMPORTANCE OF NTBFS IN THE SOFTWARE SECTOR

Software is the dynamo of the Information Communication Technology (ICT) sector as it provides the code that enables hardware products to function. Because of low barriers to entry in the software sector, it has provided the greatest opportunity for NTBF formation. Many European countries have witnessed the emergence of software clusters over the past three decades. Table 4.1 summarizes the enterprise and employment data for European high technology sectors.

Table 4.1   *Employment in high-technology manufacturing and services sectors in the Europe-19 (2000)*

	Enterprises (1000s)			Employment (1000s)		
	SMEs	LSEs	Total	SMEs	LSEs	Total
Panel A: Manufacturing Sector						
Pharmaceuticals, chemical products and man-made fibres	32	1	33	507	1319	1826
Machinery and equipment	144	2	146	1597	1421	3018
Office machinery and computers	13	0	13	75	138	213
Electrical machinery	53	1	54	555	920	1474
Radio, television and communication equipment	26	0	26	233	596	829
Medical, precision and optical instruments	86	1	87	576	378	955
Total manufacturing	**354**	**5**	**359**	**3543**	**4772**	**8315**
Panel B: Services Sector						
Computer and related activities	342	1	343	1234	364	1598
Research and development	50	1	51	208	343	551
Total Services	**392**	**2**	**394**	**1442**	**707**	**2149**
Total	**746**	**7**	**753**	**4985**	**5480**	**10465**

Source: Derived from ENSR (2002, p. 20).

*Table 4.2   Firm size and turnover in multinational companies (MNCs)
            and indigenous software companies (2000)*

	Firms	Employment	Average firm size	Sales (000s)
Irish	760	14 000	18	€1 400 000
MNCs	140	16 000	114	€8 750 000
Total	900	30 000	33	€10 150 000

Source: Derived from National Software Directorate (2001).

Forty-six per cent (342 000) of Europe's high-tech small and medium-sized enterprises (SMEs) belong to the computer and related services sector. The next highest concentration of SMEs is found in the machinery and equipment sector, which accounts for 14 per cent (144 000) of high-tech SMEs. In contrast, there are only 32 000 SMEs (4 per cent of the total) engaged in the manufacture of pharmaceuticals and chemical. Employing 1.2 million people (25 per cent), the computer and computer-related services sector is the second most important employer in the high-tech SME sector after machinery and equipment manufacturing, which employs 1.5 million people.

The Software Industry in Ireland

Ireland emerged as the location of choice for the global software industry from the mid-1990s onwards. In 2000 Ireland and the United States accounted for more than 55 per cent of OECD exports of software (OECD, 2003). According to HotOrigin (2002), the software sector accounted for 9.9 per cent of Irish GDP and 10.3 per cent of exports. The software industry in Ireland is dominated by the subsidiaries of multinational companies (MNCs). Table 4.2 shows the relative contributions of the indigenous firms and MNCs to employment and output in Ireland in 2000.

Of the sector's €10 billion in sales, €8.75 billion (86 per cent) is attributed to MNCs. There is less disparity in the relative contribution of MNCs and indigenous firms to employment within the sector. Of the 30 000 people working in the sector, 14 000 (47 per cent) were employed by indigenous firms. To put these figures in context, employment in the sector accounts for 2 per cent of the total workforce. These figures are not directly comparable with those in Table 4.1 (which include a very broad range of activities) but indicate that Ireland accounts for a very small proportion of software SMEs in the EU, representing less than 0.2 per cent of the total.

Indigenous firms are on average much smaller than their MNC

counterparts. In 2000 there were 900 firms in the Irish software sector of which 140 (16 per cent) were MNCs. MNCs had an average of 114 employees. The average for indigenous firms was 18 employees. This chapter is concerned with independent software product SMEs in the indigenous sector that would face very different financial challenges to the subsidiaries of MNCs based in Ireland.

FINANCING THE START-UP STAGE OF NTBFS

The stage model has provided the dominant paradigm in the analysis of business formation and development (Kazanjian, 1988; Kazanjian and Drazin, 1990 and Autio, 2000). The model is also dominant in the analysis of the financial development of NTBFs (Bank of England, 2001). The model holds that stages in the firm's development are paralleled by changes in its financial structure and access to finance (Roberts, 1991). Roberts (1991) identified four stages in the financial lifecycle of NTBFs: *seed*, *start-up*, *early growth* and *sustained growth*. The *seed* stage is characterized by an intensive period of research and development which is usually funded by the founders' own funds. The seed stage is followed by prototype development and testing at *start-up*, and it is this stage that is the focus of this chapter. The development of an early customer base is critical to the success of the start-up stage. During start-up the organization usually becomes more structured, and one or more of the founders will be engaged full-time in the business. It is likely that the founders' personal funds will be exhausted during this stage, and they must look elsewhere for further funding.

The NTBF represents a high risk to commercial lenders because its products are often untried or even unknown, and debtholders experience considerable difficulty in assessing product potential and founders' capabilities (Bank of England, 1996; 2001). In contrast to the standard new firm which will already be accumulating both reputational and business assets – making it easier for them to negotiate bank finance – the NTBF is usually still involved in product development and in seeking out early or reference customers. The NTBF will therefore differ from the general population of start-up firms in their financial requirements and access to finance. Further, retained profits and trade credit are less likely to feature as a source of finance at this stage for the NTBF, given its limited trading status.

An assumption in Roberts' (1991) model is that NTBFs face greater problems in debt markets than small firms generally. However, there is scant empirical evidence on the sources of financing used by NTBFs. Most

Table 4.3   Sources of funding employed by new technology-based firms at start-up in the UK and US (percentage of total)

Source of funding	UK	US
Owners' funds (including friends and family)	58	79
External sources:		
Bank loans	7	0
Venture capital	10	5
Private investors	0	7
Government grants	9	0
Strategic partners or non-financial corporations	6	6
Public stock issues	0	3
University endowments	6	0

Note: This table summarizes the findings on sources of finance at start-up for NTBFs in the US and the UK. The findings for the UK are drawn from Moore (1994), which is a study of financing in 42 high-tech products and services start-ups during 1992. The findings for the US come from Roberts (1991), which is a summary of various studies of engineering, medical and computing start-ups, conducted in the US during the 1960s, 1970s and 1980s.

studies list the sources of funds employed at start-up, but few provide information on the proportion of funding derived from each source. Table 4.3 reports the sources of funding employed by NTBFs in the UK (Moore, 1994) and the US (Roberts, 1991). It should be noted that the studies summarized in Table 4.3 were undertaken in different decades, and that the types of NTBFs surveyed vary substantially. Nonetheless, the table confirms that, as for all new firms, the founders' savings and those of family and friends are the most important source of finance employed by NTBFs at start-up. Relative to internal sources of funds, external sources play a minor role in NTBFs at start-up. Roberts (1991) reports that: 'initial capital is supplied most frequently by entrepreneurs themselves from their own savings, second by their family and friends, and third by private investors, all these being sources of capital outside of the normal channels' (Roberts, 1991, p. 141).

In the UK, venture capital, bank loans and government grants appear to be the most common outside sources of finance, while in the US, strategic partners and other private equity sources supplement funding from venture capitalists. The US study shows that commercial bank finance does not feature as a funding source in NTBFs at start-up. For the UK, Moore (1994) reports that NTBFs raised only 7 per cent of initial funding from banks, compared with 24 per cent for SMEs in general. Consistent with the predictions of stage theory as applied to NTBFs, the evidence suggests that they face greater problems in debt markets than their counterparts in other sectors at start-up.

External equity in the form of venture capital or private equity is a more important source of finance than bank loans in both the UK and the US. Venture capitalists provide 10 per cent of funding to NTBFs in the UK and 5 per cent to firms in the US. It must be noted that these two countries have well-developed venture capital markets. The venture capital industry remains underdeveloped in many countries, and as such many NTBFs around the world are unlikely to have access to venture capital at start-up. In Italy, for example, Giudici and Paleari (2000) found that only one of the 46 firms in their study raised venture capital in the early development phase, and only three firms subsequently obtained venture capital.

If private equity or venture capital is unavailable, the NTBF is likely to face serious financing constraints. Undercapitalization at start-up has been linked to poor growth performance (Roberts, 1991 and Moore, 1994). In a study examining the relation between funding and growth, Lumme et al. (1994) found that NTBFs in Cambridge (UK) grew more rapidly than their counterparts in Finland. The authors suggest that the variation in performance is related to differences in financial structure, including the quantity and composition of initial capital (defined as share capital and loans employed at start-up). The Cambridge firms started with a higher proportion of share capital and smaller levels of debt than their Finnish counterparts. Debt-funded growth, argue Lumme et al. (1994), puts the firm under more pressure than equity-funded growth because the scarce resources of the highly leveraged firm are required to finance loan and interest repayments. The authors conclude that: 'greater availability of private capital in the form of venture capital, corporate venturing funds and private investors and organisations partially explains the healthier initial capital structure and the more rapid growth of Cambridge firms' (Lumme et al., 1994, p. 91).

A fundamental criticism of the stage model is that it treats NTBFs as a homogeneous group (O'Farrell and Hitchens, 1987 and Gibb and Davies, 1991). However, not all NTBFs are the same. Product lead times vary significantly across NTBF subsectors, so the financing requirements of NTBFs differ considerably between subsectors (Bullock, 1983; Oakey, 1984, 1991 and 1995; Roberts, 1991; Moore, 1994; Bank of England, 1996 and 2001; and Hine and Kapeleris, 2007). In the software sector, product lead times are generally shorter than in other high technology sectors, and capital requirements are relatively low (Oakey, 1995; Roberts, 1991 and Hine and Kapeleris, 2007). Software development firms may therefore differ from other NTBFs, in so far as they may be able to finance the start-up process purely from internal sources. Myers (2001) points out that theories of capital structure are 'not designed to be general' and that testing them on heterogeneous samples of firms can be uninformative. We avoid the issue of heterogeneity by restricting our sample to software product firms. In the next section we draw on studies of the start-up patterns of NTBFs in the software sector in order to develop hypotheses relating to their funding.

The Impact of the Formation Process on Funding of Software Product Firms

A number of studies have looked at the formation process of NTBFs (Bullock, 1983; Segal, Quince and Partners 1985; Roberts, 1991; Tiler et al., 1993; and Clarysse et al., 2003). Bullock (1983) developed the 'soft versus hard' company start-up model to explain the formation process in NTBFs in the MIT and Stanford regions of the US. The key concept is that NTBFs face a spectrum of risks from both a financial and technological perspective. The founders can adopt a low-risk entry strategy by starting out as 'soft-start' consultancy-based service companies and over a period of time evolve or 'harden' to become product companies. 'Start-up' can occur anywhere along the development path, even as fully 'hardened' product companies, as in the case of the industry spin-out. According to Bullock, industrial spin-outs from larger companies are usually set up by teams of scientists and managers who have worked together, and most of their product development work will be completed at the time of start-up. Bullock noted that the 'soft start' became increasingly feasible in software, as low-cost computing had greatly extended the range and complexity of consultancy services that new firms in the sector could offer. This has continued to be the case in software, where increasingly the boundary between product and service companies is becoming blurred.

The 'soft start' entry strategy facilitates a very different financial life cycle than that experienced by the typical NTBF. 'Soft start' firms are more likely to rely on internal funds through the start-up and early growth phases, and they are less likely to face difficulties in debt markets as they are generating regular cash flows to cover potential loan commitments. Interestingly, according to Bullock (1983) these owner-managers prefer to on-sell their businesses rather than achieve substantial growth through stock market quotation. The concept of the 'soft start' has been validated in a number of studies (Roberts, 1991; Segal, Quince and Partners, 1985; Moore, 1994; Tiler et al., 1993; Bank of England, 1996; Clarysse et al., 2003). Tiler et al. (1993) adapt the classification to identify three separate start-up strategies in NTBFs: (1) *soft start*, where the firm is established without external capital; (2) *hard start,* where the firm starts with external financing, typically in the form of venture capital; and (3) *transitional start*, where the firms adopts a 'soft start' entry strategy with the intention of 'hardening' subsequently.

Clarysse et al. (2003) also draw on Bullock's classification to identify three types of business model adopted by research-based spin-offs in their analysis of the start-up process in European life sciences and IT industries. 'Technological SMEs are lifestyle companies set up with minimum capital and are "R&D boutiques" or "technical consulting" companies primarily targeting the local market' (Clarysse et al., 2003, p.110). Prospectors adopt a 'soft start' entry strategy, starting out as a consulting organization with the specific intention of becoming a product company. The venture capital-backed firm is a product-focused company that starts with a well-balanced team and substantial capital. Such firms are very rare in Europe but are the genesis of global NTBFs, according to the authors.

As already noted, product lead times differ substantially across NTBF subsectors, and this affects their funding requirements. Firms in the bio-technology sector, for example, are likely to face longer product lead times and take longer to reach break-even point than their counterparts in the electronic and software sectors (Oakey, 1995). The biotechnology start-up is therefore less likely than other NTBFs to be 100 per cent funded by its founders, or if it is fully funded by internal sources initially, to remain internally funded for very long. Despite the short product lead times in software development, the 'soft versus hard' model, as extended by Tiler et al. (1993), suggests that venture capital-backed firms are more likely to be product-focused from start-up compared to non-venture capital-backed firms. Given the relatively low start-up costs in the software sector, non-venture capital-backed firms should be capable of completing prototype development without access to external funding. In contrast, the model suggests that venture capital-backed firms will be more product-focused from the outset and therefore will require funding to complete prototype development. This gives rise to our first testable hypothesis:

Hypothesis 1:   At start-up, non-venture capital-backed firms are more likely than venture capital backed firms to complete prototype development without using external finance.

If non-venture capital-backed firms tend to self-fund prototype development, it follows that they will receive their first product revenues before sourcing external funds. This gives rise to Hypothesis 2:

Hypothesis 2:   Non-venture capital-backed start-ups are more likely to generate product revenues without sourcing external finance than venture capital-backed firms.

The Role of Consulting in Financing the Formation Process

The evidence from studies of the formation process of software NTBFs (Bullock, 1983; Segal, Quince and Partners, 1985; Roberts, 1991; Bhide, 1992; Clarysse et al., 2003) indicates that the 'soft start' business model is an important funding strategy for software entrepreneurs. Using consulting revenues to fund new business development is a well-established 'bootstrapping' practice, but rarely features in empirical studies of financing of SMEs, which tend to focus on formal sources such as savings, trade credit, banks loans, grants and equity. Bootstrapping refers to the founding of new ventures with modest personal funds (Bhide, 1992) or minimizing the amount of external funding required from banks and investors (Freear et al., 1995; Harrison and Mason 1997; Winborg and Landström 1997 and 2001; Harrison et al. 2004 and Ebben and Johnson 2006). Ebben and Johnson (2006) see bootstrapping as a business strategy that reduces overall capital requirements, improves cash flow and takes advantage of personal sources of finance. Bootstrapping has received scant regard in the literature until recently (Winborg and Landström 2001; Harrison et al. 2004 and Ebben and Johnson 2006).

Consultancy emerges as an important source of bootstrapping in studies of software start-ups. Two studies have looked at the role of bootstrapping and business alliances in the software sector: Freear et al. (1995) and Harrison et al. (2004). The study by Harrison et al. (2004) is an extension of the early study of software firms in Massachusetts to two regions of UK. These studies examined the role of bootstrapping for product development and business development. In total, 12 different methods of bootstrapping were identified for product development and 19 for business development. They limited the definition of consulting activities for bootstrapping to where firms turned consulting projects into commercial products. Turning consulting projects into commercial products was ranked in the top five most important bootstrapping techniques for product development in all three regions, with the exception of larger firms in Northern Ireland.

The evidence from studies of the formation process of software firms (Bullock, 1983; Segal, Quince and Partners, 1985; Roberts, 1991; Bhide, 1992 and Clarysse et al., 2003) and studies of bootstrapping methods for product development in software firms attest to the prevalence of consulting as a funding method in the sector. Consulting has two key functions as a bootstrapping strategy for product development in software product firms: it can provide valuable funds to sponsor product development, and it can be used as a source of new products when consulting projects are transformed into products.

The founders of 'soft' start-ups choose a low-risk, service-orientated start-up entry strategy and 'harden' over time to become product-orientated ventures. This soft start strategy is consistent with a self-funding strategy as it enables the founders to fund product development without accessing external finance. This suggests that non-venture capital-backed firms are more likely to adopt a soft start strategy to fund proto-type product development. We investigate whether or not non-venture capital-backed firms are more likely to have consulting revenues prior to completing prototype development than their venture capital-backed counterparts.

Hypothesis 3:   Non-venture capital-backed firms are more likely to be soft-starts than venture capital-backed firms, and engage in consulting activities prior to producing their first prototype.

METHODOLOGY AND SAMPLE CHARACTERISTICS

NTBFs are a sub-class of high technology firms. Little (1977) used the concept to distinguish between larger, well-established and smaller, newly-established high technology firms. More precisely it includes independent firms, less than 25 years old, set up to exploit an invention or technologi-cal innovation. The software sector incorporates a wide variety of activi-ties, but the most common distinction is made between software service companies and product development companies. Software development firms are primarily involved in the development and commercialization of their own products as opposed to resellers, subcontracting or services firms. Clearly the financing requirements of a company engaged in its own product development activities will be very different to that of a service-based company.

Using various sources (National Software Directory, Software Association of Ireland, lists of occupants of innovation parks, lists of participants in a national technology entrepreneurship award programme, and firms cited in specialist journals), a database of all software product firms in Ireland was compiled for this study. We identified almost 300 indigenous product software companies and 500 services companies in Ireland at the beginning of 2002, consistent with numbers identified by National Software Directorate (see Table 4.2) and a government-funded survey of the industry by private equity company HotOrigin (2001), which recorded a total of 250 product companies for 2000. Of the 298 product companies identified, seven were publicly limited companies, 19 had ceased trading and 15 had been sold, leaving 257 independent software product firms which were included in the survey. Therefore the survey is based on the entire population of independent software product firms in Ireland at the beginning of 2002.

The survey design was based on self-administered questionnaires using the tailored design method (Dillman, 1976 and 2000). The survey was administered by mail and addressed to CEOs by name. Respondents were given the choice of completing either a paper or web-based questionnaire. The number of valid returns was 117 out of a population of 257, giving a response rate of just under 46 per cent. Of the 117 firms that responded, 110 provided information on the timing and sequencing of key events in the formation process. The number of venture capital-backed and non-venture capital-backed firms in the study is similar: 56 of the 110 firms (51 per cent) for which survey data is available had not received venture capital backing and 54 (49 per cent) were funded by venture capitalists. This distribution reflects the dominance of venture capital as a source of funding for the software sector in Ireland. It is consistent with prior research for the sector, which found that only 44 per cent of software start-ups and 25 per cent of developing firms had *not* received external finance in the form of venture capital and private equity (HotOrigin, 2002).

The survey instrument asked founders to identify the month and year in which the following key events occurred: firm formation, development of first prototype, recruitment of the first employee(s), receipt of the first revenues from consulting activities and product sales, and receipt of first tranche of external funding from either banks, government, private investors or venture capitalists.

Table 4.4 summarizes the age and size distribution of the sample firms. Panel A shows that the youngest firm is less than one year old, and the oldest is 27 years. Two firms are more than 25 years old, and thus they fall beyond Little's (1977) age criterion. However as they fulfilled all of Little's other criteria, we include them. Overall, young firms are well represented in the sample. The average age is less than six years and the median is four years. The venture capital-backed firms are younger than the non-venture capital-backed; the mean age of the former was 4.8 years (median 3.5 years) at the time of the survey, and the latter group were on average 6.7 years old (median 5 years). The age structure of the venture capital backed firms most likely reflects the growth of the venture capital industry in Ireland in the late 1990s and the increased channelling of funds to start-ups through government schemes.

The table also reports data on firm size. Two measures of size are provided: employment (Panel B) and turnover (Panel C). Panel B shows

Table 4.4 Age and size distribution for venture capital and non-venture capital-backed firms

Panel A: Age (years)	Venture capital-backed (n = 54)	Non-venture capital-backed (n = 56)	Total (n = 110)
Mean	4.8	6.7	5.8
Median	3.5	5.0	4.0
Min	1.0	0.0	0.0
Max	19.0	27.0	27.0

Panel B: Size (employment)	Venture capital-backed (n = 54)	Non-venture capital-backed (n = 56)	Total (n = 110)
Total	1755.0	854.0	2609.0
Mean	32.5	15.8	24.1
Median	20.5	8.5	13.5
Min	0.0	0.0	0.0
Max	200.0	140.0	200.0

Panel C: Size (turnover)	Venture capital-backed		Non-venture capital-backed		Total	
	Number	%	Number	%	Number	%
Pre-revenue	12	23.1	9	16.1	21	19.4
<€127 000	1	1.9	12	21.4	13	12.0
€127 000–€634 999	15	28.8	11	19.7	26	24.1
€635 000–€1 269 999	7	13.5	10	17.9	17	15.7
€1 270 000–€3 809 999	11	21.2	11	19.6	22	20.4
€3 810 000 +	6	11.5	3	5.4	9	8.3
Total	52		56		108	

Note: Turnover figures were requested in Irish punts, as euro notes and coins were not introduced until 2002, but we report our findings in euros only.

employment data for 108 firms that provided information for 2002. Total employment in the full sample is 2609, or an average of 26 employees per firm (median 12.5). The venture capital-backed firms employ over twice as many people as the non-venture capital-backed firms; the former employ a total of 1755 people, giving an average of 32.5 employees per firm, and the latter a total of 854 people, giving an average of 16 employees per firm.

Turnover figures for 2001 are presented in Panel C of Table 4.4. Most respondent firms are relatively small when size is measured by sales. Almost one-third had a turnover of less than €127000, and 55.5 per cent had a turnover of less than €635000. Twenty-nine per cent of firms had a turnover in excess of €1270000, and only 8 per cent had a turnover above €3810000. There is little difference between the two groups except that the venture capital-backed firms have a higher proportion of firms recording both no turnover and turnover exceeding €3810000.

RESULTS

Table 4.5 reports the timing of the key events in the start-up process of software product firms. The mean and median number of months from start-up to the attainment of each milestone appears in columns [1] and [2] respectively. All of the means exceed the medians, indicating right-skewness in the data, therefore the discussion of the summary statistics will concentrate on medians rather than means, and the statistical testing will be non-parametric. Panel A presents the average figures for the sample overall, Panel B provides a breakdown for the non-venture capital-backed firms, and Panel C provides details for the venture capital-backed firms. The time periods are calculated from the month of formation. Some firms reported not having attained particular milestones, and this information is recorded in column [6]. All but four firms for which data are available had recruited their first employee, and 22 firms (20.5 per cent) had not acquired funding from any external source including banks, government agencies, private investors or venture capitalists.

The median time to development of first prototype for the overall sample was 12 months. This is consistent with estimates provided in prior research which suggest that product lead times in this sector are between six and twelve months (Oakey, 1995; Hine and Kapeleris, 2007). The first tranche of external funding was secured just a half month after the development of first prototype – a median of 12.5 months after start-up. First product revenues were earned a median of two months after prototype development, in month 14. Receipt of consulting revenues in month 3

Table 4.5 Timing of key events in the start-up stage in venture capital and non-venture capital-backed firms (monthly analysis)

Panel A: Overall Sample 109	[1] Mean	[2] Median	[3] Min.	[4] Max.	[5] Total attaining milestone	[6] Milestone not (yet) attained	[7] Missing
Time to first:							
a. Prototype	17	**12**	0	88	**102**	6	1
b. Employee	8	**4**	0	135	**104**	4	1
c. Consulting revenue	6.5	**3**	0	33	**85**	22	2
d. Product revenues	19	**14**	0	91	**91**	17	1
e. External funding	20	**12.5**	0	156	**84**	22	3
Panel B: Non-VC-backed = 55							
a. Prototype	16	**10**	0	88	**49**	5	1
b. Employee	11	**2**	0	135	**51**	3	1
c. Consulting revenue	4.5	**2**	0	27	**44**	10	1
d. Product revenues	18.5	**12**	0	91	**46**	8	1
e. External funding*	24	**14.5**	0	156	**32**	22	1
Panel C: VC-backed = 54							
a. Prototype	18	**12**	0	79	**53**	1	
b. Employee	6	**4**	0	28	**53**	1	
c. Consulting revenue	8.5	**6**	0	33	**41**	12	1
d. Product revenues	19	**14**	1	78	**45**	9	0
e. External funding	18	**11.5**	0	112	**52**	0	2
Panel D : T-Test							
a. Prototype	.525						
b. Employee	.153						
c. Consulting revenue	.013						
d. Product revenues	.944						
e. External funding	.334*						

Notes: Column [6], 'milestone not yet attained': firms were asked to tick a 'not applicable' box if their business had not yet reached the particular milestone.
* 22 non-VC backed firms had no external funding and are not included in this test.

marks the first transaction for the newly formed firm, and occurred one month before first hire.

The segmentation of the sample reveals important similarities and differences in the timing of these events between venture capital-backed and non-venture capital-backed firms. First, the median time to initial prototype for non-venture capital-backed firms was 10 months, and it was 12 months for the venture capital-backed firms. The t-test (p = .55) shows that the timing of prototype development does not distinguish between the two cohorts. This is an important finding in that it indicates that venture capital-backed firms do not take significantly longer to produce their prototypes than non-venture capital-backed firms in this particular sector. As already noted, product lead times are shorter in software development than in other high-tech sectors and therefore would appear to have less impact on financing requirements.

Second, the non-venture capital-backed firms earned their first revenues from consulting activities a median of four and a half months after start-up, compared to a median of eight and a half months for the venture capital-backed subgroup. The difference in the timing of consulting revenues between the groups is significant (p = .01).

Third, the venture capital-backed firms took longer to reach all milestones, with the exception of external funding. It took the venture capital-backed firms a median of 11.5 months to secure external funding, compared to a median of 14.5 months for their non-venture capital-backed counterparts. Although the t-test result (p = .334) indicates that the difference in the timing of first funding is not significant, this is misleading as 22 non-venture capital-backed firms claimed not to have secured any external funding at the time of the survey, and are therefore not included. In effect, these firms were entirely self-funded. These 22 firms were an average 76 months old at the time of the survey, which would bring up the average time to first funding significantly if they were to be included. It is clear that the timing of external funding also marks an important difference between the two subgroups, and this will become more evident when we look at the sequences of events in the next section. Together, these results suggest that as prototype development is short in software development, firms have some financial flexibility in so far as they can delay or even eschew, as in the case of 22 firms, the process of fundraising from external resources, by using revenues generated internally from consulting activities.

Hypothesis 1:   Prototype development before receipt of first external financing

There are also differences in the sequencing of events across the two cohorts. The data suggests that non-venture capital-backed firms fund prototype development using internal funds only, as first funding arrives for this cohort a median of two months after completion of first prototype.

Table 4.6 shows the sequencing of first prototype and first external funding for the whole group as well as for the venture capital and non-venture capital-backed firms. Row A of Table 4.6 shows the number of

Table 4.6   The sequencing of first prototype and first external funding

	Full sample N = 109		VC-backed N = 54		Non-VC-backed N = 55	
	No.	%	No.	%	No.	%
Panel A						
A. Prototype and external funding concurrently	4	3.8	2	4.0	2	3.7
B. Prototype before funding or without funding	56	53.8	20	40.0	36	66.7
C. Funding before prototype or without prototype	41	39.4	28	56.0	13	24.1
D. No prototype and no external funding	3	2.9	0.0	0.0	3	5.5
Total	**104**	**100**	**50**	**100**	**54**	**100**
Missing/insufficient data	5		4		1	

Panel B
Independent Sample Test
Mann–Whitney U
z = −3.154
p = .002

firms that produced their first prototype and received their first tranche of external funding in the same month. Row B shows the number of firms that either had produced a prototype before attracting funding or had not secured external funding at the time the study was undertaken (see column [6] of Table 4.5). Therefore, these firms being self-funded, as already noted, produced their prototypes before attracting external funding. Similarly, row C shows the number of companies that had secured funding before developing their first prototype or that had not developed their first prototype at the time the study was completed. There was insufficient data available to determine the sequencing of the two specified events in three cases, and information was not provided by two firms.

The table confirms the findings from Table 4.5. Fifty-six of the 104 firms for which we have data (53.8 per cent) developed their first proto-type prior to attracting any external funding. This pattern is much more evident in the non-venture capital-backed firms, where 36 out of 54 firms (66.7 per cent) had developed their first prototype prior to attracting external funding. The corresponding figure for the venture capital-backed firms was 20 (40 per cent). The test statistics for the sequencing of the key events are presented in Panel B of Table 4.6. In order to maximize the number of observations, the data was transferred from continuous to categorical, otherwise the 22 non-venture capital-backed firms that had no external funding of any kind would have to be excluded. Thus firms that had developed their first product beta before receiving external funding, or were yet to receive external funding, are combined as category 1 (Row B), and those that had accessed funding before product beta or had yet to produce their first beta are denoted category 0. The independent samples test confirms that difference in the sequencing of the two events across venture capital-backed and non-venture capital-backed firms is significant (p = .02).

The results indicate that non-venture capital-backed firms adopt a self-funding strategy for prototype development. The venture capital-backed firms appear to be more focused on attracting external financing from start-up, and it is the only milestone they achieve before their non-venture capital-backed counterparts. These findings are strongly supportive of Hypothesis 1, that non-venture capital-backed firms are more likely than venture capital-backed firms to complete prototype development without using external finance.

These findings are consistent with patterns of funding identified in growth configuration studies. Self-funding firms have been categorized in the NTBF growth configuration literature as 'soft starts' by Tiler et al. (1993), and 'technological SMEs' or 'R&D boutiques' by Clarysse et al. (2003). Firms that are highly product focused and dependent on external funds from their genesis are described as 'hard starts' (Tiler et al., 1993) or 'venture capital backed' (Clarysse et al., 2003). Many of the venture capital-backed firms in this study appear to be more focused on attracting external financing from foundation, and are more likely to access external funds in order to finance prototype development than their non-venture capital-backed counterparts. The remaining firms in the sample belong to an intermediate group – known as 'transitional starts' (Tiler et al., 1993) or 'prospectors' (Clarysse et al., 2003) – that access external funding after completing prototype development. These include 16 non-venture capital-backed firms (36 in total: 20 with no funding plus 16 receiving funding after prototype) and 20 venture capital-backed firms (see row B in Table 4.6).

Hypothesis 2:   Product revenues before receipt of first external
                    financing

Hypothesis 2 follows on from Hypothesis 1 in predicting that since non-venture capital-backed firms are more likely to produce their prototypes without accessing any kind of external funding, they are also more likely

Table 4.7   *Test statistics for differences in the median time to attainment of key events in the formation process in venture capital and non-venture capital-backed firms*

	Median months apart			Independent sample test Mann–Whitney U	
	Overall sample	VC-backed	Non VC-backed	z	p
H2: Prototype before product revenues	−1.5	−2.5	2.5	−3.658	.000
H3: Consulting revenue before prototype	9	6.0	8.0	−1.119	.263

to receive their first product revenues before obtaining external finance. Table 4.5 revealed that there was little difference in the timing of first revenues from products across the two groups (p = .944). However, when we examine the sequencing of product revenues and external funding we see a clear pattern emerging. The non-venture capital cohort received their first revenues from product sales a median of two and a half months before they received their first external funds, whilst the venture capital-backed firms received their first product revenues a median of two and a half months after attracting funding (see Table 4.7).

The results of the Mann–Whitney test are highly significant (p = .00), supporting Hypothesis 2, which predicted that non-venture capital-backed start-ups are more likely to generate product revenues without sourcing external finance than venture capital-backed firms. Again, this finding is consistent with a self-funding strategy whereby companies seek to minimize the use of external sources of finance at start-up.

Hypothesis 3:   Consulting revenues before completion of prototype development

Thus far it has been established that non-venture capital-backed firms earn revenues from consulting activity earlier in their development, but do not have significantly longer product lead times, when compared with venture capital-backed software product firms. Hypothesis 3 looks at the sequencing of prototype development and consulting revenues in the two subgroups. The venture capital-backed firms produced their first prototypes a median of six months after receiving their first consulting revenues in month 6, and the non-venture capital-backed produced theirs a median of eight months after receiving their first consulting revenues in month 2. The difference in sequencing is not significant (p = .263), indicating that consulting revenues are an important source of early funding for both cohorts. Thus Hypothesis 3 is rejected. Although the non-venture capital-backed firms earn income from consulting earlier, income from consulting is also an important source of funding for product development for the venture capital-backed firms. Whilst some firms can fund prototype development solely from internally generated funds, few firms can fund prototype development solely with external finance. This is consistent with evidence on the sources of funding employed by NTBFs at start-up (Roberts, 1991 and Moore, 1994).

CONCLUSION

The start-up stage in NTBF formation is important since policy-makers believe that the gap in the market for finance is most likely to appear at this stage. In this chapter we have investigated the relation between the key events in the start-up phase of NTBFs in venture capital-backed and non-venture capital-backed firms in the software product sector. In particular we have analysed the impact of product lead times and the availability of finance from consulting activities on the financing patterns of both cohorts at start-up. The study is one of the first seeking systematically to link the product development process to funding in NTBFs, and it highlights the heterogeneous nature of the financing patterns even within this narrowly defined sub-category – software development firms – confirming a fundamental weakness of the stage model (O'Farrell and Hitchens, 1987). It emphasizes that along with the more familiar characteristics impacting on SME financial decision-making, such as age, ownership structure and management preferences, sector is a key variable.

First, overall product lead times in the software product sector are relatively short, with firms developing their first prototypes within a year of formation. In addition, our evidence suggests that product lead times are not significantly longer in venture capital-backed than non-venture capital-backed firms in the sector. This is an important finding as it suggests that product lead times may not have the same impact on funding in the software sector as it does in other sectors. Researchers have long pointed out that shorter product lead times in software development facilitate a self-funding start-up strategy.

Second, although product lead times in venture capital and non-venture capital-backed software product firms are not significantly different, the analysis reveals fundamental differences in the funding of prototype development within the two subgroups. The non-venture capital-backed cohort relies largely on internal funding for product development, whilst the venture capital-backed firms are more likely to access external funding prior to completing the process. Some non-venture capital-backed firms accessed external funding after completing prototype development, but 22 firms had accessed no funding. Whilst two of these firms were less than one year old, the average age of these firms was six years, suggesting that they were entirely self-funding. In addition, the owners of non-venture capital-backed firms are more likely to self-fund until first product sales have been realized. Other studies have also noted the prevalence of the self-funding model amongst NTBFs (Tiler et al., 1993 and Clarysse et al., 2003). This funding pattern is consistent with the stylized version of the stage model in non-NTBFs, where start-up is funded entirely by founders. It also helps explain why 46 per cent of NTBF start-ups in the EU are in the computer and computer-related services sector.

Third, revenue from consulting is an important source of funding for prototype development in both venture capital-backed and non-venture capital-backed firms. Short product lead times facilitate a self-funding strategy which is enabled by a 'soft start' business model whereby consulting revenues are employed to fund prototype development, limiting the need for external sources of funding. Although non-venture capital-backed firms earn revenues from consultancy significantly earlier, they are no more likely to have received these revenues prior to completing prototype development than their venture capital-backed counterparts. Thus both groups rely on revenues from consulting to fund prototype development. The evidence confirms that while some firms can self-finance the product development process, fewer firms can fund prototype development solely from external sources of financing.

The analysis is subject to a number of limitations. First, it is based on a cross-section of surviving NTBFs in the software product sector. It would obviously be interesting to know how the formation process impacts on survival rates. Survivorship bias is an unavoidable pitfall of this mode of research, where firms of different ages are included in a survey-based study. Obviously one would have more confidence in the results from a survey that included failed firms. In addition, many other factors which impact on the pattern of financing adopted by software entrepreneurs are not considered here, including: team size, knowledge of how to access capital, the owners' growth orientation and preferences for ceding control in their businesses. The focus here is the timing and sequencing of key

events on the formation process on NTBFs, which has not been systematically examined in prior research.

In sum, our analysis concludes that short product lead times and 'soft
start' strategies provide founders of software product companies with
greater financial flexibility than the founders of companies in other sectors
such as biotechnology. While venture capital has proved an important
source of funding for high technology firms in Europe over the last decade,
the critical role of internal (or entrepreneurial) sources cannot be ignored.
It verifies that consulting revenues are an important source of funding for
software development. In the aftermath of the financial crisis, it appears
unlikely that there will be any major changes in the availability of bank
finance to NTBFs, at the same time as venture capital funding is predicted
to remain constrained. Internal sources of finance are likely to become
even more important in NTBF funding. Policy-makers might do well to
revisit the support schemes provided to NTBFs, paying greater attention
to schemes that focus on funds provided by the founders themselves, and
in particular on the tax treatment of the money they invest in their own
businesses. Tax incentives plans, such as the Seed Capital Scheme, which
allow founders to reclaim income tax paid in previous employment against
start-up expenses, may also be more relevant in times of increasing constraints in the market for external funds.

REFERENCES

Autio, E. (2000), 'Growth of technology-based new firms', in D.L. Sexton and H.
    Landström (eds), *Handbook of Entrepreneurship*, Oxford: Blackwell Publishers,
    pp. 329–47.
Bank of England (1996), *The Financing of Technology-based Small Firms*, London:
    Bank of England.
Bank of England (2001), *The Financing of Technology-based Small Firms*, London:
    Bank of England.
Beuselinck, C. and S. Manigart (2007), 'Public venture capital across Europe: a 15
    year perspective', in G.N. Gregoriou, M. Kooli and R. Kraeussl (eds), *Venture
    Capital in Europe*, Oxford: Elsevier, pp. 19–31.
Bhide, A.V. (1992), 'Bootstrap finance: the art of start-ups', *Harvard Business
    Review*, **70**(6), 109–17.
Bullock, M. (1983), *Academic Enterprise, Industrial Innovation and the Development
    of High Technology Financing in the United States*, London: Brand Brothers and
    Co.
Clarysse, B., A. Heirman and J.J. Degroof (2003), 'Growth paths of technology-
    based companies in life sciences and information technology', Innovation Policy
    Studies Series, European Commission Enterprise Directorate-General, Report
    no. 32.
Dillman, D. (1976), *Mail and Telephone Survey*, New York: John Wiley and Sons.

Dillman, D. (2000), *Mail and Internet Surveys*, New York: John Wiley and Sons.

Ebben, J. and A. Johnson (2006), 'Bootstrapping in small firms: an empirical analysis of change over time', *Journal of Business Venturing*, **21**(6), 851–65.

Enterprise Ireland (2006), 'Seed and venture capital programme 2000–2006: 2005 Report', Dublin: Enterprise Ireland.

Enterprise Strategy Group (2004), *Ahead of the Curve–Ireland's Place in the Global Economy*, Dublin: Enterprise Strategy Group.

European Commission (1995), *Green Paper on Innovation*, Luxembourg: Office for Official Publications of the European Communities.

European Commission (1999), 'Risk capital markets; a key to job creation in Europe. From fragmentation to integration', report prepared by Delphine Sallard, Directorate General II, Economic and Financial Affairs. *Euro Papers*, No. 32.

European Commission (2001), 'Funding of new technology-based firms by commercial banks in Europe'. *Innovation Papers*, No.7, Luxembourg: Office for Official Publications of the European Communities.

European Network for SME Research (ENSR) (2002), 'Observatory of European SMEs, 2002: high-tech SMEs in Europe', Report No. 6, prepared for Enterprise Directorate-General by KPMG Special Services and EIM Business and Policy Research in the Netherlands in cooperation with the ENSR and Intomart, Luxembourg: Office for Official Publications of the European Communities.

Freear, J., J.E. Sohl and W.E. Wetzel Jr (1995), 'Who bankrolls software entrepreneurs?', in W.D. Bygrave, B.J. Bird, S. Birley, N.C. Churchill, M. Hay, R.H. Keeley and W.E. Wetzel Jr (eds), *Frontiers of Entrepreneurship Research*, Wellesley, MA: Babson College, pp. 394–406.

Gartner, W.B. and N.M. Carter (2004), 'Overview: the start-up process', in W.B. Gartner, K.G. Shaver, N.M. Carter and P.D. Reynolds (eds), *Handbook of Entrepreneurial Dynamics: The Process of Business Creation,* Thousand Oaks, CA: Sage Publications, pp. 235–43.

Gartner, W.B., K.G. Shaver, N.M. Carter and P.D. Reynolds (2004), *Handbook of Entrepreneurial Dynamics: The Process of Business Creation*, Thousand Oaks, CA: Sage Publications.

Gibb, A.A. and L.G. Davies (1991), 'Methodological problems in the development and testing of a growth model of business enterprise development', in A.A Gibb and L.G. Davies (eds), *Recent Research in Entrepreneurship*, Aldershot: Avebury, pp. 286–321.

Giudici, G. and S. Paleari (2000), 'The provision of finance to innovation: a survey conducted among Havian technology-based small firms', *Journal of Small Business Economics*, **14**(1), 37–53.

Harrison, R.T. and C.M. Mason (1997), 'Entrepreneurial growth strategies and venture performance in the software industry', in P.D. Reynolds, W.D. Bygrave, N.M. Carter, P. Davidsson, W.B. Gartner, C.M. Mason and P.P. McDougall (eds), *Frontiers of Entrepreneurship Research*, Wellesley, MA: Babson College, pp. 448–9.

Harrison, R.T., C.M. Mason and P.L Girling (2004), 'Financial bootstrapping and venture development in the software industry', *Entrepreneurship & Regional Development*, **16**(4), 307–33.

Hine, D. and J.Kapeleris (2007), *Innovation and Entrepreneurship in Biotechnology, an International Perspective: Concepts, Theories and Cases*, Cheltenham, UK and Northampton, MA, USA: Edward Elgar Publishing.

Hogan, T. and E. Hutson (2005), 'Capital structure in new technology-based firms: evidence from the Irish software sector', *Journal of Global Finance*, **15**(3), 369–87.

Hogan, T. and E. Hutson (2006), 'The relation between key events in the development phase and the financial structure of NTBFs in the software sector', *International Entrepreneurship and Management Journal*, **2**(2), 56–72.

HotOrigin (2001), *Ireland's Emerging Software Cluster: A Hothouse of Future Stars*, Dublin: HotOrigin.

HotOrigin (2002), *Ireland's Software Cluster: Innovation – the Fuel for International Success. A Report on the Indigenous Software Sector in the Republic and Northern Ireland*, Dublin: HotOrigin.

Irish Venture Capital Association (IVCA) (2006), *The Economic Impact of Venture Capital in Ireland: 2005*, Dublin: IVCA.

Kazanjian, R.K. (1988), 'Relation of dominant problems to stages of growth in technology-based new ventures', *Academy of Management Journal*, **31**(2), 257–79.

Kazanjian, R.K. and R. Drazin (1990), 'A stage contingent model of design and growth for technology based new ventures', *Journal of Business Venturing*, **5**(3), 137–50.

Little, A.D. (1977), *New Technology-based Firms in the United Kingdom and the Federal Republic of Germany*, London: Wilton House.

Lumme, A., I. Kauranen and E. Autio (1994), 'The growth and funding mechanisms of new technology-based firms: a comparative study between the United Kingdom and Finland', in R. Oakey (ed.), *New Technology-based Firms in the 1990s+*, London: Paul Chapman Publishing, pp. 81–92.

Moore, B. (1994), 'Financial constraints to the growth and development of small high technology firms', in A. Hughes and D.J. Storey (eds), *Finance and the Small Firm*, London: Routledge, pp. 112–44.

Mulcahy, D. (2005), *Angels and IPO: Policies for Sustainable Equity Financing of Irish Small Businesses*, Trinity College Dublin: The Policy Institute.

Murray, G. and D. Dimov (2007), 'Through a glass darkly: new perspectives on the equity gap', in B. Clarysse, J. Roure and T. Schamp (eds), *Entrepreneurship and the Financial Community: Starting up and Growing New Businesses*, Cheltenham, UK and Northampton, MA, USA: Edward Elgar Publishing, pp. 161–74.

Myers, S. (2001), 'Capital structure', *Journal of Economic Perspectives*, **15**(2), 81–102.

National Software Directorate (NSD) (1997), *The Financing of High-technology Start-ups,* Dublin: National Software Directorate.

National Software Directorate (NSD) (2001), *Irish Software Industry Survey 2000,* Dublin: National Software Directorate.

Oakey, R.P. (1984), *High Technology Small Firms*, London: Frances Pinter.

Oakey, R.P. (1984), 'High Technology Small Firms: their potential for rapid industrialisation', *International Journal of Small Business*, **11**(4), 9–22.

Oakey, R.P. (1995), *High-Technology New Firms: Variable Barriers to Growth*, London: Paul Chapman.

OECD (2003), *Information Technology Outlook 2003; ICTs, E-commerce and the Information Economy*, Paris: OECD.

Oehler, A., K. Pukthuanthong, M. Rummer and T. Walker (2007), 'Venture capital in Europe: closing the gap on the US', in G.N. Gregoriou, M. Kooli and R. Kraeussl (eds), *Venture Capital in Europe*, Oxford: Elsevier, pp. 3–17.

O'Farrell, P.N. and D.M.W.N. Hitchens (1987), 'Alternative theories of small firm growth: a critical review', Research Paper No. 15, Department of Town and Country Planning, Herriot Watt University Edinburgh.

Reynolds, P.D. and B. Miller (1992), 'New firm gestation: conception, birth, and implications for research', *Journal of Business Venturing*, **7**(5), 405–17.

Roberts, E.B. (1991), *Entrepreneurs in High Technology: Lessons from MIT and Beyond*, New York: Oxford University Press.

Segal, Quince and Partners (1985), *The Cambridge Phenomenon: the Growth of High Technology Industry in a University Town*, Cambridge: Segal, Quince and Partners.

Tiler, C., S. Metcalfe and D. Connell (1993), 'Business expansion through entrepreneurship: the influence of internal and external barriers to growth', *International Journal of Technology Management*, Special publication on small firms and innovation, **8**, 119–32.

Winborg, J. and H. Landström (1997), 'Financial bootstrapping in small businesses – a resource-based view on small business finance', in P.D. Reynolds, W.D. Bygrave, N.M. Carter, P. Davidsson, W.B. Gartner, C.M. Mason and P.P. McDougall (eds), *Frontiers of Entrepreneurship Research*, Wellesley, MA: Babson College, pp. 471–85.

Winborg, J. and H. Landström (2001), 'Financial bootstrapping in small businesses: examining small business managers' resource acquisition behaviors', *Journal of Business Venturing*, **16**(3), 235–54.

5. A new approach to testing the effects of entrepreneurship education among secondary school pupils

Jan Lepoutre, Wouter Van den Berghe, Olivier Tilleuil and Hans Crijns

INTRODUCTION

Since entrepreneurship may serve as an important vehicle for economic and social prosperity, a plethora of actors in society have taken initiative to stimulate entrepreneurship through education at various stages of human development. In particular, it is argued that entrepreneurship education programmes should start at as early an age as possible (Wilson et al., 2004; World Economic Forum, 2009), because:

> to a greater or lesser degree in just about every culture there are sceptical or even hostile attitudinal barriers to entrepreneurship. [. . .] And hence the need for entrepreneurship education aimed specifically at young people, who are typically more open to self-exploration and usually more willing to challenge received wisdom and societal prejudice than are most adults. (World Economic Forum, 2009, p. 30).

Entrepreneurship education programmes for teenage pupils, however, may also be confronted with many specific challenges. For example, teenage pupils are often not allowed to start up their own companies or may not have full control over their financial situation. Furthermore, career choices may be part of some distant future for teenagers. As a result, educational initiatives aimed at stimulating entrepreneurship may be perceived by teenagers as irrelevant, or may be long forgotten by the time actual career choices have to be made (Peterman and Kennedy, 2003). The question is then what entrepreneurial outcomes can be realized with entrepreneurship programmes among teenage pupils, and how. In line with previous work that has argued in favour of entrepreneurship education programmes that match the specific characteristics of a target population (Wilson et al.,2007; Athayde, 2009), our interest in this chapter is therefore to know what characteristics of entrepreneurship education programmes are most 'effective' for teenage pupils. More specifically, our aim is to address two research questions: first, do entrepreneurship education initiatives have an impact on secondary school pupils, and how will we assess this 'impact'? And second, what types of personal and initiative characteristics influence these effects?

These challenges are added to the general methodological issues that have been raised in the context of entrepreneurship education effect measurements. A first question is whether one should evaluate the effectiveness of entrepreneurship education programmes on subjective assessments, such as the intention to start up a business or course satisfaction, or on more objective behavioural outcomes such as the actual start-up of a business or higher start-up survival or returns (McMullan et al., 2001). A second issue that is raised relates to whether entrepreneurial intentions or behaviours can be causally related to the actual entrepreneurship programme, or can only partially be attributed to having been exposed to an entrepreneurship course or programme (McMullan et al., 2001). Conversely, entrepreneurship programmes can also result in several outcomes, such as management skills (Westhead et al., 2001). A final issue relates to whether the effects of entrepreneurship programmes should be assessed shortly after a programme has ended, or whether they should be followed up over a longer time span with longitudinal studies (Henry et al., 2004). Crossing these more theoretical concerns are also more practical issues of cost and feasibility, which together make up the trade-off that has to be made to assess the effectiveness of entrepreneurship education programmes efficiently (McMullan et al., 2001).

With our chapter, we thus hope to contribute to the broader entrepreneurship education literature, by exploring the specific effects of a variety of entrepreneurship education initiative characteristics, but also to shed more specific light on these effects among secondary school pupils. Furthermore, we propose a new approach to measuring the impact of entrepreneurship education initiatives, by using not only several types of outcomes, but also by using different ways of measuring the outcomes.

THEORETICAL FRAMING AND HYPOTHESES

Entrepreneurship Education

In recent years, we have seen a slow but increasingly growing body of scholarship dedicating research on entrepreneurship education. A first stream in this literature has been mainly focused on the establishment of entrepreneurship education as a legitimately distinct profession, and takes a historical perspective on the development of the field to identify the needs and challenges that entrepreneurship education should address (Kuratko, 2005; Gibb, 2002; Solomon et al., 2002; Katz, 2003; Aronsson, 2004). A second stream of literature has been dedicated to assessing the effectiveness of entrepreneurship education, and identifying some of the factors that may play a role in determining this effectiveness (Peterman and Kennedy, 2003; Souitaris et al., 2007; Wilson et al., 2007; Athayde, 2009; Charney and Libecap, 2000). This chapter aims to contribute in particular to the second body of conversation.

The Effectiveness of Entrepreneurship Education

A number of studies have shown that entrepreneurship education pro-grammes have a significant positive impact on various proxies for entrepre-neurship, including entrepreneurial intentions, the desirability and feasibility of entrepreneurial ventures, and various competencies that are associated with entrepreneurship (Peterman and Kennedy, 2003; Souitaris et al., 2007; Wilson et al., 2007; Charney and Libecap, 2000; Athayde, 2009). In these impact studies, researchers most often draw on the psychology literature to argue that the 'intention' to start up a business is the proxy that best reflects the odds regarding whether or not a person will start a business (Krueger et al., 2000; Souitaris et al., 2007). As a result, the success of entrepreneurship education is mostly measured as a positive change in entrepreneurship as a career choice, and the majority of these studies do in fact show that entrepre-neurship education has a positive impact on such entrepreneurial intentions.

Drawing on the same psychology literature, changes in entrepreneurial intentions are subsequently further explored by using different theoretical intention models, such as the Shapero Entrepreneurial Event (SEE) model (Shapero and Sokol, 1982) or Ajzen's Theory of Planned Behaviour (TPB) (Ajzen, 1991). Whereas the SEE model predicts entrepreneurial inten-tions based on the perceived feasibility and the perceived desirability of entrepreneurship as a career choice, along with the propensity to act, the Theory of Planned Behavior models entrepreneurial intentions as a result of the attitudes toward entrepreneurship, the subjective norms held about entrepreneurship by one's important relationships, and the perceived behavioural control one has to actually follow through one's ambitions. Although a comparative study showed that the SEE model had better predictive power over the TPB model (Krueger et al., 2000), both models are successfully used in entrepreneurship education impact studies. The results of these studies, however, are somewhat inconclusive. Whereas some studies have shown that entrepreneurship education increases the desirability of entrepreneurship (Peterman and Kennedy, 2003; Athayde, 2009), others show that such initiatives have no impact on the desirability or the attitudes towards entrepreneurship (Souitaris et al., 2007). Entrepreneurship education also seems to have a positive effect on the perceived feasibility of entrepreneurship, or on entrepreneurial self-efficacy (Wilson et al., 2007), which is a similar measure, but not on the perceived behavioural control (Souitaris et al., 2007). Finally, Souitaris and his colleagues found the interesting observation that entrepreneurship education initiatives had a significant impact on the 'expectations of significant others', which they explained was the result of a small network of fellow programme participants who shared a positive disposition towards entrepreneurship as a result of the programme. Overall, however, we can conclude that results about entrepreneurship education initiatives remain inconclusive, and that more detailed research is needed to get a full understanding of the contingent effects of entrepreneurship education.

Furthermore, given the high importance expressed about student population-specific entrepreneurship education, we also lack knowledge on the impact of personal and initiative characteristics on entrepreneurial intentions and other outcomes. Whereas we know that positive entrepreneurship education impacts are stronger among pupils with a positive prior exposure to entrepreneurs (Peterman and Kennedy, 2003), among female students (Wilson et al., 2007), and when triggering inspirational events are part of the entrepreneurship education initiative (Souitaris et al., 2007), we lack a more comprehensive perspective on how these factors influence entrepreneurship education impacts at the same time.

Given the inconclusive results of entrepreneurship education impact studies, we are interested in assessing their effect on a variety of entrepreneurship outcomes. To this purpose, we are interested not only in the effect of entrepreneurship education programmes on entrepreneurial intentions, but also on their theoretical antecedents. In line with earlier research among high-school pupils, we follow the SEE model and investigate the impact of entrepreneurship education on the perceived desirability, perceived feasibility and propensity to act. Furthermore, we assess the impact of entrepreneurship education programmes on the level of creativity and a general attitude towards entrepreneurs, both identified as critical aspects of entrepreneurship (Timmons and Spinelli, 2004). We therefore tested the following hypotheses:

Hypothesis 1a: High-school pupils that have followed an entrepreneurship education programme will have higher levels of entrepreneurial intentions after than before the programme.

Hypothesis 1b: High-school pupils that have followed an entrepreneurship education programme will have higher levels of creativity after the programme than before the programme.

Hypothesis 1c: High-school pupils that have followed an entrepreneurship education programme will have a more positive attitude towards entrepreneurs after the programme than before the programme.

Hypothesis 1d: High-school pupils that have followed an entrepreneurship education programme will have higher levels of perceived desirability, perceived feasibility and propensity to act after the programme than before the programme.

Hypothesis 1e: High-school pupils that have increased their perceived feasibility, their perceived desirability and their propensity to act, will also have increased their intention to start their own business.

The next hypotheses were concerned with the impact of pedagogical methods on the entrepreneurship education programme effects. Entrepreneurship programmes may cover a wide array of initiatives and pedagogical methods, all aimed to foster entrepreneurial competencies among pupils. Such initiatives may include more passive approaches such as lectures, guest speakers or site visits to entrepreneurial companies, or more active 'experiential' programmes that include simulations, writing business plans, up to the actual setting up of a company (Hills, 1988; Gartner and Vesper, 1994; Solomon et al., 2002; Kuratko, 2005). It is often argued that for entrepreneurship education to be successful, more experiential and active hands-on approaches are necessary (Solomon et al., 2002; Aronsson, 2004; Gendron, 2004). Such approaches confront pupils with the actual practice of starting and running a business or being passionately engaged in an activity of uncertain success and thus expose the pupil to a learning experience that would be more easily internalized. We therefore test the following hypotheses:

Hypothesis 2a: The greater the intensity of an entrepreneurship education programme, the higher the increase in pupils' entrepreneurial intentions, perceived desirability, perceived feasibility, propensity to act, creativity, and attitudes towards entrepreneurs.

Hypothesis 2b: The greater the experiential nature of an
entrepreneurship education, the higher the increase in
pupils' entrepreneurial intentions, perceived desirability,
perceived feasibility, propensity to act, creativity, and
attitudes towards entrepreneurs.

Regardless of the pedagogical approach taken, the study of Souitaris
and colleagues (2007) also showed how individual benefits derived from
the entrepreneurship education programme have an influence. We therefore hypothesize:

Hypothesis 3:   The better the pupils evaluated the programme in
terms of fun and importance, the higher the increase in
pupils' entrepreneurial intentions, perceived desirability,
perceived feasibility, propensity to act, creativity, and
attitudes towards entrepreneurs.

METHODS

Procedures

In order to test for the effects of the entrepreneurship education programmes, we adopted an unusual approach. Instead of using a traditional
pre-test – post-test control group design, we combined two different
methods at the same time, to independently assess the evolution of the
pupils. More specifically, we used a retrospective pre-test – post-test design
on the one hand, in which we used the different programme participant
groups as control groups for each other, and a perceived change measure
on the other. In contrast to pre-test – post-test designs, retrospective pre-
test – post-test designs assess the 'before' (pre-) and 'after' (post-) situation
at the same time, namely at the end of the programme. We argue that such
an approach may be more appropriate than pre-test – post-test assessments, as these may suffer from response shift biases (Howard and Dailey,
1979; Sprangers and Hoogstraten, 1989; Lam and Bengo, 2003; Pratt et
al., 2000; Hill and Betz, 2005), and as such under- or overrated the impacts
of entrepreneurship education programmes.

Response shift biases occur when a person's subjective (internal) *measurement scale* for assessing a particular phenomenon at one point in time
(e.g., feasibility to start a firm) may be different before and after a particular
intervention. For example, the insights of an entrepreneurship programme
may (and preferably do) produce a direct impact on how 'entrepreneurship'

is assessed, and how one self-perceives one's ability and desirability regarding entrepreneurship. Respondents asked to self-assess their ability and desirability towards entrepreneurship may thus use different subjective measurement scales before and after the programme. As a result, concluding that a respondent may have felt no impact of a programme because of a self-assessed 'very high' feasibility for entrepreneurship both before and after the programme may in fact be a wrong representation of what actually happened. Looking back, this same respondent could maybe assess his or her ability in the past as 'low', despite the fact that he or she answered 'very high' at that time. In order to avoid this bias, impact study methodology suggests to use a combination of post-test–retrospective pre-tests on the one hand, in which one's status at the beginning (retrospectively) and the end of the programme is measured at the same time, and self-perceived change on the other hand. This methodology is an often used method in impact studies, especially in the context of impact evaluation of educational interventions, recreation or medical treatments (Sibthorp et al., 2007; Schwartz and Rapkin, 2004; Lam and Bengo, 2003).

In our survey, we asked all respondents to reflect back to the same 'pre-test' moment, since we asked them about a particular status 'at the beginning of the schoolyear'. The 'post-test' moment differed among respondents, as respondents were only asked to complete a survey once they had finished participating in the entrepreneurship education programme.

Programmes

We conducted the study among pupils that participated in 21 entrepreneurship education programmes that are implemented in the Flemish part of Belgium. Out of 23 initiatives that were identified as part of a larger inventory of entrepreneurship education initiatives in Flanders (Van den Berghe, 2007) and that were subsequently invited to participate in the research, these 21 participating initiatives cover the large majority of existing initiatives in Flanders today. We were surprised to see that this was not only reflecting a broad coverage of our study in terms of the existing offer of entrepreneurship education initiatives, but also that they covered a broad participation of entrepreneurship education initiatives by Flemish schools. Together, the 21 initiatives are present in 78 per cent of the schools, which indicates that entrepreneurship education is gaining a significant penetration among secondary schools (650 in total). This, however, does not necessarily mean that 78 per cent of all pupils have contact with such a programme. Table 5.1 shows the 21 programmes, their penetration in Flemish schools, and their pedagogical characteristics in terms of intensity and experiential focus. A programme was classified

Table 5.1   The entrepreneurship programmes and their characteristics

Name of the programme (organization)	Schools in the programme	Respon-dents	Main peda-gogical methodology	Intensity[a]	Experiential[b]
Young Enterprise (Vlajo)	230	297	Student enterprise	I	H
Entrepreneur in the Classroom (VKW)	214	810	Guest lecture	S	L
Dream-Day (Dream)	145	446	Guest lecture/ company visit	S	L
Jieha! (Vlajo)	124	124	Student enterprise	I	H
Practice Firm (Cofep)	72	501	Simulation game	I	M
The World at your Feet (KVIV)	68	153	Guest lecture	S	L
Learn Enterprise (UNIZO)	54	111	Student enterprise	I	H
COOS (DBO)	50	25	Competition	S	L
Ecoman (HUB)	47	359	Simulation game	M	M
Prize Entrepreneurial School (UNIZO)	46	50	Competition	M	M
Virtual Office (WEB)	43	15	Simulation game	I	M
Promising Entrepreneur (DBO)	31	24	Business plan competition	S	L
TMF Stressfactor (Deadline)	25	60	Organizing event	M	H
The Inventors– class edition (Flanders DC)	24	20	Workshop	M	M
NFTE-course (NFTE)	16	56	Business plan and lectures	I	H
Flanders DC Fellows (Flanders DC)	12	15	Guest lecture	S	L

Table 5.1   (continued)

Name of the programme (organization)	Schools in the programme	Respon-dents	Main peda-gogical methodology	Intensity[a]	Experiential[b]
Company visits East-Flanders (VOKA)	11	3	Company visit	S	L
All-in All-out Limburg (VOKA)	7	28	Guest lecture/ company visit	S	L
Project Entrepre-neurship (HUB)	7	9	Simulation game	M	M
Flying Starters Brigade Antwerp (VOKA)	7	24	Guest lecture/ company visit	S	L
Economic Discoveries (VOKA)	7	0	Guest lecture/ company visit	S	L

Notes:
[a]   I = intense, M = intermediate, S = short.
[b]   H = high, M = intermediate, L = low.

as having low intensity when the time dedicated was limited to a couple of hours up to a day, intermediate when several days were taken, and intense when it lasted several weeks or even months. The experientiality of a programme was assessed based on the level of hands-on tasks that needed to be executed. A programme had low experientiality when it consisted only of a lecture or a seminar, intermediate when it included some activity such as a company visit or a game, and high when it involved running an actual business or event. All programmes took place in the period between January and May 2009, and participants were asked to complete the survey right after the programme finished.

Participants

In order to garner survey participants, we asked the coordinators of each of these entrepreneurship programmes to contact all the teachers they worked with in their programmes and to ask the teachers to distribute a survey among their pupils. We asked the programme coordinators only to submit the survey request when the programme was finished, so that the post-test measurement was indeed taken after the programme was finished. As a result of this approach, a total of 3130 pupils answered the questionnaire. From these 3130 responses, we selected only the last four years of high-school. After data cleaning, this left us with 2160 responses. From these 2160 responses, 46 per cent were from boys, and 54 per cent from girls.

Intention and SEE

We adopted an adapted version of the intention and SEE questionnaire as proposed by Krueger (1993) and Krueger and colleagues (2000). The adaptations consisted of rephrasing the questions such that they could all fit the same 5-point Likert scale that ranged from 'totally disagree' to 'totally agree'. As a result, the intention question, for example, changed from 'estimate the probability you'll start your own business in the next 5 years' to 'the likelihood that I will ever run my own business is very high'. We adapted each of the five 'perceived feasibility' questions and each of the three 'perceived desirability' questions in a similar way. For the 'propensity to act' measure, we adopted nine questions from the 20 'desirability of control' (Burger, 1985) measures. Table 5.2 summarizes the questions as they were asked in the survey.

Other Dependent Variables: Creativity and Attitude Towards Entrepreneurs

In order to measure creativity, we adopted a shortened version of the 'Problem solving' part of the Self-Description Questionnaire (Marsh and O'Neill, 1984). This questionnaire has been used in earlier research on creativity, and in particular related to motivation profiles of pupils (Sheldon, 1995). The attitude towards entrepreneurs was measured using two measures from the Gallup Eurobarometer survey, which investigated the image of entrepreneurs across various countries in Europe and around the world.

Evaluation of the Activity

In order to evaluate the activity, we designed four questions aimed at capturing both whether the pupils found the activity fun and whether they found it important. As such, we deviate from the 'trigger-event' approach as used by Souitaris and colleagues (2007), but our aim was more on

Table 5.2   Measurement instruments for survey questionnaire

Entrepreneurial intention (5-point scale: totally disagree – totally agree), adapted from Krueger (1993)

---

1. The likelihood that I will ever run my own business is very high.

SEE-model variables (5-point scale: totally disagree – totally agree), adapted from Krueger (1993) and Krueger et al. (2000)

Perceived feasibility (Cronbach's α: t1 = 0.58, t2 = 0.58)

---

1. I think it would be very cool to start my own business.
2. I would love to start my own business.
3. If I would start my own business, I would be constantly afraid to lose all my money. (-)

Perceived desirability (Cronbach's α: t1 = 0.65, t2 = 0.63)

---

1. I know what it takes to start a business.
2. I feel sure enough of myself to start my own business at some point in the future.
3. If I would start my own business, it would certainly be a success.
4. It looks very hard to me to start your own business. (-)
5. If I would start my own business, I would definitely be overworked. (-)

Propensity to act (Cronbach's α: t1 = 0.65, t2 = 0.65)

---

1. I'd rather make my own mistakes than listen to someone else's orders.
2. I would rather someone else take over the leadership role when I'm involved in a group project. (-)
3. I like to get a good idea of what a job is all about before I begin. (-)
4. I'd rather not have too much responsibility. (-)
5. I enjoy making my own decisions.
6. I consider myself to be generally more capable of handling situations than others are.
7. When I see a problem, I prefer to do something about it rather than sit by and let it continue.
8. Others usually know what is best for me. (-)
9. I like to wait and see if someone else is going to solve a problem so that I don't have to be bothered with it. (-)

Creativity (5-point scale: totally disagree – totally agree), adapted from Marsh and O'Neill (1984)

'Problem solving' (Cronbach's α: t1 = 0.59, t2 = 0.60)

1. I can often see better ways of doing routine tasks.
2. I am good at combining ideas in ways that others have not tried.
3. I am not very original in my ideas thoughts and actions. (-)
4. I am never able to think up answers to problems that haven't already been figured out. (-)

Table 5.2   (continued)

Attitude towards entrepreneurs (Flash Eurobarometer, 2007)

Image of entrepreneurship (Cronbach's α: t1 = 0.70, t2 = 0.73)
1. Entrepreneurs are job creators.
2. Entrepreneurship is the basis of wealth creation, benefiting us all.

---

obtaining a broader evaluation of the programme from the pupil than merely the inspiration received from the programme.

Control Variables

In order to control for other potential factors that interfere with the effects of the programme initiatives, we controlled for gender, age, breadth and positiveness of exposure, motivational profile and the initial values of the pupils at t1.

Data Analysis

In order to test our first hypotheses regarding whether the programmes had an effect on entrepreneurial intentions and its related predictor variables, and on creativity and attitudes towards entrepreneurs, we conducted a series of paired t-tests with the retrospective pre-test (t1) and post-test (t2) values of each of these variables. Table 5.3 summarizes the results of these t-tests. Furthermore, Table 5.3 also reports the direct measurements of perceived change, and their difference and correlation with the calculated retrospective pre-test – post-test differences. In order to test Hypothesis 1e, we employed a correlation analysis, as summarized in Table 5.4.

In order to test for the differences in effects between the programs, we employed three analyses. First, we used the correlation analysis in Table 5.4 to test whether an increase in intensity, experientiality or a positive personal evaluation of the programme was significantly associated with an increase in entrepreneurial intentions and its predictive variables, and creativity and the attitudes towards entrepreneurs. Second, we used a step-wise hierarchical regression (Table 5.5) to test whether these correlations held while controlling for additional predictive variables. Finally, given that both intensity and experientiality were ordinal variables, we also used a one-way ANOVA to test for differences between the means of each of the categories (Table 5.6).

Table 5.3 T-test for programme effects through retrospective pre-test and perceived change methodology

	Method 1: Retrospective pre-test-values		T-test	Method 2: Perceived change	Mean	T-test	Correlation
	t1	t2	t2–t1	Due to the programme, I have a/it's become …	t2–t1	M1–M2	M1/M2
Intention to start own business	2.95	2.75	.20**	'higher chance of starting my own business'	2.89	–2.69**	.238**
Creativity	3.31	3.42	.11**	'more creative'	2.9	–2.79**	.117**
Attitude towards entrepreneurs	3.67	3.85	.19**	N/A	N/A	N/A	N/A
Perceived feasibility	2.81	3.01	.19**	'more feasible to start my own business'	3.11	–2.92**	.183**
Perceived desirability	3.07	3.18	.11**	'more desirable to start my own business'	3.02	–2.92**	.233**
Propensity to act	3.32	3.58	.26**	'better in solving problems' 'faster in taking initiative' 'more confident I can realize my own goals'	2.93 3.07 3.31	–2.66** –2.81** –3.05**	.104** .133** .109**

Note: **p < 0.001.

Finally, we used the correlation and the hierarchical regression analysis to test the influence of the programme evaluation on the change in entrepreneurial intention, creativity, perceived feasibility, perceived desirability and propensity to act.

RESULTS

Hypotheses 1a–1e

Using the paired t-tests to compare pre- with post-test results, the results revealed significant difference between t1 and t2 for entrepreneurial intentions and its predictor variables, creativity and attitudes towards entrepreneurs, confirming Hypotheses 1a, 1b, 1c and 1d. Comparing the direct measurements of perceived change, and their difference and correlation with the calculated retrospective pre-test – post-test differences, our findings suggest that the perceived change measures are consistently and significantly higher than the actual calculated t2–t1 differences. This finding is in line with the predictions of Lam and Bengo (2003). The perceived changes are nevertheless also all significantly correlated with the actual calculated differences, indicating that both measurements are related to each other despite their substantial differences. Given that Lam and Bengo (2003) argue that these results are due to a smaller bias in retrospective pre-test – post-test designs, we only used the data collected with these measures in the rest of our analysis. Furthermore, as expected, a change in perceived feasibility, perceived desirability and propensity to act was significantly related to an increased intention to start one's own business. Therefore, Hypothesis 1e was accepted.

Hypotheses 2a–b and 3

The correlation Table in Table 5.4 indicates a significant and positive association between both the intensity and the experientiality of the programmes, and the change in entrepreneurial intention, creathvitq, perceived feasibility, perceived desirability and propensity to act. From our data, however, we were lot able to prove that more intensive and more experiential programmes had stronger effects on changes in attitudes towards entrepreneurs. As such, these results would suggest an acceptance of Hypotheses 2a and 2b for all variables except the attitudd tosards entrepreneurs. Using the hierarchical regression analysis, these correlations lost their significance for all variables but the impact of experientiality on

Table 5.4   Descriptive statistics and Pearson correlations

		Mean	SD	1	2	3	4	5	6	7	8
1	Intention (t1)	2.95	1.19	1							
2	Creativity(t1)	3.42	.61	.225**	1						
3	Attitude towards entrepreneurs (t1)	3.85	.69	.195**	.195**	.177**	1				
4	Perceived feasibility (t1)	3.01	.61	.583**	.295**	.121**	1				
5	Perceived desirability (t1)	3.18	.84	.668**	.216**	.179**	.562**	1			
6	Propensity to act (t1)	3.58	.50	.276**	.495**	.231**	.326**	.284**	1		
7	Intention (t2)	2.75	1.17	.776**	.177**	.122**	.467**	.543**	.199**	1	
8	Creativity (t2)	3.31	.60	.171**	.827**	.121**	.249**	.168**	.410**	.190**	1
9	Attitude towards entrepreneurs (t2)	3.67	.73	.144**	.147**	.733**	.075**	.115**	.187**	.178**	.168**
10	Perceived feasibility (t2)	2.81	.64	.437**	.209**	.048**	.707**	.444**	.192**	.570**	.255**
11	Perceived desirability (t2)	3.07	.83	.576**	.182**	.128**	.476**	.797**	.211**	.629**	.194**
12	Propensity to act (t2)	3.32	.40	.211**	.399**	.187**	.258**	.218**	.741**	.236**	.445**
13	Intention (t2–t1)	.20	.79	.357**	.076**	.116**	.187**	.205**	.124**	-.312**	-.023
14	Creativity (t2t1)	.11	.36	.099**	.321**	.096**	.092**	.094**	.159**	-.013	-.267**
15	Attitude towards entrepreneurs (t2–t1)	.19	.52	.056**	.024	.293**	.057**	.076**	.039	-.089**	-.078**
16	Perceived feasibility (t2–t1)	.19	.48	.163**	.102**	.091**	.336**	.127**	.164**	-.164**	-.021
17	Perceived desirability (t2–t1)	.11	.53	.170**	.066**	.086**	.152**	.349**	.131**	-.114**	-.035
18	Propensity to act (t2–t1)	.26	.34	.159**	.256**	.115**	.180**	.167**	.596**	.014	.075**
19	Intensity	.64	.78	.041	.019	.008	.072**	.044*	.029	.012	-.017
20	Experientiality	.59	.76	.039	.035	.021	.063**	.047*	.042*	.006	-.011
21	Evaluation of the activity	3.51	.81	.173**	.126**	.202**	.144**	.186**	.150**	.088**	.050

Notes: * Significant at the 0.05 level; ** significant at the 0.01 level.

9	10	11	12	13	14	15	16	17	18	19	20	21
1												
.099**	1											
.151**	.550**	1										
.208**	.267**	.225**	1									
−.045*	−.186**	−.065**	−.029	1								
−.027	−.071**	−.016	−.066**	.168**	1							
−.436**	−.075**	−.043*	−.046*	.216**	.165**	1						
−.038	−.428**	−.124**	−.027	.487**	.213**	.173**	1					
−.054*	−.149**	−.287**	−.003	.426**	.175**	.187**	.393**	1				
.028	−.033	.043*	−.098**	.217**	.314**	.112**	.277**	.200**	1			
−.011	−.002	.002	.003	.046*	.064**	.024	.093**	.063**	.043**	1		
.001	.006	.009	.016	.051*	.078**	.026	.071**	.060**	.046**	.842**	1	
.134**	.039	.118**	.048	.129**	.127**	.075**	.132**	.116**	.176**	.091**	.085**	1

Table 5.5 Hierarchical regression models for the evolution of intentions, creativity attitude towards entrepreneurs and predictor variables before and after the programmes (N = 2160)

	Intention (t2–t1)		Creativity (t2–t1)		Attitude towards entrepreneurs (t2–t1)		Perceived feasibility (t2–t1)		Perceived desirability (t2–t1)		Propensity to act (t2–t1)	
	Step 1	Step 2	Step 1	Step 2	Step 1	Step 2	Step 1	Step 2	Step 1	Step 2	Step 1	Step 2
Step 1: control variables												
Gender	-0.048		-0.082	-0.076	-0.102	-0.097			-0.083	-0.076		
Age	-0.086	-0.074					0.060					
Grade	0.059	0.050					-0.065	-0.060				
Economics major					0.076	0.077	0.062	0.045				
Intrinsic motivation			0.175	0.153	0.117	0.098	0.043		0.057		0.208	0.181
Extrinsic motivation	0.099	0.104	-0.058	-0.055	-0.065	-0.062	0.064	0.069	0.057	0.063	-0.054	-0.049
T1 values of dependent variable	-0.338	-0.349	-0.289	-0.290	-0.463	-0.477	-0.440	-0.444	-0.310	-0.324	-0.132	-0.135
Step 2: predictor variables												
Intensity												
Experientiality				0.090								
Evaluation of the activity		0.145		0.109		0.115		0.133		0.144		0.141
R square	0.119	0.141	0.100	0.117	0.217	0.230	0.193	0.217	0.098	0.122	0.056	0.076
Adjusted R square	0.116	0.137	0.097	0.113	0.215	0.226	0.190	0.213	0.095	0.117	0.052	0.071
R Square Change		0.022		0.017		0.013		0.024		0.023		0.020

Table 5.6   *ANOVA of differences between levels of intensity, experientiality and evaluation of the activity on the intention, creativity, attitude towards entrepreneurs and predictor variables*

	Intensity			Experientiality			Evaluation of the activity		
	F	Sig	Eta²	F	Sig	Eta²	F	Sig	Eta²
Intention	2.252	.105	.002	2.821	.060	.003	3.166	.000	.025
Creativity	4.495	.011	.004	6.683	.001	.006	3.101	.000	.025
Attitude towards entrepreneurs	.691	.501	.001	1.024	.359	.001	1.560	.067	.013
Feasibility	9.640	.000	.009	6.570	.001	.006	3.335	.000	.026
Desirability	4.295	.014	.004	4.120	.016	.004	2.602	.000	.021
Propensity to act	2.419	.089	.002	2.235	.107	.002	6.487	.000	.050

changes in creativity, when we control for gender, age and grade, major and type of motivation profile (intrinsic vs. extrinsic). In other words, these findings would indicate that we should reject Hypothesis 2a, and only partly accept Hypothesis 2b for creativity. However, the regression analyses with intensity and experientiality as independent variables are based on the assumption that they are continuous variables. Since this assumption may be violated, we therefore did an additional test using a one-way ANOVA to assess the significance of the differences between the three levels of intensity and experientiality. As Table 5.6 indicates, the three intensity and experientiality levels differ significantly ($p \leq .05$) from one another for differences in creativity, perceived feasibility and perceived desirability, and marginally significantly ($p \leq 0.1$) for differences in entrepreneurial intention and propensity to act. The intensity and experientiality does not seem to have an effect on the differences in attitude towards entrepreneurs. As a result, we reject Hypotheses 2a and 2b for attitude towards entrepreneurs at the .1-level, and for attitude towards entrepreneurs, entrepreneurial intention and propensity to act at the .05-level.

Finally, using the correlation and the hierarchical regression analysis, we found a significant impact of the evaluation of the programme on the change in entrepreneurial intention, creativity, perceived feasibility, perceived desirability and propensity to act. As a result, we do not reject Hypothesis 3.

DISCUSSION

The main focus of this chapter is to assess whether entrepreneurship education programmes have an effect on the entrepreneurial intent, creativity and attitude towards entrepreneurs among teenage pupils, and whether the effect of such programmes differs depending on such objective programme characteristics as intensity and experientiality or subjective programme evaluations. We addressed these questions by using a combination of a retrospective pre-test – post-test and perceived change research design.

Our results first show that, in general, there are significant differences between the pre- and post-test phase, as indicated by both the retrospective pre-test – post-test differences and the self-perceived changes. Our findings are thus in line with earlier studies on the effects of entrepreneurship education programmes, but nevertheless present some differences as well. First, our results confirm earlier analyses that, in general, entrepreneurial intentions change significantly as a result of entrepreneurship education programmes (Peterman and Kennedy, 2003; Souitaris et al., 2007; Wilson et al., 2007; Charney and Libecap, 2000; Athayde, 2009). However, our data reinforce the notion that entrepreneurship programmes also have a significant effect on the self-perceived feasibility of starting up a company (Peterman and Kennedy, 2003; Wilson et al., 2007), for which Souitaris and colleagues (2007) did not find confirmation in their data. Furthermore, we also found confirmation for the impact of entrepreneurship education programmes on the perceived desirability (Peterman and Kennedy, 2003), propensity to act (Athayde, 2009), creativity (Athayde, 2009) and a positive attitude towards entrepreneurs. As we do not have an explicit control group in our research design, one could argue that these significant retrospective pre-test – post-test differences may be due to either a natural progress made by pupils during a school year, or as a result of a bias in the response as a result of the natural tendencies of people to answer in a way that reflects progress (Hill and Betz, 2005). However, given that we have two methods indicating the same direction, we can assume that the programmes do have an impact.

In order to further explore the significance of entrepreneurship education programmes, we can use our comparisons between different programme types as control groups for one another. Doing so indicates that the more intensive (time-consuming) and the more experiential the programmes become, the more effective they become in stimulating shifts in perceived desirability, perceived feasibility and creativity. Although with less significance, more intense and more experiential programmes also have higher impacts on entrepreneurial intentions and propensity to act. The only variable on which differences in intensity and experientiality do not seem to have an effect is on attitude towards entrepreneurs. These findings also reinforce the tenet in much of the entrepreneurship education literature that entrepreneurship education is particularly successful when it employs a more hands-on experiential learning approach (Solomon et al., 2002; Kuratko, 2005; Aronsson, 2004; Izquierdo, 2008). Despite the many difficulties that may be involved in engaging students in real-life experiences of starting up and running a business or any kind of organization or project, our findings suggest that overcoming these challenges is well worth the effort.

Finally, the finding that the evaluation of the programme is a significant and stronger predictor for the changes made in all of the variables of interest than the programme characteristics puts further emphasis on the role of tweaking these entrepreneurship programmes as much as possible to what pupils find fun and important. Furthermore, given that passion and emotion are increasingly acknowledged as having a vital role in various aspects of entrepreneurship (Baron, 2008; Cardon et al., 2009), such reaffirmed attention to the emotional aspects of entrepreneurship may well be one of the most important contributions of entrepreneurship education research (Souitaris et al., 2007).

LIMITATIONS OF THE RESEARCH

Although we were very careful in ensuring rigour in both the design, the execution and the analysis of the research in this chapter, we believe the generalizability of our findings may be limited in some ways. First, although we maintain that the retrospective pre-test – post-test design is a more appropriate way of investigating concepts that may change across time, our research design does not allow for confirming or disconfirming this hypothesis. In order to fully understand the impact of retrospective bias on entrepreneurship education impact studies research, future research should therefore use a combination of pre-test – post-test and retrospective pre-test – post-test design to test to what extent both methods differ and which one is preferred under what conditions.

Second, Cronbach's alpha values for perceived feasibility and creativity may in some ways be just below accepted levels for use in research (0.6). Future research could therefore assess whether our findings also hold, or even have better predictive power, when more complete questionnaires are used. One problem that researchers may face in this context is the balance between survey length and data quality, since pupils may be reluctant complete questionnaires if they are too long.

Third, since most students were asked to complete the questionnaire voluntarily, our sampling technique may involve a selection bias on those students that had a positive experience with the entrepreneurship programme. Although we tried to cover this both by explicitly taking it into account as a predictor variable in our research, and by offering respondents cinema tickets if they participated in the survey, future research could change the sampling technique to a more focused approach using only three types of programmes in randomly selected schools and then asking all students to fill in the survey.

CONCLUSION

As entrepreneurship is increasingly important in our societies today, entrepreneurship education programmes in secondary schools offer a tool to instil entrepreneurial attitudes and competencies among pupils at a young age. With our research, we have demonstrated not only that such programmes are effective, but also that their effect depends on the intensity and the experientiality of the programme itself and how it is evaluated by the pupils. Whereas higher levels of intensity and experientiality have some positive impact on the change in entrepreneurial intent, creativity, perceived desirability, perceived feasibility and propensity to act, it is in particular the evaluation of the programme by the pupil that has a positive impact on the change in these variables.

With these findings, we contribute to a better understanding of entrepreneurship education among younger students. To date, research on entrepreneurship education for this age group is greatly lacking, even though the importance of starting with entrepreneurship education at an early age is widely acknowledged. Given that attitudes are often formed in younger phases of life, our research shows that – at least in the short term – entrepreneurship education programmes do have an effect on changing entrepreneurial attitudes and intentions. In addition, our findings suggest that these effects are stronger when the programmes are more experiential, more time-intensive, and when more attention is paid to making the programmes fun and showing the relevance to a person's personal development. As such, policy-makers, teachers and programme developers alike can use our findings as a point of reflection and improve the effectiveness of entrepreneurship education programmes if deemed necessary.

From our research we also see several avenues for further research. Maintaining that it is best for entrepreneurship education to start at an early age, we should also continue our efforts to see what entrepreneurship education would look like for even younger age groups, what different effects they may generate, and how the effects of entrepreneurship education can be measured at such a young age. By the same token, research into the long-term effects of secondary school entrepreneurship education programmes would also shed light on whether the impact of entrepreneurship education programmes is lasting. While we are getting an increasingly more fine-grained picture about the effects of graduate entrepreneurship education programmes, having a more long-term perspective on how a sequence of programmes and educational efforts impacts the attitudes, feasibility and performance of entrepreneurship among people is a challenging but necessary research agenda if we want to understand the full spectrum of initiatives that may help people to discover their potential entrepreneurial futures.

Secondly, we reiterate the potential of retrospective pre-tests to deal with the methodological inconsistency that may exist when the subjective interpretations of the very concepts that are measured pre- and post-treatment are different. In order to further substantiate the potential of the retrospective pre-test for entrepreneurship education programmes evaluations, however, it would need to be compared with a traditional pre-test measurement, which was not available in our current research design. Again, we believe that future research could shed more light on this methodological issue.

In summary, we hope our research has provided ground for further exploration of the effects of entrepreneurship education and may inspire teachers and policy-makers alike to foster the appropriate environments for successful entrepreneurship education.

REFERENCES

Ajzen, I. (1991), 'The theory of planned behavior', *Organizational Behavior and Human Decision Processes*, **50**, 179–211.

Aronsson, M. (2004), 'Education matters – but does entrepreneurship education? An interview with David Birch', *Academy of Management Learning and Education*, **3**, 289–92.

Athayde, R. (2009),. 'Measuring enterprise potential in young people', *Entrepreneurship Theory and Practice*, **33**, 481–500.

Baron, R.A. (2008), 'The role of affect in the entrepreneurial process', *The Academy of Management Review*, **33**, 328–40.

Burger, J.M. (1985), 'Desire for control and achievement-related behaviors', *Journal of Personality and Social Psychology,* **48**, 1520–533.

Cardon, M.S., J. Wincent, J. Singh, and M. Drnovsek, (2009), 'The nature and experience of entrepreneurial passion', *The Academy of Management Review (AMR),* **34**, 511–32.

Charney, A. and G.D. Libecap (2000), *The Impact of Entrepreneurship Education:*

An Evaluation of the Berger Entrepreneurship Program at the University of Arizona, 1985–1999 Tucson, AZ: University of Arizona.

Flash Eurobarometer (2007), 'Entrepreneurship survey of the EU) (25 member states), United States, Iceland and Norway', Analytics report, Rep. no. Flash EB series no. 192, Brussels: The Gallup Organization.

Gartner, W.B. and K.H. Vesper (1994), 'Experiments in entrepreneurship education: successes and failures', *Journal of Business Venturing*, **9**, 179–87

Gendron, G. (2004), 'Practitioners' perspectives on entrepreneurship education: an interview with Steve Case, Matt Goldman, Tom Golisano, Geraldine Lay Bourne, Jeff Taylor and Alan Webber', *Academy of Management Learning and Teaching*, **3**, 302–14.

Gibb, A. (2002) 'In pursuit of a new "enterprise" and "entrepreneurship" paradigm for learning: creative destruction, new values, new ways of doing things and new combinations of knowledge', *International Journal of Management Reviews*, **4**, 233–69.

Henry, C., F.M. Hill, and C.M. Leitch (2004), 'The effectiveness of training for new business creation: a longitudinal study', *International Small Business Journal*, **22**, 249–72.

Hill, L.G. and D.L. Betz (2005), 'Revisiting the retrospective pretest', *American Journal of Evaluation*, **26**, 501–17.

Hills, G.E. (1988), 'Variations in university entrepreneurship education: an empirical study of an evolving field', *Journal of Business Venturing*, **3**, 109–22.

Howard, G.S. and P.R. Dailey (1979), 'Response-shift bias source of contamination of self-report measures', *Journal of Applied Psychology*, **64**, 144–50.

Izquierdo, E.E. (2008), 'Impact assessment of an educational intervention based on the constructivist paradigm on the development of entrepreneurial competencies in university students', Unpublished dissertation, Ghent: Ghent University.

Katz, J.A. (2003), 'The chronology and intellectual trajectory of American entrepreneurship education 1876–1999', *Journal of Business Venturing*, **18**, 283–300.

Krueger, N.F. (1993), 'The impact of prior entrepreneurial exposure on perceptions of new venture feasibility and desirability', *Entrepreneurship Theory and Practice*, **18**, 5–21.

Krueger, N.F., M.D. Reilly and A.L. Carsrud (2000), 'Competing models of entrepreneurial intentions', *Journal of Business Venturing*, **15**, 411–32.

Kuratko, D.F. (2005), 'The emergence of entrepreneurship education: development, trends, and challenges', *Entrepreneurship Theory and Practice*, **29**, 577–98.

Lam, T.C.M. and P. Bengo (2003), 'A comparison of three retrospective self-reporting methods of measuring change in instructional practic', *American Journal of Evaluation*, **24**, 65–80.

Marsh, H.W. and R. O'Neill (1984), 'Self Description Questionnaire III: the construct validity of multidimensional self-concept ratings by late adolescents', *Journal of Educational Measurement*, 153–74.

McMullan, E., J.J. Chrisman and K. Vesper (2001), 'Some problems in using subjective measures of effectiveness to evaluate entrepreneurial assistance programs', *Entrepreneurship Theory and Practice*, **26**, 37–55.

Peterman, N.E. and J. Kennedy (2003), 'Enterprise education: influencing students perceptions of entrepreneurship', *Entrepreneurship Theory and Practice*, **28**, 129–44.

Pratt, C.C., W.M. McGuigan, and A.R. Katzev (2000), 'Measuring program outcomes: using retrospective pretest methodology', *American Journal of Evaluation,* **21**, 341–49.

Schwartz, C.E. and B.D. Rapkin (2004), 'Reconsidering the psychometrics of quality of life assessment in light of response shift and appraisal', *Health and Quality of Life Outcomes,* **2**, 16.

Shapero, A. and L. Sokol (1982), 'The social dimensions of entrepreneurship', in C.A. Kent, D.L. Sexton, and K.H. Vesper (eds), *The Encyclopedia of Entrepreneurship,* . Englewood Cliffs, NJ: Prentice-Hall, pp. 72–90.

Sheldon, K.M. (1995), 'Creativity and self-determination in personality', *Creativity Research Journal,* **8**, 25–36.

Sibthorp, J., K. Paisley, J. Gookin and P. Ward (2007), 'Addressing response-shift bias: retrospective pretests in recreation research and evaluation', *Journal of Leisure Research,* **39**, 295–315.

Solomon, G.T., S. Duffy, and A. Tarabishy (2002). 'The state of entrepreneurship education in the United States: a nationwide survey and analysis', *International Journal of Entrepreneurship,* **1**, 1–22.

Souitaris, V., S. Zerbinati, and A. Al-Laham (2007), 'Do entrepreneurship programmes raise entrepreneurial intention of science and engineering students? The effect of learning, inspiration and resources', *Journal of Business Venturing,* **22**, 566–91.

Sprangers, M. and J. Hoogstraten (1989), 'Pretesting effects in retrospective pretest-posttest designs', *Journal of Applied Psychology,* **74**, 265–72.

Timmons, J.A. and S. Spinelli, (2004), *New Venture Creation: Entrepreneurship for the 21st Century*, 6th edn, New York: McGraw-Hill.

Van den Berghe, W. (2007). *Ondernemend Leren en Leren Ondernemen,* Brussels: Koning Boudewijnstichting.

Westhead, P., D.J. Storey & F. Martin (2001), 'Outcomes reported, by students who participated in the 1994 Shell Technology Enterprise Programme', *Entrepreneurship and Regional Development,* **13**, 163–85.

Wilson, F., J. Kickul and D. Marlino, (2007), 'Gender, entrepreneurial self-efficacy, and entrepreneurial career intentions: implications for entrepreneurship education', *Entrepreneurship Theory and Practice,* **31**, 387–406.

Wilson, F., D. Marlino and J. Kickul (2004). 'Our entrepreneurial future: examining the diverse attitudes and motivations of teens across gender and ethnic identity', *Journal of Developmental Entrepreneurship,* **9**, 177–97.

World Economic Forum (2009), *Educating the Next Wave of Entrepreneurs: Unlocking Entrepreneurial Capabilities to Meet the Challenges of the 21st Century,* Geneva, World Economic Forum.

6. Effects of regional human capital structure on business entry: a comparison of independent start-ups and new subsidiaries in different industries

Kenta Ikeuchi and Hiroyuki Okamuro

INTRODUCTION

The start-up of new businesses increases innovation and competition and creates local employment. Therefore, start-up activities have been encouraged and supported by various programmes in many countries. However, even in Japan, where the start-up ratio[1] has been lower than the closure ratio[2] since the late 1980s, considerable efforts aimed at increasing the entry of start-ups have hitherto not met with much success (Okamuro and Kobayashi, 2006).

Business start-ups are important for both national and regional economies. In order to comprehensively consider the impact of business start-ups on the regional economy, we find it appropriate to distinguish between new business entries of independent start-ups and subsidiaries of existing firms. The former type depends basically on the decision of the people living or working in the region regarding setting up independent businesses, which means the regional structure of human capital is expected to play a significant role. The latter type is based on decisions by the top management of existing firms, which could be located outside the region, regarding where to locate new subsidiaries. In this case, the regional level of demand and cost may be more important than the human capital structure. Bosma et al. (2008) investigate differences in the regional determinants of independent start-ups and new subsidiaries, focusing on agglomeration effects and comparing manufacturing and service sectors.

The effects of human capital structure on entry may differ considerably across sectors and industries. Industries differ in their sensitivity to regional supply and demand (market) conditions as well as in the required levels and types of human capital. However, few studies have examined inter-industry differences of entry, apart from some studies comparing the manufacturing and service sectors. Okamuro (2008) compares the regional determinants of start-ups in high-tech versus low-tech industries in the manufacturing sector, finding that the agglomeration of special- ized human capital and knowledge is important. In addition, Acs and Armington (2006) examine the differences in the regional determinants of entry among various sectors (manufacturing, retail trade, local market, distribution and business services), focusing on educational requirements and market segments.

However, in their analysis of the regional determinants of entry, these studies do not differentiate between independent start-ups and new sub- sidiaries of existing firms. Within the same sector, regional factors may differ between the types of start-ups. As mentioned earlier, we may assume that the decisions on independent start-ups are mainly based on human capital structure, while the location of new subsidiaries is determined by considerations of demand and cost factors. Moreover, regional factors of start-ups may vary across sectors and industries, depending on whether we focus on independent start-ups or new subsidiaries. For example, the location choice of new subsidiaries would not necessarily depend on local demand conditions in manufacturing industries with wide, possibly foreign, markets, while it would be influenced by the human capital in the region in the case of knowledge-intensive services.

The aim of this chapter is, therefore, to investigate the impact of regional human capital structure on the start-up ratio using Japanese data at the prefecture level, differentiating between independent start-ups and new subsidiaries of existing firms. Moreover, we will compare the effects of regional human capital structure on entry across different industries and sectors. Since these issues have not been explicitly explored by existing studies, this chapter makes a major contribution to the literature by ana- lysing them. One policy implication that could be derived from our study is that regional policies to activate business start-ups should recognize the differences between encouraging local entrepreneurship and attracting new subsidiaries. In addition, these differences may vary even within the service sector according to technological intensity.

The remainder of this chapter is organized as follows. The second section reviews the previous literature on regional variations of the start-up ratio. On the basis of the literature review, the third section pro- vides our hypotheses for the empirical analysis. In the fourth section, we present our research framework to capture the determinants of regional differences in the entry of independent start-ups and new subsidiaries. The fifth section provides the estimation results and discusses them. The final section provides concluding remarks.

LITERATURE REVIEW

Determinants of regional entry have been investigated since the 1990s in several countries using various kinds of regional variables, including demand factors, cost factors, business agglomeration, labour force structure, industry structure and some other factors (see, for example, Okamuro and Kobayashi, 2005, for a detailed survey of the relevant literature).

Several studies demonstrate that the start-up ratio is higher in regions with a higher level and growth of regional demand measured by the size and growth of population or income (e.g., Audretsch and Fritsch, 1994a; Davidsson et al., 1994; Reynolds et al., 1995; Acs and Armington, 2004). It is also empirically established that the start-up ratio is negatively correlated with the level of factor costs, especially with wage level (Gerlach and Wagner, 1994; Santarelli and Piergiovanni, 1995; Audretsch and Vivarelli, 1996). Moreover, several studies indicate that the start-up ratio is positively affected by agglomeration, measured by population or business density (Audretsch and Fritsch, 1994a; Davidsson et al., 1994; Acs and Armington, 2004). With regard to the industry structure, previous studies concur that a smaller share of the manufacturing sector and a larger share of the service sector have positive effects on the start-up ratio (Evans and Leighton, 1989; Reynolds et al., 1995; Egeln et al., 1997).

With regard to labour force structure, numerous studies focus on the effects of the qualitative and quantitative composition of regional labour force as well as the impact of the employment situation on the start-up ratio. The qualitative composition denotes the endowment of a highly educated or skilled labour force (we will address this in detail later), while the quantitative composition is mainly measured by the age structure of the labour force (Evans and Leighton, 1989; Reynolds et al., 1995; Egeln et al., 1997). As for the effect of the unemployment ratio on the start-up ratio, there are contrasting views (the push hypothesis suggesting a positive impact and the pull hypothesis suggesting a negative impact), both of which find empirical support.[3]

The impact of the qualitative composition of the regional labour force with regard to education, job experience and technical skills has attracted considerable attention from the human capital perspective. Several studies demonstrate that the ratio of white-collar to blue-collar workers (Keeble and Walker, 1994; Fotopoulos and Spence, 1999) and the proportions of college graduates (Guesnier, 1994; Armington and Acs, 2002; Acs and

Armington, 2004) and the workforce in professional and managerial occupations (Guesnier, 1994; Hart and Gudgin, 1994) have positive effects on the start-up ratio.

Such a regional labour force structure proxies the agglomeration of human capital in the regions. Following Becker (1975), the previous literature distinguishes between the generic and specific components of human capital. Generic human capital is related to the general knowledge acquired by founders through formal education and professional experience. Specific human capital comprises capabilities that founders can directly apply to the entrepreneurial jobs in new businesses and that can be obtained through prior work experience in the same industry (industry-specific human capital) or through managerial and self-employment experience (entrepreneur-specific human capital) (Colombo and Grilli, 2005). Therefore, we may expect that regions that show a higher ratio of highly educated labour force with rich professional, managerial or specific work experience would be characterized by larger agglomeration of human capital.

Why and how does such regional human capital structure positively affect the start-up of new businesses? Acs and Armington (2004, 2006) indicate the following three reasons. First, the agglomeration of a highly educated and skilled labour force generates entrepreneurs with new ideas for creating new businesses (Glaeser et al., 1992). Second, it also promotes local knowledge spillovers, by which new start-ups are initiated and sustained (Reynolds et al., 1995). Third, it facilitates the founders of new firms to search for and hire skilled labour (Rauch, 1993).

A recent trend of research on regional variations of the start-up ratio is to differentiate between and compare start-up types, such as high- versus low-tech (Okamuro, 2008) and independent businesses versus new subsidiaries (Bosma et al., 2008). On the basis of micro data of start-ups in the Japanese manufacturing sector, Okamuro (2008) shows that regions characterized by agglomerations of highly educated and specialized human capital, as well as research institutes and high-tech industries, attract high-tech start-ups (those in high-tech industries), while a high unemployment ratio would draw only low-tech start-ups (push hypothesis).

Bosma et al. (2008) is practically the first study that directly addresses and empirically investigates the determinants of location choice of subsidiaries in comparison to independent start-ups. Using a Dutch regional database, they find that localization economies positively affect independent business start-ups, while urbanization economies stimulate the entry of new subsidiaries. However, they do not explicitly consider the effects of regional human capital, although agglomeration economies also include general benefits such as access to a highly qualified labour pool.

Bosma et al. (2008) argue that the incentives for establishing a firm in a particular region are essentially different for independent start-ups and new subsidiaries. A founder of an independent firm will decide whether or not to start a business, comparing the expected utility of a business start-up with that of remaining an employee. In contrast, founders of new subsidiaries may not necessarily work themselves in these subsidiaries, and thus will choose the best location for the subsidiaries, considering several regional characteristics such as demand and cost factors. Thus, we may expect that, among various regional factors, the regional structure of human capital affects the entry of independent start-ups more strongly than that of new subsidiaries. In this sense, it is important to compare the effect of regional human capital structure between independent start-ups and new subsidiaries.

Moreover, policy measures to stimulate start-ups by inhabitants and to attract new subsidiaries, especially of firms located outside the region, may be quite different. Therefore, in the current study, we will explore different impacts of human capital on the entry of independent businesses and subsidiaries, founded on the basic models of Bosma et al. (2008) along with the concepts of Okamuro (2008).

Several previous studies compare the factors of regional entry in the manufacturing and service sectors (Audretsch and Fritsch, 1994a; Hart and Gudgin, 1994; Keeble and Walker, 1994; Audretsch and Vivarelli, 1996; Bosma et al., 2008) and in high- versus low-tech industries in the manufacturing sector (Nerlinger, 1998; Okamuro, 2008). Inter-industry comparison within the manufacturing or service sectors has not been conducted, except by Armington and Acs (2002) and Acs and Armington (2004), who performed sub-sample analyses in the service sector. In contrast to these studies, our research not only compares manufacturing and service sectors but also distinguishes between relatively high- and low-tech industries in the service sector. Thus, another contribution of this chapter is to compare different industries in the service sector, differentiating between independent start-ups and subsidiaries.

HYPOTHESES

Regional human capital structure might have different impacts on independent start-ups and new subsidiaries for the following reasons. On the one hand, the regional structure of human capital is expected to play a significant role for independent start-ups because they depend on the decisions of people living or working in the region.[4] On the other hand, location choices of new subsidiaries are based on the decisions by the top management of the existing firms, which could be located outside the region. In this case, the regional level of demand and cost may be more important than the regional human capital structure, because the heads of new subsidiaries often come from other regions, especially the headquarters.

As the measures of regional human capital structure, we focus on the ratio of college graduates and the ratio of the workers in professional and technical occupations to the labour force. According to the above discussion on human capital based on Becker (1975), both measures relate to generic human capital.

With regard to the ratio of college graduates, previous studies such as Colombo and Grilli (2005) argue that highly educated workers are likely to be more capable ('capability theory') and earn higher incomes ('wealth effect') than others. They may have good ideas and projects for their new businesses and thus expect a high return from independent start-ups, on the one hand, and may be financially less constrained, on the other. Hence, they are more likely to start new businesses than others. However, previous studies for Japan demonstrate that highly educated persons are more reluctant to start their own businesses than others (e.g. Small and Medium Enterprise Agency, 2002), because, especially under the traditional Japanese employment system, they are aware of the high opportunity cost of quitting the current job to start a business.

Thus, the effect of high education on the regional entry of independent start-ups can be either positive or negative. Which of these contrasting effects is stronger than the other at the regional level is therefore an empirical question. Consequently, we propose the following hypotheses with regard to the entry of independent start-ups.

Hypothesis 1a: The agglomeration of *college graduates* at the prefecture level has a positive impact on the entry rate of independent start-ups in the prefecture.

Hypothesis 1b: The agglomeration of *college graduates* at the prefecture level has a negative impact on the entry rate of independent start-ups in the prefecture.

The top managers of the subsidiaries of existing firms are not necessarily recruited from among the inhabitants of the region where the subsidiaries are located. If the firms are located outside the region, the top managers of the subsidiaries are also often appointed from outside the region. Hence, in this regard, the availability of highly educated workers in the region is not expected to matter much for the entry of subsidiaries.

However, in the case of local firms, the top managers of new subsidiaries are usually recruited from among local workers or managers. Moreover, even firms located outside the region recruit (at least partly) local workers as the employees for their subsidiaries. In these cases, regions that can provide many highly educated and skilled workers would attract the entry of subsidiaries.[5] Therefore, we expect a positive impact of college graduates also on the entry of subsidiaries, which is formulated in the following hypothesis.

Hypothesis 2:   The agglomeration of *college graduates* at the prefecture level has a positive impact on the entry rate of subsidiaries in the prefecture.

According to the Japan Standard Occupation Classification, professional and technical occupations include various types of scientists and engineers, medical and health-care services, social welfare services, legal services and business support services (see note 6). People engaged in these occupations may not only have the potential to start new businesses (especially high-tech ventures or specialized service firms) by themselves, but also can be employed in new high-tech ventures or service firms. Moreover, they (especially those in legal and business support services) can also provide founders of new businesses with professional support. Thus, we postulate that the agglomeration of the workers in professional and technical occupations positively affects the entry of independent start-ups.

With regard to subsidiaries, even if professional workers such as engineers are required, they can be recruited from other regions or brought from the headquarters or other subsidiaries. Moreover, unlike the de novo start-up of independent firms, the entry of new subsidiaries may not require local professional support. Therefore, we do not expect any positive relationship between the regional structure of professional and technical workers and the entry of new subsidiaries.

Hypothesis 3:   The agglomeration of professional and technical workers at the prefecture level has a positive impact only on the entry rate of independent start-ups in the prefecture.

We test these hypotheses not only with a sample of all industries but also with sub-samples of manufacturing and service sectors. These sectors may differ in their sensitivity to regional supply and demand (market) conditions as well as in the required levels and types of human capital. We also examine whether or not the effects of regional human capital are different between high- and low-tech industries in the service sector. In high-tech (research-intensive) industries such as the information and communication industry, firms generally face rapid technological development. To survive technological competition, entrepreneurs in high-tech industries require highly educated and skilled workers to a larger extent than those in low-tech industries.

EMPIRICAL MODEL AND DATA

We estimate the impact of various regional factors on the entry rate of independent start-ups and new subsidiaries for each industry sector in the sample. Relying on Bosma et al. (2008), we employ the seemingly unrelated regression (SUR) method, which assumes correlation between the error terms of two regression models, because variables affecting the entries of both independent businesses and subsidiaries might be omitted. By the SUR estimation procedure, regression models for both types of entries are simultaneously estimated, and asymptotically more efficient estimators (i.e. more efficient than the OLS estimator) can be obtained (Zellner, 1962; 1963). Moreover, as mentioned above, we estimate the same models for each industry sector in the sample and compare the results.

Following Bosma et al. (2008), we estimate the following model:

$$\ln SR^{\text{Ind}} = \alpha_0^{\text{Ind}} + \alpha_1^{\text{Ind}} H + \mathbf{x}' \boldsymbol{\gamma}^{\text{Ind}} + e^{\text{Ind}},$$
$$\ln SR^{\text{Sub}} = \alpha_0^{\text{Sub}} + \alpha_1^{\text{Sub}} H + \mathbf{x}' \boldsymbol{\gamma}^{\text{Sub}} + e^{\text{Sub}},$$
$$cor(e^{\text{Ind}}, e^{\text{Sub}}) = \rho.$$

The dependent variables are the entry rates of independent establishment (SR^{Ind}) and of new subsidiaries (SR^{Sub}) in natural logarithms. Following Bosma et al. (2008), we use the variables of the workforce and the stock of existing establishments to measure and control for the effect of economic size in the regions. In other words, we apply the 'labour market approach' to independent start-ups and the 'ecological approach' to new subsidiaries (c.f. Audretsch and Fritsch, 1994b).

As the main subject of this chapter, we examine the effects of regional human capital structure (H) on the entry rate of independent start-ups and new subsidiaries. As the variables for regional human capital structure, we use the ratio of highly educated workforce (the ratio of college graduates) and the ratio of the workforce in professional and technical occupations. The other determinants of entry ($\mathbf{x}$) comprise demand and supply factors (population growth rate, wage rate and unemployment rate) and a measure of agglomeration economies.

Regional Entry in Japan

We use pooled regional data at the prefecture level from four periods (1996–1999, 1999–2001, 2001–2004 and 2004–2006). With 47 prefectures in Japan, we have, at most, 188 observations in our pooled sample. In general, a prefecture in Japan is, on average, smaller than a state in the US but larger than a county or city. Thus, it may be too large an area to represent the local (labour) market. However, we cannot obtain appropriate data for a narrower regional classification level (i.e. of the 'municipality'), which is the main reason for the use of the prefecture-level data.

Table 6.1 shows the definitions and the descriptive statistics of the variables used for our regressions. Regional start-up data are obtained from the e-Stat Database of the Establishment and Enterprise Census. The number of regional independent start-ups in Japan from 1996 to 2006 is, on average, 4600 per prefecture, annually, which is more than the number of new subsidiaries (2400 on average). These numbers vary significantly among regions; the maximum number of regional start-ups is more than 60 times the minimum.

To control for the effects of regional economic size, we use the regional workforce and stock of establishments, obtained from the Establishment and Enterprise Census, as proxies for regional economic size. As shown in Table 6.1, the entry rate of independent start-ups is, on average, 4.16 per 1000 workers and ranges from 2.00 to 14.16 across prefectures, while that of new subsidiaries is, on average, 1.7 per cent of the existing establishments and ranges from 0.58 per cent to 3.45 per cent across prefectures. Thus, although the entry rate in Japan is at the lowest level among OECD countries in recent years, the entry rates of both independent start-ups and new subsidiaries are significantly different among regions in Japan.

In addition, the ratio of the number of new subsidiaries to the total number of entries at the national level increased from 32.6 per cent in the period 1996–1999 to 37.5 per cent in the period 2004–2006. This ratio and its trend are almost the same as those in the Netherlands (Bosma et al., 2008). An increase in this ratio can also be observed at the prefecture level. It ranges from 15.3 per cent to 41.5 per cent across prefectures in the period 1996–1999 and from 21.7 per cent to 45.1 per cent in the period 2004–2006.

The number of entries and the rate of entry also differ between industries. Table 6.1 shows the industrial composition of regional independent start-ups and new subsidiaries. The entry rates both of independent start-ups and new subsidiaries are higher in the service sector than in manufacturing. Within the service sector, they are relatively lower in the information and communication industry, compared to commercial establishments and the restaurant industry.

Table 6.1   Definitions of the variables and sample statistics

	No. of obs.	Mean	S.D.	Min.	Max.
N^{Ind} = Number of independent start-ups per year (per 1000 establishments)					
Overall industry	188	4.60	5.73	0.63	44.75
Manufacturing sector	188	0.28	0.39	0.03	2.97
Service sector	188	3.85	4.89	0.51	38.38
Information & communication	94	0.08	0.30	0.01	2.61
Commerce & restaurants	94	1.81	1.98	0.27	13.42
N^{sub} = Number of new subsidiaries per year (per 1000 establishments)					
Overall industry	188	2.40	2.97	0.34	20.73
Manufacturing sector	188	0.11	0.15	0.01	0.99
Service sector	188	2.09	2.61	0.30	18.62
Information & communication	94	0.07	0.13	0.01	1.00
Commerce & restaurants	94	1.17	1.44	0.19	9.67
WF = Work force (1000 workforce)	188	1161.54	1347.17	228.67	8416.06
ES = Number of existing establishments (per 1000 establishments)					
Overall industry	188	130.41	126.09	27.91	759.21
Manufacturing sector	188	14.26	16.54	1.91	97.46
Service sector	188	100.98	99.83	22.28	595.23
Information & communication	94	1.22	2.75	0.18	18.83
Commerce & restaurants	94	54.27	51.34	12.37	299.27
SR^{Ind} = Entry rate of independent start-ups = $1000 \times N^{Ind}/WF$					
Overall industry	188	4.16	1.87	2.00	14.16
Manufacturing sector	188	0.24	0.13	0.07	0.62
Service sector	188	3.45	1.59	1.66	12.72
Information & communication	94	0.04	0.04	0.01	0.34
Commerce & restaurants	94	1.75	0.84	0.88	7.29

Table 6.1   (continued)

	No. of obs.	Mean	S.D.	Min.	Max.
SR^{sub} = Entry rate of new subsidiaries = $100 \times N^{sub}/ES$					
Overall industry	188	1.70	0.68	0.58	3.45
Manufacturing sector	188	0.79	0.40	0.18	1.97
Service sector	188	1.92	0.75	0.64	3.83
Information & communication	94	5.93	2.52	1.99	13.69
Commerce & restaurants	94	1.95	0.72	0.82	3.79
CollegeGrad = 100 ×college graduates/ workforce (in 2000)	188	12.23	3.74	7.18	24.19
Expert = 100×number of workers in professional and technical occupations/workforce	188	12.79	1.38	10.10	16.97
Wage = Wage rate (100 yen per hour)	188	2.06	0.27	1.55	2.93
PopGrowth = % growth between (t-4) and (t-1)	188	−0.05	1.07	−2.66	2.80
Unemp = Unemployment rate (%)	188	4.74	1.30	2.52	11.40
Localization = 1000×number of existing establishments/regional					
Overall industry	188	49.70	6.52	30.80	64.93
Manufacturing sector	188	5.15	2.16	2.07	12.09
Service sector	188	38.26	4.74	24.77	50.41
Information & communication	94	0.34	0.20	0.13	1.55
Commerce & restaurants	94	20.91	2.85	12.73	26.88

Independent Variables

In order to test our hypotheses on the relationship between regional human capital structure and regional new business start-ups, as mentioned in the previous section, we use the proportions of college graduates (*CollegeGrad*) and workers in professional and technical occupations[6]

(*Expert*) to the entire workforce in each prefecture; these were obtained from the Population Census. As shown in Table 6.1, the mean values of both *CollegeGrad* and *Expert* are approximately 12 per cent–13 per cent, while the regional variations of these variables are different. The proportion of college graduates ranges from 7.2 per cent to 24.2 per cent across regions (standard deviation is 3.7), while that of expert workers ranges from 10.1 per cent to 17.0 per cent (standard deviation is 1.4).

We also include in the estimation models several control variables as additional determinants of regional start-up rate. The definitions and descriptive statistics of these variables are summarized in Table 6.1. Following Bosma et al. (2008), we include the population growth rate (*PopGrowth*), the natural logarithm of average wage rate (*Wage*) and the unemployment rate (*Unemp*) as demand and supply factors for regional entrepreneurship[7] and the ratio of establishment stock (*ES*) of each industry to the population as a measure of 'localization economy' (*Localization*).

We also consider including the population density of each prefecture as a proxy for *urbanization economy* as another agglomeration factor, following Bosma et al. (2008). However, since the correlation between population density and *CollegeGrad* is very high (0.721), we do not include this proxy for urbanization economy in the estimation models in order to avoid multicollinearity.

We expect the coefficients of the variables *PopGrowth* and *Localization* will be positive. For the independent start-up rate, the coefficient of the variable *Unemp* is expected to be positive according to the 'push hypothesis' and negative according to the 'pull hypothesis', while it is expected to be negative (also according to 'pull hypothesis') or insignificant for new subsidiaries.

The effect of the variable *Wage* on the entry rate of subsidiaries would be negative, since a higher wage rate implies a higher cost to hire employees for new subsidiaries from the local labour market. Further, the effect of the wage rate on the independent start-up rate would be negative since the regional wage rate should directly reflect a potential entrepreneur's opportunity cost of quitting the current job to start a new business.

However, the regional wage rate is highly correlated with the college graduates ratio (*CollegeGrad*) in our dataset (see Table 6.2). Since the productivity of highly educated workers would be relatively high and the wage rate offered for such productive workers would also be high, we would not be able to distinguish the opportunity cost effects of new business start-ups for highly educated workers from the effects of wage rate. For this reason, we include the variable *Wage* only in the equation for

Table 6.2 Correlation coefficients of the variables

		\multicolumn{5}{c}{$\ln SR^{Ind}$}				
		(1)	(2)	(3)	(4)	(5)
$\ln SR^{Ind}$						
Overall industry	(1)	1.000				
Manufacturing sector	(2)	0.748	1.000			
Service sector	(3)	0.996	0.699	1.000		
Information & communication	(4)	0.685	0.478	0.697	1.000	
Commerce & restaurants	(5)	0.969	0.592	0.978	0.604	1.000
$\ln SR^{sub}$						
Overall industry	(6)	0.716	0.568	0.708	0.675	0.642
Manufacturing sector	(7)	0.688	0.451	0.683	0.580	0.608
Service sector	(8)	0.682	0.590	0.669	0.650	0.619
Information & communication	(9)	0.782	0.596	0.770	0.531	0.696
Commerce & restaurants	(10)	0.665	0.500	0.659	0.645	0.536
CollegeGrad	(a)	−0.073	0.107	−0.063	0.327	−0.205
Expert	(b)	0.217	0.051	0.252	0.449	0.148
ln (wage)	(c)	−0.208	0.124	−0.214	0.122	−0.448
PopGrowth	(d)	−0.123	0.021	−0.116	0.161	−0.313
Unemp	(e)	0.478	0.130	0.531	0.520	0.746
Localization (of own industry)	(f)	−0.120	0.335	0.027	0.562	0.006

		\multicolumn{5}{c}{$\ln SR^{Sub}$}				
		(6)	(7)	(8)	(9)	(10)
$\ln SR^{Sub}$						
Overall industry	(6)	1.000				
Manufacturing sector	(7)	0.886	1.000			
Service sector	(8)	0.993	0.851	1.000		
Information & communication	(9)	0.875	0.726	0.874	1.000	
Commerce & restaurants	(10)	0.976	0.826	0.975	0.817	1.000

Table 6.2   (continued)

		InSR^{Sub}				
		(6)	(7)	(8)	(9)	(10)
CollegeGrad	(a)	0.222	0.028	0.232	0.025	0.313
Expert	(b)	0.288	0.175	0.259	0.082	0.237
In *(wage)*	(c)	0.129	−0.026	0.155	−0.143	0.133
PopGrowth	(d)	0.008	−0.032	0.008	−0.171	0.104
Unemp	(e)	0.316	0.296	0.266	0.441	0.348
Localization (of own industry)	(f)	−0.454	−0.474	−0.410	−0.175	−0.585
		(a)	(b)	(c)	(d)	(e)
CollegeGrad	(a)	1.000				
Expert	(b)	0.699	1.000			
In *(wage)*	(c)	0.842	0.412	1.000		
PopGrowth	(d)	0.655	0.313	0.622	1.000	
Unemp	(e)	0.083	0.434	−0.108	−0.006	1.000
Localization	(f)					
Overall industry		−0.322	−0.384	−0.155	−0.139	−0.267
Manufacturing sector		0.165	--0.287	0.384	0.202	−0.441
Service sector		−0.356	0.224	−0.285	−0.192	−0.001
Information & communication		0.433	0.373	0.414	0.411	0.049
Commerce & restaurants		−0.480	−0.271	−0.361	−0.303	−0.009

the entry rate of new subsidiaries (SR^{Sub}) as a basic specification. We will then check the robustness of the estimation results of the basic models by excluding *Wage* from the equation SR^{Sub}.

Finally, dummy variables for the periods 1999–2001, 2001–2004 and 2004–2006 (period dummies: the baseline reference is the period 1996–1999) are included in the estimation models in order to control for the time-variant differences of start-up ratio in each prefecture.

ESTIMATION RESULTS

SUR estimation results of the overall industry (excluding the primary sector) are shown in Tables 6.3a and 6.3b. For each specification, the results of the equations for the entry rates of independent establishments

Table 6.3a   SUR estimation results for overall industry

Specification	I(a)			I(b)		
Industry	Overall industry			Overall industry		
Dependent variable	lnSR^{Ind}	lnSR^{Sub}	VIF	lnSR^{Ind}	lnSR^{Sub}	VIF
Constant	−6.891***	−4.6***		−6.891***	−4.787***	
	[0.129]	[0.197]		[0.129]	[0.132]	
CollegeGrad	−0.039***	0.036***	8.3	−0.039***	0.026***	2.1
	[0.005]	[0.009]		[0.005]	[0.005]	
Expert	0.122***	−0.015	3.1	0.122***	−0.005	2.3
	[0.013]	[0.016]		[0.013]	[0.014]	
ln(*Wage Rate*)		−0.271	4.9			
		[0.212]				
Period dummy	Yes	Yes	1.3	Yes	Yes	1.2
N	188	188		188	188	
R squared	0.841	0.832		0.841	0.831	
Correlation between residuals of both equations:	0.016			0.046		
Breusch–Pagan test of independence:	0.0			0.4		

Specification	I(c)			I(d)		
Industry	Overall industry			Overall industry		
Dependent variable	lnSR^{Ind}	lnSR^{Sub}	VIF	lnSR^{Ind}	lnSR^{Sub}	VIF
Constant	−5.79***	−4.761***		−6.388***	−5.201***	
	[0.056]	[0.08]		[0.133]	[0.123]	
CollegeGrad	−0.008**	0.03***	3.6			
	[0.004]	[0.006]				
Expert				0.041***	0.003***	1.3
				[0.011]	[0.011]	
ln(*Wage Rate*)		−0.196	3.6		0.426***	1.3
		[0.183]			[0.112]	
Period dummy	Yes	Yes	1.1	Yes	Yes	1.1

and subsidiaries are shown in the first column (lnSR^{Ind}) and second column (lnSR^{Sub}) respectively, and the scores of the variation inflation factor (VIF) for each independent variable are also shown in the third column to check if a multicollinearity problem occurs. [8]

In specification I(a), in which the natural logarithm of the wage rate

Table 6.3a   (continued)

Specification	I(c)			I(d)		
Industry	Overall industry			Overall industry		
Dependent variable	lnSR^{Ind}	lnSR^{Sub}	VIF	lnSR^{Ind}	lnSR^{Sub}	VIF
N	188	188		188	188	
R squared	0.768	0.832		0.780	0.819	
Correlation between residuals of both equations:		−0.018			0.003	
Breusch–Pagan test of independence:		0.1			0.0	

Specification	I(e)			I(f)		
Industry	Overall industry			Overall industry		
Dependent variable	lnSR^{Ind}	lnSR^{Sub}	VIF	lnSR^{Ind}	lnSR^{Sub}	VIF
Constant	−5.791***	−4.83***		−6.388***	−5.116***	
	[0.056]	[0.047]		[0.133]	[0.125]	
CollegeGrad	−0.008**	0.025***	1.0			
	[0.004]	[0.003]				
Expert				0.041***	0.048***	1.1
				[0.011]	[0.01]	1.1
Period dummy	Yes	Yes	1.0	Yes	Yes	
N	188	188		188	188	
R squared	0.768	0.831		0.780	0.804	
Correlation between residuals of both equations:		0.023			−0.158	
Breusch–Pagan test of independence:		0.1			4.7**	

Notes:
Standard errors are shown in brackets.
*** $p < .01$, ** $p < .05$.
Sample periods: 1996–1999, 1999–2001, 2001–2004 and 2004–2006.

is included in the equation for the entry rate of subsidiaries, the VIF score for *CollegeGrad* is 8.3. This indicates that the correlation between *CollegeGrad* and the other independent variable may cause multicollinearity. Thus, for a robustness check, we estimate other specifications in which

Table 6.3b   *SUR estimation results for overall industry (with control variables)*

Specification	I(g)			I(h)		
Industry	Overall industry			Overall industry		
Dependent variable	$\ln SR^{Ind}$	$\ln SR^{Sub}$	VIF	$\ln SR^{Ind}$	$\ln SR^{Sub}$	VIF
Constant	−6.984***	−3.825***		−6.984***	−3.901***	
	[0.121]	[0.204]		[0.121]	[0.172]	
CollegeGrad	−0.026***	0.02**	9.8	−0.026***	0.015**	4.0
	[0.004]	[0.009]		[0.004]	[0.006]	
Expert	0.56***	−0.024	3.7	0.056***	−0.019	3.1
	[0.01]	[0.015]		[0.01]	[0.014]	
ln(Wage Rate)		−0.135	5.1			
		[0.192]				
PopGrowth	0.013	0.038**	2.5	0.013	0.037**	2.4
	[0.011]	[0.016]		[0.011]	[0.016]	
Unemp	0.12***	0.015	1.7	0.12***	0.016	1.7
	[0.008]	[0.011]		[0.008]	[0.011]	
Localization	0.004***	−0.012***	1.4	0.004***	−0.012***	1.3
	[0.001]	[0.002]		[0.001]	[0.002]	
Period dummy	Yes	Yes	2.1	Yes	Yes	1.9
N	188	188		188	188	
R squared	0.937	0.872		0.937	0.872	
Correlation between residuals of both equations:	−0.067			−0.044		
Breusch–Pagan test of independence:	0.9			0.4		

Notes:
Standard errors are shown in brackets.
*** $p < .01$, ** $p < .05$.
Sample periods: 1996–1999, 1999–2001, 2001–2004 and 2004–2006.

the variables highly correlated with *CollegeGrad* are excluded. In specification I(b), I(e) and I(f), the wage rate is excluded. In specification I(c), I(d), I(e) and I(f), *CollegeGrad* and *Expert* are included interchangeably. Furthermore, we confirm that results do not change even after including the other control variables in Table 6.3b. The difference between specification I(g) and I(h) arises from the inclusion or exclusion of the wage rate.

For all specifications, the coefficient of *CollegeGrad* for independent start-ups is negative and significant at least at the 5 per cent level;

the coefficients of *Expert* for independent start-ups and *CollegeGrad* for new subsidiaries are positive and significant at the 1 per cent level. These results support Hypothesis 1a, Hypothesis 2 and Hypothesis 3. According to these results, an agglomeration of a highly educated workforce attracts new subsidiaries, on the one hand, but decreases the independent start-up rate, on the other hand, while an agglomeration of workers in professional and technical occupations promotes regional entrepreneurship.

With regard to the effect of control variables, an increase in the wage level has an overall negative but not significant effect, while the population growth and unemployment rate have positive impacts on both types of start-up rates. However, the effect of population growth is significant only for the entry rate of subsidiaries, while the effect of the unemployment rate is significant only for the ratio of independent start-ups. Similar to the results of Bosma et al. (2008), we find a significant and positive impact of localization economies only on independent start-ups.

Manufacturing and Service Industries

Tables 6.4a and 6.4b show the estimation results for the manufacturing industry and the service industry. We find some differences in the determinants of entry between the manufacturing and service sectors. In the manufacturing industry, the proportion of college graduates (*CollegeGrad*) positively affects independent start-ups, while this human capital structure has no significant effects on new subsidiaries; the coefficient of *Expert* for independent start-ups is negative and significant. These results support Hypothesis 1a but do not support Hypothesis 2 and Hypothesis 3. This implies that the agglomeration of highly educated workforce (rather than the professional and technical workforce) promotes regional entrepreneurship in the manufacturing sector, but regional human capital structures, contrary to our expectation, do not influence the decision on the location of new subsidiaries.

In the service industry, the results are the same as those for the industry as a whole. The proportion of college graduates (*CollegeGrad*) has a negative and significant effect on the entry rate of independent establishments and a positive and significant effect on new subsidiaries at the 1 per cent level. The proportion of professional and technical workers (*Expert*) has a positive and significant effect on the independent start-up rate at the 1 per cent level. These results are consistent with Hypothesis 1b, Hypothesis 2 and Hypothesis 3. It implies that in the service sector an agglomeration of highly educated workforce attracts new subsidiaries, while workers in professional and technical occupations promote regional entrepreneurship.

Table 6.4a   SUR estimation results for the manufacturing and service sectors

Specification	II(a)					II(b)				
Industry	Manufacturing		Service			Manufacturing		Service		
Dependent variable	InSR^Ind	InSR^Sub	InSR^Ind	InSR^Sub	VIF	InSR^Ind	InSR^Sub	InSR^Ind	InSR^Sub	VIF
Equation	(i)	(ii)	(iii)	(iv)		(i)	(ii)	(iii)	(iv)	
Constant	−8.209***	−5.611***	−7.257***	−4.4***		−8.209***	−5.656***	−7.257***	−4.44***	
	[0.226]	[0.335]	[0.139]	[0.173]		[0.226]	[0.248]	[0.139]	[0.123]	
CollegeGrad	0.039***	0.004	−0.043***	0.034***	8.3	0.039***	0.001	−0.043***	0.032***	2.1
	[0.008]	[0.015]	[0.005]	[0.008]		[0.008]	[0.009]	[0.005]	[0.005]	
Expert	−0.092***	0.008	0.142***	−0.03**	3.1	−0.092***	0.011	0.142***	−0.028**	2.3
	[0.023]	[0.028]	[0.014]	[0.014]		[0.023]	[0.026]	[0.014]	[0.013]	
ln(Wage Rate)		−0.065		−0.058	4.9					
		[0.325]		[0.176]						
Period dummy	Yes	Yes	Yes	Yes	1.3	Yes	Yes	Yes	Yes	1.2

	(i)	(ii)	(iii)	(iv)		(i)	(ii)	(iii)	(iv)
N	188	188	188	188		188	188	188	188
R squared	0.693	0.654	0.813	0.848		0.693	0.653	0.813	0.848
Correlation of the residuals with the equation:									
(i)	1.000	−0.503	0.331	−0.448		1.000	−0.502	0.331	−0.447
(ii)	−0.503	1.000	0.129	0.648		−0.502	1.000	0.133	0.649
(iii)	0.331	0.129	1.000	−0.006		0.331	0.133	1.000	0.001
(iv)	−0.448	0.648	−0.006	1.000		−0.447	0.649	0.001	1.000
Breusch–Pagan test of independence:	187.9***					188.1***			

Notes:
Standard errors are shown in brackets.
*** $p < .01$, ** $p < .05$.
Sample periods: 1996–1999, 1999–2001, 2001–2004 and 2004–2006.

137

Table 6.4b *SUR estimation results for the manufacturing and service sectors*

Specification	II(a)					II(b)				
Industry	Manufacturing		Service			Manufacturing		Service		
Dependent variable	$\ln SR^{Ind}$	$\ln SR^{Sub}$	$\ln SR^{Ind}$	$\ln SR^{Sub}$	VIF	$\ln SR^{Ind}$	$\ln SR^{Sub}$	$\ln SR^{Ind}$	$\ln SR^{Sub}$	VIF
Equation	(i)	(ii)	(iii)	(iv)		(i)	(ii)	(iii)	(iv)	
Constant	−8.125**	−5.319***	−7.04***	−4.296***		−8.125***	−5.504***	−7.04***	−4.399***	
	[0.226]	[0.319]	[0.085]	[0.171]		[0.226]	[0.239]	[0.085]	[0.123]	
CollegeGrad	0.043***	−0.014	−0.029***	0.028***	9.5	0.043***	−0.024**	−0.029***	0.022***	4.0
	[0.011]	[0.016]	[0.004]	[0.009]		[0.011]	[0.012]	[0.004]	[0.006]	
Expert	−0.121***	0.003	0.063***	−0.028*	3.7	−0.121***	0.012	0.063***	−0.023	3.1
	[0.027]	[0.03]	[0.01]	[0.016]		[0.027]	[0.028]	[0.01]	[0.015]	
$\ln(Wage\ Rate)$		−0.269		−0.15	5.0					
		[0.308]		[0.173]						
PopGrowth	0.008	0.131***	0.008	0.046***	2.4	0.008	0.129***	0.008	0.045***	2.4
	[0.03]	[0.032]	[0.011]	[0.017]		[0.03]	[0.032]	[0.011]	[0.016]	
Unemp	0.05**	0.022	0.135***	−0.001	1.7	0.05**	0.024	0.135***	0.000	1.7
	[0.021]	[0.022]	[0.008]	[0.012]		[0.021]	[0.022]	[0.008]	[0.011]	
Period dummy	Yes	Yes	Yes	Yes	1.9	Yes	Yes	Yes	Yes	1.7

N	188	188	188	188	188	188	188	188
R squared	0.703	0.692	0.933	0.855	0.703	0.689	0.933	0.854
Correlation of the residuals with the equation:								
(i)	1.000	-0.577	0.311	-0.480	1.000	-0.575	0.311	-0.479
(ii)	-0.577	1.000	-0.015	0.628	-0.575	1.000	0.005	0.631
(iii)	0.311	-0.015	1.000	-0.105	0.311	0.005	1.000	-0.084
(iv)	-0.480	0.628	-0.105	1.000	-0.479	0.631	-0.084	1.000
Breusch–Pagan test of independence:				200.4***				199.6***

Notes:
Standard errors are shown in brackets.
*** $p < .01$, ** $p < .05$
* $p < .10$.
Sample periods: 2001–2004 and 2004–2006.

Table 6.4c SUR estimation for the manufacturing and service sectors (controlled for localization economy)

Specification	II(a)						II(b)					
Industry	Manufacturing			Service			Manufacturing			Service		
Dependent variable	$InSR^{Ind}$	$InSR^{Sub}$	VIF	$InSR^{Ind}$	$InSR^{Sub}$	VIF	$InSR^{Ind}$	$InSR^{Sub}$	VIF	$InSR^{Ind}$	$InSR^{Sub}$	VIF
Equation	(i)	(ii)		(iii)	(iv)		(i)	(ii)		(iii)	(iv)	
Constant	-10.018***	-4.02***		-7.357***	-3.724***		-10.014***	-3.813***		-7.359***	-3.837***	
	[0.183]	[0.255]		[0.106]	[0.188]		[0.183]	[0.203]		[0.106]	[0.148]	
CollegeGrad	-0.003	0.005	9.5	-0.025***	0.022**	9.9	-0.003	0.017**	4.7	-0.025***	0.016***	4.2
	[0.008]	[0.012]		[0.004]	[0.009]		[0.008]	[0.009]		[0.004]	[0.006]	
Expert	0.005	-0.092***	4.1	0.061***	-0.024	3.7	0.005	-0.1***	3.8	0.061***	-0.019	3.1
	[0.019]	[0.022]		[0.01]	[0.015]		[0.019]	[0.021]		[0.01]	[0.014]	
ln(Wage Rate)		0.378	5.3		-0.168	5.0						
		[0.268]			[0.181]							
PopGrowth	0.012	0.122***	2.4	0.014	0.036**	2.5	0.012	0.125***	2.4	0.014	0.035**	2.5
	[0.02]	[0.022]		[0.011]	[0.016]		[0.02]	[0.022]		[0.011]	[0.016]	
Unemp	0.096***	-0.016	1.8	0.013***	0.009	1.8	0.096***	-0.018	1.8	0.13***	0.01	1.8
	[0.014]	[0.015]		[0.008]	[0.011]		[0.014]	[0.015]		[0.008]	[0.011]	

140

Localization of own industry	0.125*** [0.007]	−0.115*** [0.008] 1.7	0.008*** [0.002]	−0.014*** [0.002] 1.4	0.125*** [0.007]	−0.112*** [0.008] 1.6	0.008*** [0.002]	−0.014*** [0.002] 1.4
Period dummy	Yes	Yes 1.9	Yes	Yes 2.3	Yes	Yes 1.7	Yes	Yes 2.0
N	188	188	188	188	188	188	188	188
R squared	0.873	0.856	0.936	0.869	0.873	0.854	0.936	0.869
Correlation of residuals with the equation:								
(i)	1.000	−0.013	0.500	−0.273	1.000	−0.044	0.499	−0.254
(ii)	−0.013	1.000	0.061	0.521	−0.044	1.000	0.019	0.524
(iii)	0.500	0.061	1.000	−0.039	0.499	0.019	1.000	−0.010
(iv)	−0.273	0.521	−0.039	1.000	−0.254	0.524	−0.010	1.000
Breusch–Pagan test of independence:	113.0***				111.2***			

Notes:
Standard errors are shown in brackets.
*** $p < .01$, ** $p < .05$.
Sample periods: 1996–1999, 1999–2001, 2001–2004 and 2004–2006.

141

High- and Low-tech Service Industries

To check the robustness of the results for the service sector, we focus on two subsectors with regard to technological intensity: information and communications and the commerce and restaurant subsectors. The R&D intensity of the information and communication industry is the highest (0.74 per cent) in the service sector,[9] according to the Input–Output Tables of 2005. In contrast, the R&D intensity of the commerce and restaurant industry is only 0.22 per cent. Thus, we regard the information and communication industry as a high-tech industry and compare the results of this industry and the commerce and restaurant industry.[10]

Table 6.5 shows the estimation results for these two industries in the service sector.[11] In both subsectors, the effects of the proportion of professional and technical workers (*Expert*) on independent start-ups are positive and significant at the 1 per cent level. These results are consistent with Hypothesis 3. We find that human capital has a different effect on start-ups both in a high- and low-tech service: the coefficient of *CollegeGrad* is significantly negative for independent start-ups but significantly positive for new subsidiaries in the commerce and restaurant industry; while the coefficients of *CollegeGrad* are not significant for both types of start-ups in the information and communication industry. Thus, Hypothesis 1b and Hypothesis 2 are supported only in a relatively low-tech (commerce and restaurant) industry.

CONCLUSION

This chapter investigated the determinants of regional business entry distinguishing between independent start-ups and subsidiaries, with a special focus on the effects of regional human capital. This is the major contribution of this chapter. Another contribution to the literature is that it compares the determinants of regional entry between the manufacturing and service sectors as well as across subsectors within the service sector. For the empirical analyses, pooled data of 47 Japanese prefectures for four observation periods are used.

The estimation results of SUR indicate considerable differences in the impact of regional factors between independent start-ups and subsidiaries as well as among different industries. Table 6.6 summarizes the empirical tests of the hypotheses. First, the ratio of college graduates is correlated negatively with independent start-ups (Hypothesis 1b) and positively with the entry of subsidiaries (Hypothesis 2). Second, the ratio of professional and technical workers positively affects independent start-ups but not

Table 6.5a SUR estimation results for high- and low-tech service industries

Specification	II(a)					II(b)				
Industry	Info & communication		Commerce & restaurants			Info & communication		Commerce & restaurants		
Dependent variable	lnSR^{Ind}	lnSR^{Sub}	lnSR^{Ind}	lnSR^{Sub}	VIF	lnSR^{Ind}	lnSR^{Sub}	lnSR^{Ind}	lnSR^{Sub}	VIF
Equation	(i)	(ii)	(iii)	(iv)		(i)	(ii)	(iii)	(iv)	
Constant	-12.829*** [0.461]	-3.292*** [0.388]	-8.047*** [0.244]	-4.237*** [0.313]		-12.829*** [0.461]	-3.424*** [0.259]	-8.047*** [0.244]	-4.463*** [0.208]	
CollegeGrad	0.007 [0.016]	0.007 [0.018]	-0.063*** [0.008]	0.048*** [0.014]	8.3	0.007 [0.016]	0.000 [0.009]	-0.063*** [0.008]	0.036*** [0.007]	2.1
Expert	0.161*** [0.044]	0.005 [0.029]	0.162*** [0.024]	-0.033 [0.023]	3.1	0.161*** [0.044]	0.012 [0.025]	0.162*** [0.024]	-0.021 [0.02]	2.3
ln (WageRate)		-0.179 [0.392]		-0.307 [0.316]	4.9					
Period dummy	Yes	Yes	Yes	Yes	1.3	Yes	Yes	Yes	Yes	1.2

143

Table 6.5a (continued)

Specification	II(a)					II(b)				
Industry	Info & communication		Commerce & restaurants		VIF	Info & communication		Commerce & restaurants		VIF
Dependent variable	lnSR^Ind	lnSR^Sub	lnSR^Ind	lnSR^Sub		lnSR^Ind	lnSR^Sub	lnSR^Ind	lnSR^Sub	
Equation	(i)	(ii)	(iii)	(iv)		(i)	(ii)	(iii)	(iv)	
N	94	94	94	94		94	94	94	94	
R squared	0.535	0.739	0.724	0.776		0.535	0.737	0.724	0.775	
Correlation of residuals with the equation:										
(i)	1.000	0.003	0.369	0.200		1.000	0.003	0.369	0.197	
(ii)	0.003	1.000	0.219	0.432		0.003	1.000	0.231	0.439	
(iii)	0.369	0.219	1.000	0.050		0.369	0.231	1.000	0.077	
(iv)	0.200	0.432	0.050	1.000		0.197	0.439	0.077	1.000	
Breusch–Pagan test of independence:	38.8***					40.2***				

Notes:
Standard errors are shown in brackets.
***p < .01
Sample periods: 2001–2004 and 2004–2006.

Table 6.5b SUR estimation results for high- and low-tech service industries (with basic control variables)

Specification	III(a)					III(b)				
Industry	Info & communication		Commerce & restaurants			Info & communication		Commerce & restaurants		
Dependent variable	lnSR^{Ind}	lnSR^{Sub}	lnSR^{Ind}	lnSR^{Sub}	VIF	lnSR^{Ind}	lnSR^{Sub}	lnSR^{Ind}	lnSR^{Sub}	VIF
Equation	(i)	(ii)	(iii)	(iv)		(i)	(ii)	(iii)	(iv)	
Constant	−12.57***	−3.053***	−7.875***	−3.95***		−12.57***	−3.338***	−7.875***	−4.352***	
	[0.435]	[0.382]	[0.162]	[0.303]		[0.435]	[0.252]	[0.162]	[0.202]	
CollegeGrad	0.001	0.021	−0.042***	0.045***	9.5	0.001	0.008	−0.042***	0.026***	4.0
	[0.021]	[0.018]	[0.008]	[0.015]		[0.021]	[0.012]	[0.008]	[0.01]	
Expert	0.106**	−0.038	0.074***	−0.048*	3.7	0.106**	−0.026	0.074***	−0.03	3.1
	[0.048]	[0.03]	[0.018]	[0.024]		[0.048]	[0.028]	[0.018]	[0.022]	
ln (WageRate)		−0.384		−0.541*	5.0					
		[0.385]		[0.303]						
PopGrowth	0.092*	0.012	0.002	0.061**	2.4	0.092*	0.008	0.002	0.056**	2.4
	[0.052]	[0.03]	[0.019]	[0.024]		[0.052]	[0.03]	[0.019]	[0.024]	
Unemp	0.113***	0.063***	0.147***	0.024	1.7	0.113***	0.065***	0.147***	0.028	1.7
	[0.036]	[0.021]	[0.014]	[0.017]		[0.036]	[0.021]	[0.014]	[0.017]	
Period dummy	Yes	Yes	Yes	Yes	1.9	Yes	Yes	Yes	Yes	1.7

Table 6.5b   (continued)

Specification	III(a)					III(b)				
Industry	Info & communication		Commerce & restaurants		VIF	Info & communication		Commerce & restaurants		VIF
Dependent variable	$lnSR^{Ind}$	$lnSR^{Sub}$	$lnSR^{Ind}$	$lnSR^{Sub}$		$lnSR^{Ind}$	$lnSR^{Sub}$	$lnSR^{Ind}$	$lnSR^{Sub}$	
Equation	(i)	(ii)	(iii)	(iv)		(i)	(ii)	(iii)	(iv)	
N	94	94	94	94		94	94	94	94	
R squared	0.607	0.767	0.885	0.799		0.607	0.765	0.885	0.798	
Correlation of residuals with the equation:										
(i)	1.000	-0.131	0.168	0.095		1.000	-0.133	0.369	0.090	
(ii)	-0.131	1.000	-0.062	0.397		0.003	1.000	0.231	0.403	
(iii)	0.168	-0.062	1.000	-0.218		0.369	-0.027	1.000	0.077	
(iv)	0.095	0.397	-0.218	1.000		0.197	0.403	-0.155	1.000	
Breusch–Pagan test of independence:	24.7***					22.7***				

Notes:
Standard errors are shown in brackets.
***p < .01, **p < .05, *p < .10
Sample periods: 2001–2004 and 2004–2006.

Table 6.5c   SUR estimation results for high- and low-tech service industries (controlled for localization economy)

Specification	III(a)						III(b)					
Industry	Info & communication			Commerce & restaurants			Info & communication			Commerce & restaurants		
Dependent variable	lnSR^Ind	lnSR^Sub	VIF	lnSR^Ind	lnSR^Sub	VIF	lnSR^Ind	lnSR^Sub	VIF	lnSR^Ind	lnSR^Sub	VIF
Equation	(i)	(ii)		(iii)	(iv)		(i)	(ii)		(iii)	(iv)	
Constant	-12.483*** [0.272]	-3.218*** [0.375]		-8.19*** [0.201]	-3.51*** [0.305]		-12.483*** [0.272]	-3.363*** [0.245]		-8.192*** [0.201]	-3.692*** [0.235]	
CollegeGrad	-0.014 [0.013]	0.019 [0.018]	10.0	-0.036*** [0.008]	0.024*** [0.014]	10.8	-0.014 [0.013]	0.012 [0.012]	4.5	-0.036*** [0.008]	0.014*** [0.009]	4.9
Expert	0.071** [0.03]	-0.022 [0.03]	3.6	0.07*** [0.017]	-0.038* [0.022]	3.5	0.071** [0.03]	-0.016 [0.027]	2.9	0.07*** [0.017]	-0.021 [0.02]	2.9
ln (WageRate)		-0.194 [0.379]	5.3		-0.261* [0.279]	5.3						
PopGrowth	0.037* [0.033]	0.025 [0.03]	2.6	0.006 [0.019]	0.051** [0.022]	2.6	0.037* [0.033]	0.023 [0.029]	2.6	0.006 [0.019]	0.048** [0.022]	2.5
Unemp	0.108*** [0.023]	0.065*** [0.021]	1.5	0.144*** [0.013]	0.032 [0.016]	1.5	0.108*** [0.023]	0.066*** [0.021]	1.5	0.144*** [0.013]	0.034 [0.015]	1.5
Localization of own industry	1.609*** [0.132]	-0.445*** [0.12]	1.3	0.014*** [0.006]	-0.3** [0.007]	1.6	1.608*** [0.132]	-0.45*** [0.118]	1.3	0.015*** [0.006]	-0.03*** [0.007]	1.6
Period dummy	Yes	Yes	1.4	Yes	Yes	1.6	Yes	Yes	1.4	Yes	Yes	1.6

Table 6.5c (continued)

Specification	III(a)						III(b)					
Industry	Info & communication		VIF	Commerce & restaurants		VIF	Info & communication		VIF	Commerce & restaurants		VIF
Dependent variable	$InSR^{Ind}$	$InSR^{Sub}$		$InSR^{Ind}$	$InSR^{Sub}$		$InSR^{Ind}$	$InSR^{Sub}$		$InSR^{Ind}$	$InSR^{Sub}$	
Equation	(i)	(ii)		(iii)	(iv)		(i)	(ii)		(iii)	(iv)	
N	94	94		94	94		94	94		94	94	
R squared	0.848	0.777		0.894	0.799		0.848	0.776		0.894	0.834	
Correlation of residuals with the equation:												
(i)	1.000	0.103		0.307	0.185		1.000	0.109		0.307	0.198	
(ii)	0.103	1.000		-0.049	0.430		0.109	1.000		-0.029	0.432	
(iii)	0.307	-0.049		1.000	-0.080		0.307	-0.029		1.000	-0.042	
(iv)	0.185	0.430		-0.080	1.000		0.198	0.432		-0.042	1.000	
Breusch–Pagan test of independence:			31.3***						31.5***			

Notes:
Standard errors are shown in brackets.
***p < .01, **p < .05, *p < .10
Sample periods: 2001–2004 and 2004–2006.

the entry of subsidiaries (Hypothesis 3). Third, the relationships between regional human capital structure and the entry of independent start-ups and new subsidiaries are different across industries. We find that the determinants of entry differ not only between the manufacturing and service sectors but also within the service sector. Moreover, the differences of the determinants between the types of start-up vary across sectors.

The negative relationship between the ratios of college graduates and independent start-ups (for the overall industry and the service sector) is consistent with the previous empirical evidence for Japan (e.g., Small and Medium Enterprise Agency, 2002; Okamuro, 2008), but not with the results from other countries (Guesnier, 1994; Armington and Acs, 2002; Acs and Armington, 2004). This suggests that highly educated workers in Japan regard the opportunity cost of quitting their current job as considerably higher than the expected returns from independence.

The estimation results for the manufacturing sector are not only different from, but almost contrasting to those for the service sector. For manufacturing, the ratio of college graduates is correlated positively with

Table 6.6   Summary of empirical estimations

Type of human capital (independent variable)		College graduates			Professional and technical workers	
Types of start-up (dependent variable)		Independent start-ups		New subsidiaries	Independent start-ups	New subsidiaries
Hypothesis		1a	1b	2	3	
Expected sign		+	−	+	+	
Results	Overall industry		−	+	+	
	Manufacturing sector	+			−	
	Service sector		−	+	+	
	High-tech service industry				+	
	Low-tech service industry		−	+	+	

Note: The + and − signs indicate significantly positive and negative relationships, respectively, while blank cells indicate insignificant relationships.

the ratio of independent start-ups. This may imply that high education (particularly in the natural sciences) is especially important for independent start-up in the manufacturing sector, or that highly educated workers in the manufacturing sector do not have high opportunity cost of self-employment, assuming that the founders of manufacturing firms come from the manufacturing sector.

Moreover, for the manufacturing sector, we find that the ratio of college graduates has no significant effect on start-ups of new subsidiaries (which does not support Hypothesis 2) and that the ratio of professional and technical workers has a negative effect on independent start-ups (contrary to Hypothesis 3). The latter results are different from the previous studies (Guesnier, 1994; Hart and Gudgin, 1994) that find a positive relationship for the manufacturing sector. It may be attributed to the definition of professional and technical occupations in Japan that covers numerous skills in the service sector. It is also noteworthy that our results on the effect of the unemployment ratio on the ratio of independent start-ups clearly support the push hypothesis, similar to the results of previous studies in Japan.

However, some limitations of the present study need to be addressed in future research. First, for the manufacturing sector, we find different results from the overall industry and the service sector. There might also be some heterogeneity among manufacturing industries, which means that a more detailed industry and occupation classification is needed in order to test the hypotheses more concretely. Second, although we found positive relationships between the regional structure of human capital and the ratio of independent start-ups, these relationships can be explained by two possibilities. One possibility is that entrepreneurs have accumulated their human capital within the regions, but another is the migration of high-skilled workers (e.g., Ritsila and Ovaskainen, 2001). Presently, on the basis of the data available in this study, we are unable to clarify these possibilities.

Despite these limitations, this study suggests that regional policies to activate business start-ups should recognize the differences between encouraging local entrepreneurship and attracting new subsidiaries. These differences may vary even within the service sector according to technological intensity (or innovativeness).

ACKNOWLEDGEMENTS

The authors are grateful for the financial support received from the Japan Society for the Promotion of Science (JSPS) under Grant-in-Aid for Scientific Research (A) (No. 20243018) for this study. An earlier version of this chapter was presented at the RENT (Research in Entrepreneurship and Small Business) XXIII Conference in Budapest, Hungary, in November 2009 and at the DIME (Dynamics of Institutions and Markets in Europe) Workshop: Industrial Dynamics and Economic Geography in Utrecht, the Netherlands, in September 2010. We thank the participants of this conference and two anonymous reviewers for their comments and suggestions.

NOTES

1. The start-up ratio refers to the number of new businesses in a given time as a proportion of the total business stock.
2. The closure ratio refers to the number of closing businesses in a given time period as a proportion of the total business stock.
3. For example, Evans and Leighton (1990) and Storey (1991) find evidence for the push hypothesis, while Reynolds et al. (1995) and Carree (2002) support the pull hypothesis.
4. Prior research shows that most founders start new businesses in their own region (Figueiredo et al., 2002; Stam, 2007).
5. In this respect, location decisions on subsidiaries are similar to those on foreign plants by multinational companies. Coughlin and Segev (2000), for example, find positive effects of educational attainment on the location choice of multinational companies.
6. According to the Standard Occupation Classification of Japan, 'professional and technical occupations' include various types of scientists and engineers; medical and health-care services, such as doctors, pharmacists and nurses; social welfare services; legal services, such as lawyers; business support services, such as accountants and management consultants; and teachers and artists.
7. We calculated the population growth rate and the unemployment rate from the Population Census, and the average wage rate from the Basic Survey on Wage Structure (Wage Census), at the prefecture level.
8. The VIF is a measure of the degree of multicollinearity of each independent variable in regression analysis. A common rule of thumb is the VIF of larger than 5 (or 10) is a sign of severe multicollinearity. However, some problems of this rule are also pointed out (O'Brien, 2007).
9. The R&D intensity of a certain industry is defined as the ratio of its R&D expenditure to its total output.
10. Other service industries include various industries with different levels of technology intensity, such as research institutes, postal service, medical service, education, social work, advertising, machine maintenance, amusement, barbers and laundries. Because of data limitations, we cannot divide them in further detail. For that reason, we exclude this industry from detailed analysis to test the hypotheses.
11. Because of limitations of data, this analysis is restricted to two observation periods, 2001–2004 and 2004–2006.

REFERENCES

Acs, Z.J. and C. Armington (2004), 'The impact of geographic differences in human capital on service firm formation ratio', *Journal of Urban Economics*, **56**, 244–78.

Acs, Z.J. and C. Armington, (2006), *Entrepreneurship, Geography, and American Economic Growth*, New York: Cambridge University Press.

Armington, C. and Z.J. Acs (2002), 'The determinants of regional variation in new firm formation', *Regional Studies*, **36**, 373–86.

Audretsch, D.B. and M. Fritsch (1994a), 'The geography of firm births in Germany', *Regional Studies*, **28**(4), 359–65.

Audretsch, D.B. and M. Fritsch (1994b), 'On the measurement of entry rates', *Empirica*, **21**, 105–13.

Audretsch, D.B. and M. Vivarelli (1996), 'Determinants of new-firm start-ups in Italy', *Empirica*, **23**(1), 91–105.

Becker, G.S. (1975), *Human Capital*, New York: National Bureau of Economic Research.

Bosma, N., A. van Stel and K. Suddle (2008), 'The geography of new firm formation: evidence from independent start-ups and new subsidiaries in the Netherlands', *International Entrepreneurship and Management Journal*, **4**(2), 129–46.

Carree, M.A. (2002), 'Does unemployment affect the number of establishments? A regional analysis for US states', *Regional Studies*, **36**(2), 389–98.

Colombo, M.G. and L. Grilli (2005), 'Founders' human capital and the growth of new technology-based firms: a competence-based view', *Research Policy*, **34**, 795–816.

Coughlin, C.C. and E. Segev (2000), 'Location determinants of new foreign-owned manufacturing plants', *Journal of Regional Science*, **40**(2), 323–51.

Davidsson, P., L. Lindmark and C. Olofsson (1994), 'New firm formation and regional development in Sweden', *Regional Studies*, **28**, 395–410.

Egeln, J., G. Licht and F. Steil (1997), 'Firm foundations and the role of financial constraints', *Small Business Economics*, **9**, 137–50.

Evans, D.S. and L.S. Leighton (1989), 'The determinants of changes in US self-employment, 1968–1987', *Small Business Economics*, **1**(2), 111–19.

Evans, D.S. and L.S. Leighton (1990), 'Small business formation by unemployed and employed workers', *Small Business Economics*, **2**(4), 319–30.

Figueiredo, O., P. Guimaraes and D. Woodward (2002), 'Home-field advantage: location decisions of Portuguese entrepreneurs', *Journal of Urban Economics*, **52**, 341–61.

Fotopoulos, G. and N. Spence (1999), 'Spatial variations in new manufacturing plant openings: some empirical evidence from Greece', *Regional Studies*, **33**, 219–29.

Gerlach, K. and J. Wagner (1994), 'Regional differences in small firm entry in manufacturing industries: Lower Saxony, 1979–1991', *Entrepreneurship and Regional Development*, **6**, 30–80.

Glaeser, E.L., H. Kallal, J.A. Scheinkman and A. Shleifer (1992), 'Growth in cities', *Journal of Political Economy*, **100**(6), 1126–52.

Guesnier, B. (1994), 'Regional variations in new firm formation in France', *Regional Studies*, **28**(4), 347–58.

Hart, M. and G. Gudgin (1994), 'Spatial variations in new firm formation in the Republic of Ireland, 1980–1990', *Regional Studies*, **28**(4), 367–80.

Keeble, D. and S. Walker (1994), 'New firms, small firms, and dead firms: spatial patterns and determinants in the United Kingdom', *Regional Studies*, **28**(4), 411–27.

Nerlinger, E.A. (1998), *Standorte und Entwicklung Junger Innovativer Unternehmen: Empirische Ergebnisse für West-Deutschland*, Baden-Baden: Nomos.

O'Brien, R.M. (2007), 'A caution regarding rules of thumb for variance inflation factors', *Quality & Quantity*, **41**(5), 673–90.

Okamuro, H. (2008), 'How different are the regional factors of high-tech and low-tech start-ups? Evidence from Japanese manufacturing industries', *International Entrepreneurship and Management Journal*, **4**(2), 199–215.

Okamuro, H. and N. Kobayashi (2005), 'Determinants of regional variations in the start-up ratio: evidence from Japan', COE/RES Discussion Paper Series No. 115, Hitotsubashi University.

Okamuro, H. and N. Kobayashi (2006), 'The impact of regional factors on the start-up ratio in Japan', *Journal of Small Business Management*, **44**(2), 310–13.

Rauch, J.E. (1993), 'Productivity gains from geographic concentration of human capital: next term evidence from the cities', *Journal of Urban Economics*, **34**(3), 380–400.

Reynolds, P.D., B. Miller and W.R. Maki (1995), 'Explaining regional variation in business births and deaths: US 1976–88', *Small Business Economics*, **7**(5), 389–407.

Ritsila, J. and M. Ovaskainen (2001), 'Migration and regional centralization of human capital', *Applied Economics*, **33**(3), 317–25.

Santarelli, E. and R. Piergiovanni (1995), 'The determinants of firm start-up and entry in Italian producer services', *Small Business Economics*, **7**, 221–30.

Small and Medium Enterprise Agency (2002), *White Paper on Small and Medium Enterprises in Japan 2002*, Gyosei (in Japanese).

Stam, E. (2007), 'Why butterflies don't leave: locational behavior of entrepreneurial firms', *Economic Geography*, **83**(1), 27–50.

Storey, D.J. (1991), 'The birth of firms – does unemployment matter? A review of the evidence', *Small Business Economics*, **3**, 161–78.

Zellner, A. (1962), 'An efficient method of estimating seemingly unrelated regressions and tests for aggregation bias', *Journal of the American Statistical Association*, **57**(298), 348–68.

Zellner, A. (1963), 'Estimators for seemingly unrelated regression equations: some exact finite sample results', *Journal of the American Statistical Association*, **58**(304), 977–92.

7. Cross-border cooperation between enterprises as a form of international entrepreneurship

David Smallbone, Mirela Xheneti and Friederike Welter

INTRODUCTION

This chapter is concerned with cross-border cooperation between enterprises in EU border regions. For entrepreneurs, such cooperation can offer an opportunity to access new markets and/or sources of supply, as well as giving possible access to sources of capital, labour and/or know-how. At the same time, the nature and extent of these opportunities will vary according to factors that include the respective levels of development on the two sides of the border; the hard/soft nature of the border; the external environment for entrepreneurship; and characteristics of firms themselves. As a consequence, the nature and extent of this type of cross-border activity is affected by the heterogeneity of border regions, in terms of formal and social institutional structures, linguistics and ethnicity, all of which can influence economic processes long after the demise of formal and physical borders (Huber, 2003; Perkmann, 2005; 2003). In an EU context, this means that where the process of EU enlargement has removed formal institutional barriers to cross-border cooperation between two member states, it may take time to show any effect because of the perpetuation of informal institutional barriers.

Since cross-border entrepreneurship involves firms operating across national borders, it is, by definition, a form of internationalization. The aim of this chapter is to assess the extent to which the phenomenon reflects characteristics and processes identified in the literature concerned with internationalization of firms. Firm-level internationalization has grown rapidly in recent decades, reflected in the increasing internationalization of product, labour and capital markets. The process is driven by increasing competitive pressures on the one hand and increasing access to foreign sales and supply opportunities, on the other, facilitated by developments in information and communications technology. Changes in the external operating environment have affected firms of all sizes, although size-related characteristics can affect the nature and extent of the impact on enterprises, as well as the ability of firms to identify, cope with and respond to the changes. Nevertheless, firm-level internationalization is no longer confined to large enterprises, although the internationalization literature still tends to be dominated by a large enterprise paradigm.

The chapter draws on empirical evidence from two contrasting regions: Florina, which is a Greek region with a 'hard', external EU border with the Former Yugoslav Republic of Macedonia (FYROM); and Görlitz, which is a German region with a 'soft' internal EU border with Poland, following Poland's accession to the EU. This will enable us to assess the role of formal and informal barriers to cross-border entrepreneurship (CBE), since external borders are subject to a full range of border controls whereas in the case of 'soft' borders, any barriers to cross-border activity tend to be cultural.

Following this introduction, the rest of the chapter is divided into four main sections. The second section is a review of relevant literature, which is subsequently used to guide analysis of the empirical data. The third section presents the methodology of the study including profiles of the case study regions and of the samples of the enterprises interviewed. In the fourth, fifth and sixth data and findings from Florina (Greece) and Görlitz (Germany) is presented. The final section summarises the main findings and conclusions from the analysis.

INTERNATIONALIZATION LITERATURE

In this section, we briefly review the main theoretical approaches used to analyse the internationalization of SMEs identified in the previous literature, emphasizing where this seems potentially relevant to cross-border activity. This is followed by a review of a number of potentially relevant empirical studies.

For many years the internationalization of firms was typically viewed as a process made up of a series of stages where, having initiated the process of internationalization, companies then slowly penetrate more distant markets. For example, in the so-called Uppsala model, firms initially target geographically close markets and use less committed modes of entry, such as exporting. Over time they increase their foreign market knowledge through experience, which they subsequently use to increase their foreign commitments in markets that are more psychically distant. Psychic distance refers to the factors that prevent or disturb the flow of information between a firm and its markets, including differing cultures, language, political systems, level of education and level of industrial development (Johanson and Vahlne, 1977, p. 24). Since cross-border entrepreneurial activity involves firms operating in geographically close regions, this aspect of the Uppsala model would seem to have potential application if cross-border activity represents the first stage of a process. At the same time, the Uppsala model has been criticized for not being able to explain two issues: (i) why firms take the decision to internationalize and (ii) how the movement from one stage to the other takes place (Anderson, 1993). Answering such questions requires a more process-oriented perspective. Critics of this approach often point to the experience of 'born globals' to emphasize the limitations of applying a linear approach to a dynamic, non-linear process.

International entrepreneurship was once a field narrowly focusing on the study of international new ventures, although it has broadened over time to include a wider range of international entrepreneurial activities. This is reflected in broad definitions of what constitutes international entrepreneurship, such as 'the combination of innovative, proactive and risk-seeking behaviour that crosses national borders and is intended to create value in organisations' (McDougall and Oviatt, 2000, p. 903). Defined in this way, international entrepreneurship would appear potentially relevant to the phenomenon under study, although not all the cross-border activity examined can accurately be described as innovative.

The international entrepreneurship literature draws on a number of specific approaches such as the resource-based approach, the network approach and the strategic choice approach (Wright et al., 2007). Whilst the unique resources a firm may possess may help to achieve a differential advantage in foreign markets, formal and/or informal networks act as important mechanisms to overcome the resource constraints that firms may encounter (Young et al., 2003). Since borders sometimes divide regions with a common culture and/or shared ethnic ties into two, there are a priori reasons for suggesting that formal and informal networks may be one of the mechanisms used by entrepreneurs to identify and exploit opportunities for cross-border cooperation.

The demise of trade barriers has made internationalization a necessity for many firms that want to remain competitive in the market, regardless of their size and age. This provides a context for the strategic choice approach of internationalization, which claims that the pursuit and exploitation of competitive advantage and value creation are at the core of the activities of a firm (Hitt and Ireland, 2000). The strategic choice perspective is a potentially important driver of cross-border entrepreneurial activity. It incorporates: first, O'Farrell et al.'s (1998) emphasis on the need for a flexible theoretical approach to explain internationalization in SMEs, paying particular attention to the influence of the home region context for foreign market decisions; secondly, Young et al.'s (2003) emphasis on the characteristics of and developments in the international economic, legal/ institutional, and political/social environment and the challenges and opportunities they offer; and thirdly, Jones and Coviello's (2005) emphasis on the need to incorporate entrepreneurial behaviour into our models of internationalization, whilst drawing on multiple theoretical perspectives. The approach adopted in the chapter recognizes the need for the conceptual base to be eclectic whilst emphasizing the behavioural dimension.

Empirical evidence has drawn attention to some of the distinctive features that characterize SME internationalization. They usually supply international markets from a domestic base through direct and indirect exporting and sales/service subsidiaries, for resource-based reasons, which may also explain why they often prefer some form of cooperation with a local firm rather than undertake a stand-alone investment in a greenfield site. For example, an UNCTAD survey of SMEs involved in FDI showed that more than half of their investment involved some form of partnership between the investing company and a domestic SME (UNCTAD, 1998).

There is also evidence that when SMEs invest abroad independently (i.e. rather than being linked to the decisions of other firms within a cluster), they tend to invest in geographically close regions. The cross-border activity featuring in the chapter is a good illustration of this. The reasons include more limited information fields and greater resource constraints compared with larger firms, but they can also be influenced by cultural and historical ties. This can be illustrated with reference to the results of a study undertaken in Austria's north-east border regions, where a survey of 545 Austrian SMEs showed that 21 per cent had already started cross-border activities and a further 15 per cent expressed interest in doing so. The main motives were entry to new product and labour markets, gaining additional market potential and cost reduction. The types of cooperation that had developed included subcontracting, licensing and production partnerships, and to a lesser extent, types of direct investment such as joint ventures, or acquisition of enterprises in neighbouring countries. Significantly, the partners of most SMEs were local, that is, within 100 kilometres (RWI, 2000).

In another study of Austrian and Danish SMEs, forging networks with East European partners was found to be a key driver, linked to a desire to open up new sales opportunities (Meyer et al., 2000). Although SMEs can face resource-related constraints and knowledge gaps when seeking to internationalize, Austrian SME managers referred to building knowledge initially through exporting, which was then followed by FDI, suggesting that a stages approach may be used partly for resource-based reasons. This is potentially relevant to the cross-border activity examined in this chapter, although a more process-orientated view is needed in order to identify how knowledge is acquired, as well as insight into the time dimension of these processes. SMEs may display an incremental approach to foreign market development, as the evidence described above demonstrates, based on deepening commitment and investment as firms gain international market knowledge and experience. Targeting neighbouring cross-border markets with which psychic distance is low can be an initial step in this process.

In summary, the chapter investigates cross-border entrepreneurship in EU border regions as a particular form of internationalization, in order to assess the extent to which existing theories of internationalization are appropriate in explaining the phenomenon, and in what respects. This is explored empirically by examining the entrepreneurs' rationale for entering the cross-border region, their motivations for taking such a decision, their subsequent experience and the ways they interact with both the domestic and international environment. By doing so, we aim to place cross-border entrepreneurship within the context of the emerging literature on the internationalization of SMEs.

METHODOLOGY OF THE STUDY

Empirically, the chapter draws on case material from a recently completed project on cross-border cooperation in border regions in Bulgaria, Estonia, Germany, Greece, Finland and Poland[1] (www.crossbordercoop. net). The chapter uses empirical data from two of the 12 border regions included in the study: Görlitz in Germany, which now has a 'soft' internal EU border with Poland; and Florina in Greece, which has a 'hard' external EU border with FYROM. A short profile of each of them is presented below. This is followed by a description of the characteristics of the samples of enterprises interviewed.

Regional Profile of Florina

Florina is located in the region of Western Macedonia in Greece, bordering with the Former Yugoslav Republic of Macedonia (FYROM) to the north and Albania to the east. The regional economy is small in size and faces extensive economic problems, including low levels of GDP, high unemployment and absence of investment activities. The region is mainly agricultural with only limited manufacturing activity in small units in the food and drinks industry and in the field of electric power production based on lignite. The business sector in Florina, as elsewhere in Greece, is characterized by small enterprises. Despite a ratio of two new firm births for each one that closes down, these are mostly small-sized and family-owned entities, which are unable to exploit the opportunities arising in the neighbouring Balkan markets. The low level of FDI has also been a hindrance to the creation of larger sized enterprises.

The border dividing Greece from the FYROM is a 'hard' external border of the EU, with associated controls over the movement of goods, services and people, representing a formal institutional barrier to cross-border activity. But as in other border regions, historical and cultural factors are an important part of the external environment alongside political and economic influences. In fact, commercial exchanges with the northern side of the border, particularly with Bitola and Prilep, were common until 1994 when the Greek state imposed an embargo as a result of the dispute over use of the name 'Macedonia'. As a result, consumers and entrepreneurs turned away from the FYROM towards other markets and sources of supply, such as Bulgaria and Turkey, and these links are still not fully restored.

The FYROM proclaimed its independence in 1991. From the beginning, Greece opposed the use of the official name 'Republic of Macedonia' stating that its use implied intentions of nationalist and expansionist policies. This dispute is still unresolved and in most cases acts as a constraining factor for the development of CBE. Another feature of Florina is the existence of an important Slav-speaking (bilingual) population, which is a result of population movements and exchanges during and after the dissolution of the Ottoman Empire (1912–14). This part of the population has kinship ties across the border in the FYROM. The same applies to some Greek-speaking people on the FYROM side of the border, who have links with the Greek side (Vogiatzis et al., 2008).

Regional Profile of Görlitz

The second case region is an example of a soft border region, where the border divides two EU member states: Germany and Poland. In this case, the expectation is that cross-border entrepreneurship has been facilitated by the removal of most border controls. Görlitz is the easternmost town in Germany, situated on the river Neisse. The Treaty of Potsdam divided Görlitz into a German part on the western side of the Neisse and a Polish part named Zgorzelec, making it a good example of where a border has artificially divided what was previously a single functional unit. The impact of the political division was intensified by the displacement of Germans and Poles. The German inhabitants of the town and the region were forced to move behind the newly established border to Görlitz, while the eastern part of Görlitz was taken over by the Soviet military. The inhabitants of the new Polish town were mostly resettled from pre-war eastern parts of Poland (today Ukraine and Belarus), or settled from Central Poland. From then on, the border constituted not only a national border but also a cultural and linguistic one, and the towns also differed enormously in terms of their economies. Görlitz hosted the main industries while Zgorzelec 'inherited' some municipal utility works and a few manufacturing workshops (Adamczuk and Rymarczyk, 2003).

The collapse of the former Soviet Union and the events it triggered offered prospects for a new rise of Görlitz as an intermediary between the East and the West of Europe. Since 1989 the border has been open and visa-free, facilitating an increase in cross-border traffic. In 1991, the German and Polish governments signed a 'treaty on good neigh-bourhood relations and friendly co-operation'. From an economic perspective, both cities have to deal with the disadvantage of being geographically located between the much larger cities of Dresden (Germany) and Wroclaw (Poland), which attract investors and skilled workers. The GDP per capita of Görlitz has continually been below the level of Germany as a whole, although from 2002 to 2003 it increased by about 5.5 per cent. In 2003, Görlitz showed the strongest economic development of the administrative district of Dresden, of which it is part. Historically, Görlitz has been an important location for the textile, optical, electronic and metal industry, as well as for vehicle construction and engineering. It is characterized by small enterprises and its main competencies are in the fields of machine construction, logistics and railway engineering. Enterprises in ICT and biotechnology have also settled in the region (Welter et al., 2008). However, the overall number of enterprises in the region is low. Many companies from the region have become insolvent because of the pressure of competition on the world market, although Görlitz has recently shown a comparatively high entre-preneurial propensity.

Sample Characteristics[2]

The empirical data from these regions mainly comprise the results of in-depth interviews conducted with representatives of enterprises involved in cross-border entrepreneurial activity in the two border regions. The enter-prises were purposively selected in order to reflect the variety of cross-border activity present in the regions. The selection was informed by a series of meetings with regional stakeholders, as comprehensive databases of cross-border entrepreneurial activity did not exist. A semi-structured schedule was used as a basis for the interviews, covering topics that included: characteristics of the firm and the entrepreneur; the involvement of the enterprise in cross-border entrepreneurial activity; characteristics of foreign partners; and the nature of any previous experience of cross-border entrepreneurial activity. The data gathered were mainly qualitative in nature, thereby enabling a process-oriented view to be obtained of CBE. A total of 20 interviews were conducted in each of the border regions, including some enterprises that had previous experience of CBE that was subsequently discontinued. The analysis aims to present cross-region patterns in order to make evident the distinctive features and similarities of CBE in different borders in line with case study research (Eisenhardt, 1989).

The businesses interviewed in Florina had almost all been operating for over a decade. They operate in manufacturing (nine businesses), trading (eight businesses) and services (two businesses). Their main market is the domestic market in Greece, although some produce goods for export in various European countries. Businesses interviewed were mainly micro (8 enterprises) or small (6 enterprises) and had a turnover of less than 2 million euros in 2006.

Enterprises interviewed in Görlitz were all well established in the German market. However, some have only been set up after the year 2000 to take advantage of the border location of Görlitz and the growth of demand for certain products or services in neighbouring Poland. They are mainly micro and small-sized enterprises but, unlike Florina, more are operating in technology and knowledge-intensive industries. This draws attention to the need to recognize the role of the national as well as the regional context. Sample businesses in Görlitz operate in services (ten enterprises), manufacturing (nine enterprises) and trade (one enterprise). They are mainly focused on the German and Polish markets but some manufacturers trade in other European and/or broader geographical markets.

In both regions, interviewed enterprises started their cooperation with their cross-border counterparts after the collapse of communism, in order to take advantage of the new market for their products and services and the new sources of labour and supplies. In the case of Görlitz, the Polish market became more appealing after EU enlargement because of the removal of border controls over the movement of goods and services. Not all entrepreneurs included in the sample are currently involved in CBE. Some have exited cooperation, whilst others talked about their failed attempts.

FORMS OF CROSS-BORDER COOPERATION AND THEIR RATIONALE

The internationalization literature recognizes the wide variety of methods available to SMEs in entering international markets (Wright et al., 2007), suggesting that the mode of entry is affected by the motivations of the owner-manager of the business, his/her attitudes towards risk-taking and control, and the resources available to the business. The entry modes of Florina and Görlitz entrepreneurs had some common characteristics, but also some differences. The most common entry mode for Florina entrepreneurs was subcontracting, although some firms were selling into the FYROM market through various distribution links and some had established their presence through a franchise agreement or by setting up a subsidiary (see the Appendix tables). The review of the different forms of CBE and entrepreneurs' motivations shows that engagement in cross-border entrepreneurial activities has been incremental in some cases, triggered by a combination of changes in the external environment and increased resources or knowledge accumulation by enterprises over time. There are certainly cases that fit with the stages approach of the Uppsala model, mainly operating in traditional sectors.

The FYROM is attractive to Greek producers of labour-intensive goods, such as clothing manufacturers. Cross-border entrepreneurs in this industry appear to have been alert in identifying and acting upon entrepreneurial opportunities in their cross-border regions. For many entrepreneurs, the location of their production processes has changed several times in recent years following labour market changes, reflecting the price sensitivity of the markets in which they were operating. Networking appeared to be an important resource for Greek entrepreneurs, since in a number of cases they were relying on their Greek networks in the FYROM to make informed decisions about their international production activities.

Cooperation with enterprises on the Macedonian side of the border is seen as a way of maintaining price competitiveness in existing markets, especially for products that are highly price elastic, such as clothes. The cheap labour force and proximity to Greece have been the main factors contributing to engagement in cross-border cooperation with FYROM. Although subcontracting in the clothing sector is an international phenomenon, some interviewees stressed the time savings associated with close proximity to their subcontractors in the cross-border region (see Box 7.1). Clothing manufacturers operate on the basis of subcontracting, or what was referred to as the 'passive completion' method, according to which the international partner is only asked to contribute to part of the production process, such as the sewing of already cut fabrics. Many

BOX 7.1   A GREEK CLOTHING FIRM
            SUBCONTRACTING TO FYROM TO
            REDUCE COSTS

Florina E2 is a clothing manufacturer that has rented its own production unit in FYROM in Gevgeli, which is a town near the border
with Greece. Their subsidiary in FYROM also subcontracts part of
the production process to other FYROM enterprises located in
Strumica, illustrating the network of inter-firm linkages that CBE
can involve. The entrepreneur mentioned:

The most important deriving benefit is time saving, since due to the proximity between the two countries, textile imports and exports are delivered
very fast. This is a considerable advantage compared to other clothing
manufacturers that subcontract their production to Ukraine for example.
Hence, we have shorter delivery times that never exceed four weeks
from the moment we receive an order.

clothing manufacturers have links with more than one subcontractor
across the border in order to better respond to seasonal fluctuations in
demand.

When cross-border operations involved trading activity, the FYROM
market was not considered to be a major contributor to business sales,
although there was recognition that there might be potential for this in the
future as purchasing power in the FYROM rises. Five out of the six businesses interviewed that had stopped cooperation with the other side of the
border were traders of goods. Initially, the Macedonian market lacked a
large number of products that the Greek traders could supply. However,
this type of cross-border trading can be short-lived as it is often highly
dependent on specific trading conditions (e.g. relative prices), which may
change over time for a variety of reasons.

While in Florina cost reduction through subcontracting was the dominant form of cross-border activity, Görlitz was characterized by a wider
range of activity. Although some of the Görlitz entrepreneurs are engaged
in cross-border operations as part of an attempt to reduce costs, by subcontracting part of their production processes to Polish partners, others
are seeking to take advantage of new sales opportunities in the Polish
market that have emerged, following Poland's accession to the EU. In
view of the relative strength of the Polish market compared with FYROM,
it is not surprising that CBE of this type is more common in Görlitz than
in Florina and apparently more sustainable. In addition, there are some

---

BOX 7.2   A SMALL POLISH BUSINESS SERVICES
PROVIDER IDENTIFYING CROSS-
BORDER BUSINESS OPPORTUNITIES

Görlitz E9 was initially created to offer estate services to German companies wanting to move their business operations to Poland. However, disappointed by the small number of German SMEs that were looking to locate in Poland after its accession to the EU, it decided to expand its services by offering Polish companies a post box service. Because of the arrangements of the German labour market, Polish craftsmen have to register a trade in order to become active in Germany. Consequently, Polish entrepreneurs register their firms in Görlitz at the address of Görlitz E9. They receive an address, a post box, a telephone extension and someone who picks up any incoming mail and inquiries for them. This service is used by many companies because they cannot afford their own office space in Germany. When these companies grow, Görlitz E9 assists them in finding larger office space. This case shows that at the heart of a cross-border entrepreneurial activity is the ability of an entrepreneur to look for business opportunities created as a result of border proximity and the EU enlargement. It emphasizes the entrepreneurship component that is essential in CBE.

---

cases of enterprises establishing cross-border links in order to better serve the needs of their German customers already located in Poland. However, other companies have preferred to enter the Polish market initially through links with Polish distributors, who organize the distribution of goods and services for their German partners. For some companies, this is an important source of revenue for the company and a process which was boosted by Poland's accession to the EU and the associated reduction in waiting times at the border.

For example, CBE was central to the business model of four German enterprises. Three of them offer services that are specifically aimed at assisting German companies in their cross-border activities in Poland, such as legal, customs' services and real estate services for German companies that lack Polish language skills. One of these companies is described in detail in Box 7.2. The fourth company is a travel agency that, since its inception, decided to use Polish bus operators for its tours because of the cost advantages. All these companies see proximity to the border as an important advantage alongside their ability to speak the Polish language and familiarity with the regulatory framework in Poland, enabling them to engage effectively in CBE. The forms of cross-border activities in Görlitz vary and, despite some cases where the links across the border were for cost reduction reasons, the dominant theme for CBE investigated in this region is the attraction of the large Polish market on the doorstep, which, following accession, suddenly became more accessible.

The findings described above suggest that entering a cross-border region to access markets and/or low-cost supplies requires fewer resources than more distant international entry. This applies to all types of cross-border entrepreneurship identified in Florina, where proximity reduces the time taken to receive supplies from subcontractors. In the case of German enterprises, they have been quick to respond to the opportunities that the large Polish market across the border have presented. The larger, more resourceful enterprises tended to set up their own subsidiaries, whilst other firms have established subcontracting links or links with distributors to benefit from cheaper labour in the first case and from a larger market for their own products in the second. The extent of the interest of German enterprises in the Polish market was also illustrated by the cases of those enterprises that were set up specifically to serve the demand for legal, customs or real estate services from German companies in Poland. Thus in some respects, cross-border entrepreneurial activity shares a common driver with those motives that drive wider internationalization, namely cost reduction or new market development. But in other respects, cross-border activity has distinct features associated with geographical proximity, such as time saving and/or the effects of the border itself in creating specific business opportunities.

THE ROLE OF THE EXTERNAL ENVIRONMENT

The economic, institutional and social environment can pose both challenges and opportunities for the entrepreneur. The influence of the external environment on cross-border activity in the regions was experienced in various ways, although there are differences between 'hard' and 'soft' borders in terms of whether the barriers are associated with formal or informal institutions. As mentioned earlier, the collapse of communism opened up opportunities for entrepreneurs in both Florina and Görlitz. They were able to benefit from cheaper sources of labour, supply part of production and also benefit from increased demand for their products in their neighbouring markets. However, in the case of Florina, political relations between the countries, changes in the regulatory environment

---

BOX 7.3   A GREEK ENTERPRISE SHOWING CONSIDERABLE ADAPTIVE CAPABILITY IN ITS CROSS-BORDER ACTIVITY

Florina 18 is a micro business which has been trading in construction materials since 1990. In the early 1990s, the entrepreneur was approached by individuals across the border, who were looking to buy specific materials not available at the time in the FYROM market. The retailing companies that Florina E18 was cooperating with also started to sell into the Serbian market. This was attractive for Florina E18 because it could reach two new markets within a short period of time. However, the cross-border activities encountered various problems, as the respondent mentioned:

The main reason was that I did not have time to monitor and control the developments. I had to spend all of my time arranging the exports. Especially during the embargo I received my money through Frankfurt, while the products were shipped through Bulgaria. There were delays and most of my time I would try to get my money. This included a great risk for me, especially when larger orders were transported. I could not risk it any more.

The case of Florina E18 illustrates how the external environment can influence entrepreneurial decisions related to CBE. However, given that market conditions and especially the regulatory environment have improved recently with FYROM being an EU candidate country, this entrepreneur is considering entering the Macedonian market again. Knowledge of the area and networks to rely on have contributed to the decision.

---

that occurred as part of the process of transformation of the FYROM, and burdensome customs procedures, posed a number of challenges to entrepreneurs seeking to exploit cross-border opportunities. Where entrepreneurs have experienced difficulties in their cross-border entrepreneurial activities as a result of regulatory issues, a strong business case provided an incentive for entrepreneurs to deal with these successfully. Florina entrepreneurs mentioned problems related to customs' bureaucracy, as well as contract validity and enforcement. Whilst many interviewees had found a way to deal with problems of this nature, others stopped the cooperation altogether, as in the case of the enterprise described in Box 7.3.

Not surprisingly, in the case of Görlitz, problems of a regulatory nature started to diminish after the accession of Poland to the EU, since the customs regime was harmonized and the border crossing of goods and services facilitated. However, some entrepreneurs that entered Poland before these changes occurred reported ending their cooperation or failing in their attempts to enter the Polish market, because of the conditions with respect to border controls that pertained at the time. While the current regulatory framework is not seen as problematic, some entrepreneurs perceive that its implementation by the Polish authorities is still an issue, suggesting that informal institutional influences are slower to change than formal ones. Some entrepreneurs relate this to a history of centralized decision-making during communism which they think is still evident in the behaviour of some Polish officials. For example, Görlitz E05 believes that although Polish law has adjusted to the EU regulations, many people in Poland are not fully acquainted with these regulations. According to him, it will take a long time before this change is complete.

One specific issue facing entrepreneurs when operating across borders relates to 'contract enforcement'. According to entrepreneurs it is difficult to solve problems of this nature, particularly when the cross-border partner is located outside one of the old EU member states. In such circumstances, the difficulties in making legal claims about payment obligations not being met have pushed many entrepreneurs to base their cooperation on cash payments, because of the alleged unwillingness of the Polish courts to take effective action.

Another common theme in both regions was the perception of the work culture in the region across the border and the need to introduce quality management controls to deal with this. Whilst this can be a problem in any outsourcing situation, spatial proximity can make it easier to implement quality controls when the partner is located in the cross-border region (see Box 7.4). The general belief amongst Greek entrepreneurs was that their cross-border partners have inherited a 'laid back' and 'not accountable' work culture, whilst German entrepreneurs mentioned the lack of trust and reliability of the quality of work of their Polish partners. Entrepreneurs in both regions have put in place systems of quality control and direct management to ensure products are delivered on time. Whilst this involves extra costs, for most SMEs the proximity between the two regions either side of the border helps to alleviate them.

Any form of international business activity brings a number of uncertainties related to the characteristics of the market, the regulatory environment and most importantly the partner the business is working with. For enterprises that are located in peripheral, less developed regions of a country, engagement in a neighbouring cross-border region

---

BOX 7.4   ENTREPRENEURS EMPHASIZE THE BENEFITS OF SPATIAL PROXIMITY IN CROSS-BORDER COOPERATION

Nevertheless, you need to control them very tightly and this is why many of our employees here in Thessaloniki constantly commute there. We have people supervising the production even of the subcontracting companies. This has to do with the mentality of the locals and the regime they used to live under until recently. They need to have someone controlling them, but apart from that, we don't have any other problems. (Florina, E2)

Punctuality of delivery is facilitated by the given spatial proximity of the enterprises and is regulated by simple rules such as 'goods on time ensure quick payment'. The German enterprise makes use of certain control mechanism (i.e. announces visits by the German director in the Polish site) in order to secure the quality of the Polish products. (Görlitz E1)

---

can be attractive, although navigating a 'hard' external border is not without cost, particularly where the cross-border neighbour is in an economy in transition. On the other hand, the fact that Görlitz has a soft border with Poland creates huge potential advantages for cross-border entrepreneurship especially when it comes to the transport of goods and services. Above all, it has reduced many of the uncertainties that relate to operating in an environment where rules and regulations are not the same as those in the EU. Generally, cooperation with partners in a neighbouring cross-border region is easier and less costly to control than collaboration based on longer distance collaboration, because personal contact is easier. In this regard, whilst often driven by similar aims as wider internationalization, cross-border entrepreneurial activity is distinguished by the specific opportunities provided by spatial proximity.

NETWORKING AND PSYCHIC DISTANCE

Some previous literature on the internationalization of SMEs has suggested that the ability of entrepreneurs to engage in personal and extended networking can help to identify international opportunities, gain resources, improve strategic positions, learn new skills and cope with technological changes (McDougall and Oviatt, 2003). This is especially the case for small businesses that have a limited internal resource base to rely on. The cases

---

**BOX 7.5   LANGUAGE AS A BARRIER OR
FACILITATOR TO CROSS-BORDER
COOPERATION**

Both the cultural disparities in Poland and the linguistic obstacles constitute challenges for the collaboration, as the local decision-makers do often not speak German or English. The younger generation is more open, has another mentality and has foreign language knowledge. (Görlitz E14)

Especially the knowledge of the Polish language facilitates my work in Poland. The language is also important when the German and the Polish partners go out at night together and converse on a rather private level. (Görlitz E6)

---

of the Florina and Görlitz regions show the importance that entrepreneurs attach to issues such as language and culture as a means of developing close links with their partners. Greek entrepreneurs expressed a perception of proximity in cultural and linguistic terms with partners from the FYROM, suggesting that psychic distance was low. This was regardless of whether or not the interviewee belonged to the Slavic minority in Florina. They considered these factors to be crucial in building relationships based on trust that were considered essential for successful business cooperation. Building personal contacts and relating to cross-border partners in a more personal way is also facilitated by language skills. German entrepreneurs, for example, emphasized the role of language as an obstacle to or facilitator of cross-border entrepreneurship; they dealt with this problem by either employing Poles in their firms or by gaining Polish language skills themselves (see Box 7 5).

The time dimension was also important in shaping entrepreneurial perceptions of psychic distance and accumulating the knowledge and contacts that were necessary to establish further presence in the cross-border region. This is especially the case in small businesses that often rely on informal agreements. The informal contacts and the knowledge of a language act as important resources that small businesses can rely on for future internationalization. The experience of cross-border entrepreneurship can be particularly fruitful in developing a wider knowledge of the institutional and cultural environment, which facilitates identifying and acting on opportunities in the future, as part of an incremental approach to internationalization.

The role of personal networking is especially evident in the case of

Florina enterprises, who emphasized its role as a resource for entrepreneurs at different stages of development of their cross-border activity, from the identification of opportunities in the cross-border market, or supply base, to awareness about the institutional and cultural environment, and, most importantly, the positive outcome of their cross-border activities (see Box 7.6). In both regions language is of great significance in building personal relationships that many small businesses rely on to establish or develop their presence in cross-border locations.

CONCLUSIONS

As competitive pressures on firms increase, entrepreneurs are encouraged to look for new opportunities to reduce costs and boost revenues. This is contributing to increasing internationalization, in so far as these opportunities are identified and exploited abroad, whether this involves distant locations or 'border-hopping', as in the case of the cross-border cooperation featured in this chapter. Empirically, the chapter has provided evidence of a form of internationalization, which has hitherto been under-researched. SMEs located in Europe's border regions, which by definition are at the periphery of their national territories and, in some cases, of the EU's internal market, are often at a locational disadvantage compared with some of their European competitors. In such circumstances, cross-border cooperation with foreign enterprises may offer a means of compensating for their peripherality. The empirical results presented in the chapter suggest that the collapse of communism has presented new opportunities for cross-border entrepreneurship. Analysis of the experience of SMEs in Florina and Görlitz demonstrates how these opportunities are affected by a combination of external environmental characteristics on the one hand and the entrepreneurship of individuals on the other.

The evidence also demonstrates how the nature, extent and direction of cross-border entrepreneurial activity is affected by the respective development levels on the two sides of the border. This affects both market opportunities on the demand side and (indirectly) the capacity of firms to take advantage of them on the supply side. In addition, changes in relative price levels over time can lead to some cross-border activity being transient. This particularly affects trading activity, which can be very sensitive to changes in price levels and in the nature of border regimes. Cross-border differences in levels of economic development affect opportunities for outward and inward international activities. Both Florina and Görlitz are relatively developed in relation to the regions on the other side of their

BOX 7.6 PERSONAL NETWORKS AS A
RESOURCE FOR ENTREPRENEURS
AT DIFFERENT STAGES OF
CROSS-BORDER ACTIVITY

Florina E11, the wooden furniture business that has export and subcontracting links with FYROM illustrates this well. The entrepreneur mentions the common language and kinship ties on the other side of the border:

There are some cultural aspects that constitute positive factors for our cooperation and, consequently, trust building. We are familiar to them and so are they; there are kinships on the other side of the borders, it is also the language, this local Slavic idiom we speak here, that allows us to come closer. All these enhance trust building and allowed us to come close to them in a short period of time, as well as to develop friendly relations with our collaborators from the other side of the borders.

The same entrepreneur considered the process of cross-border entrepreneurship as a learning process that leads to a better understanding of partners, markets and institutional environment, or essential factors when deciding to strengthen business presence in an international market:

Of course we learn a lot of things from this collaboration. We generally become familiar with their mentality and the market conditions there. This surely contributes to our future likely collaborations, after we positively view our extension in their market. Up to now everything has functioned well, therefore it creates some positive future potential for us and augments trust building.

Görlitz E4 manufactures orthopaedic products and offers additional services to individual customers. It builds on a history of 105 years in the field which has helped in building a presence in the Polish market. The company already operates a subsidiary there that acts as a medical supply store, offering a fitting service to Polish customers. This five-year presence in the market has increased their understanding of the needs of the Polish market and the lack of competition for such products there. This has triggered their interest in persevering with the Polish market, setting up an orthopaedics workshop and an apprenticeship school in Poland because of the need for skilled people in the area.

borders, which means that their international activities are predominantly of an outward nature, such as exporting, subcontracting, exploiting cheap labour costs and/or the demand for goods that are unavailable in the cross-border market.

The ability to exploit cross-border business opportunities is affected by the nature of the border itself. Crossing a 'hard', external border of the EU, such as between Greece and the FYROM, involves navigating a range of border controls, customs duties and a visa regime. Whilst these formal institutional barriers may be absent in the case of a 'soft' internal border, such as that between Germany and Poland, the attitudes of officials and cultural and historical influences can still act as barriers, at least in the short term, and differences in legal systems and practices can also result in ongoing implementation problems even if regulations are harmonized.

The empirical data also point to the role of network links as resources for cross-border cooperation to develop and as a basis for the type of trust-based relationships to evolve that can be so important in facilitating effective inter-enterprise cooperation. Language can be a key factor in enabling personal relationships with foreign partners to develop and evolve, particularly when part of a wider cultural affinity. Finally, a consistent implicit theme throughout is the entrepreneurship involved in cross-border activity. Firms engaged in cross-border activity tend to be the more active, entrepreneurial firms, particularly those that are involved in exploiting cross-border markets. Whilst some firms are put off by negative, early experiences and uncertainties, particularly where these focus on frustrations with regulatory and customs regimes across hard borders, others persevere to overcome such difficulties. In any type of border region, firms build on their initial entry incrementally, as their knowledge and experience of the cross-border market increases.

One of the key aims of the chapter was to assess the extent to which cross-border cooperation between enterprises shares characteristics and processes identified in the literature concerned with the internationalization of SMEs, since this affects the appropriateness of existing theories of internationalization for explaining the phenomenon. The overall conclusion is that whilst there are many similarities, cross-border entrepreneurship also has some distinctive features, mainly associated with the potential advantages of spatial proximity to the foreign partner. The similarities include the key drivers, which focus on accessing new markets on the one hand and seeking ways of reducing production costs on the other, through, for example, externalizing some or all of their production. There are also similarities in some of the processes involved, such as the emphasis on personal networking in some cases, at different stages of the identification and exploitation of cross-border opportunities. There is also evidence of an incremental approach, particularly in the Görlitz region, although so far this mainly involves geographic market extension to other parts of Germany rather than further afield. At the same time, the spatial proximity that is implicit in cross-border activity was reported to contribute to shorter turnaround times for subcontracted work and greater opportunities for close management control over quality processes that is more difficult over longer distances.

In terms of theories of internationalization, our analysis supports the need for eclecticism, providing evidence to support several theoretical perspectives, but particularly the incremental, resource-based and network approaches, with aspects of a strategic choice perspective helpful in conceptualizing the drivers. The use of a variety of collaborative arrangements with other firms as a means of engaging in cross-border activity reflects the effect of the limited internal resource base of SMEs on their approach to exploiting foreign business opportunities. The emphasis on the benefits of proximity to the neighbouring border region may be taken as further evidence to support a resource-based approach, with entrepreneurs' responses pointing to the importance of 'psychic' as well as physical distance. Proximity facilitates the maintenance of personal contacts, which was a consistent theme in the interviews with entrepreneurs in both regions.

Finally, the focus on cross-border activity in the chapter has drawn attention to the nature of the border as an issue facing SMEs when assessing the scope for identifying and exploiting business opportunities on the other side, with hard external borders presenting greater challenges. Clearly, the enlargement of the EU presents a good opportunity to examine these influences. Softening of the border between Germany and Poland, for example, is less than 10 years old, and regulatory harmonization is still evolving, at least in implementation. Nevertheless, over time, it is likely that cross-border entrepreneurial activity will grow in this region as the institutional deficiencies are rectified. Whilst cultural barriers may remain for some entrepreneurs, increasing economic integration within the EU internal market is likely to make cross-border cooperation increasingly commonplace for SMEs in soft border regions, such as Görlitz. Whilst some may argue that this makes cross-border cooperation by SMEs across soft borders a qualitatively different phenomenon from wider internationalization, because of the combination of lower barrier effects of distance and the absence of tariff and customs barriers, it raises the question as to whether the existing literature on SME internationalization pays sufficient attention to the nature of (national) borders, which can be very variable in their enabling/constraining influence on internationalization processes.

NOTES

1. Financed by the EU's Framework VI Programme, the project was entitled: 'Challenges and prospects of cross-border cooperation in the context of EU enlargement' (CBCED). It involved partners in seven EU countries and detailed empirical investigation in 12 case study regions (CSRs): Imatra and Tornio in Finland; Görlitz and Hochfranken in Germany; Biala Podlaska and Zgorzelec in Poland; Florina and Serres in Greece; Kyustendil and Petrich in Bulgaria; and Narva and Setomaa in Estonia.
2. See Tables 7A.1 and 7A.2, in the Appendix, for a detailed description of the characteristics of firms in the sample.

REFERENCES

Adamczuk, F. and J. Rymarczyk (2003), 'Local aspects of European integration: the example of Zgorzelec/Görlitz cross-border cooperation', in G. Dieckheuer (ed.), *Eastward Enlargement of the European Union*, Frankfurt: Peter Lang, pp. 137–46.

Anderson, O. (1993), 'On the internationalisation process of firms: a critical analysis', *Journal of International Business Studies*, **24**(2), 209–31.

Dana, L-P., M.B. Bajramovic, and R.W. Wright (2005), 'The new paradigm of multipolar competition and its implications for entrepreneurship research in Europe', in A. Fayolle, P. Kyro. and J. Ulijn (eds), *Entrepreneurship Research in Europe: Outcomes and Perspectives*, Cheltenham UK and Northampton, MA, USA: Edward Elgar Publishing, pp. 102–21.

Eisenhardt, K.M (1989), 'Building theories from case study research', *The Academy of management Review*, **14**(4), 532–50.

Hitt, M.A, and R.D. Ireland (2000), 'The intersection of entrepreneurship and strategic management research', in D.L. Sexton and H.A. Landström (eds), *Handbook of Entrepreurship*, Oxford: Blackwell, pp. 45–63.

Huber, P.B. (2003), 'On the determinants of cross-border cooperation of Austrian Firms with Central and Eastern European partners', *Regional Studies*, **37**(9), 947–55.

Johanson, J. and J.E. Vahlne (1977), 'The internationalization process of the firm: a model of knowledge development and increasing foreign market commitments', *Journal of International Business Studies*, **8**(1), 23–32.

Jones, M. and N. Coviello (2005), 'Internationalisation: conceptualising an entrepreneurial process of behaviour in time', *Journal of International Business Studies*, **36**, 284–303.

Labrianidis, L. (1996) 'Subcontracting in Greek manufacturing and the opening of the Balkan markets', *Cyprus Journal of Economics*, **9**(1), 29–45.

McDougall, P.P. and B.M. Oviatt (2000), 'International entrepreneurship: the intersection of two research paths', *Academy of Management Journal*, **3**(5), 902–6.

McDougall, P.P. and B.M. Oviatt (2003), 'Some fundamental issues in international entrepreneurship', available from http://www.usasbe.org/knowledge/whitepapers/index.asp, accessed 8 October 2009.

Meyer, K., A. Tind and M. Jacobsen (2000), 'National internationalisation processes: SME on the way to Eastern Europe', Working Paper No. 37, June, Centre for East European Studies Copenhagen Business School.

Niebuhr, A. and S. Stiller (2004), 'Integration effects in border regions: a survey of economic theory and empirical studies', *Review of Regional Research*, **24**, 3–21.

O'Farrell, P., P. Wood, and J. Zheng (1998), 'Regional influences on foreign market development by business service companies: elements of a strategic context explanation', *Regional Studies*, **32**, 31–48.

Perkmann, M. (2003), 'Cross border regions in Europe: significance and drivers of regional cross border cooperation', *European Urban and Regional Planning Studies*, **10**(2), 153–71.

Perkmann, M. (2005), 'Cross-border cooperation as policy entrepreneurship: explaining the variable success of european cross-border regions', CSGR Working Paper No. 166/05, Warwick.

RWI Essen (2000), 'Impact of enlargement of the European Union on small and medium-sized enterprises in the union', final report to DG Enterprise, November, in cooperation with the European Policies Research Centre, University of Strathclyde, Glasgow.

UNCTAD (1998), 'Handbook on foreign direct investment by small and medium-sized enterprises: lessons from Asia', United Nations Conference on Trade and Development.

Vogiatzis, N., D. Gkintidis, A. Kyriaki, C. Giannopoulou and G. Agelopoulos, (2008), 'Regional summary report: florina-pella, Greece', CBCED Project Deliverable 11, Thessaloniki: University of Macedonia, available at http://cross-bordercoop.net/Publications/RSR_Florina%20.pdf.

Welter, F., N. Veleva, S. Kolb, F. Schewitzer an Hack, B. Heubner and R. Luhmer (2008), 'Regional summary report: Görlitz, Germany', CBCED Project Deliverable 11, Siegen: Siegen University, available at http://crossbordercoop. net/Publications/RSR_Görlitz.pdf.

Westhead, P., M. Wright and D. Ucbasaran (2001) 'Think global, act local: international market selection strategies reported by rural and urban firms', Discussion Paper, Institute for Enterprise and Innovation, Nottingham University Business School.

Wright, M., P. Westhead and D. Ucbasaran (2007), 'Internationalisation of small and medium sized enterprises (SMEs) and international entrepreneurship: a critique and policy implications', *Regional Studies*, **41**(7), 1013–29.

Young, S., P. Dimitratos and L. Dana (2003), 'International entrepreneurship research: what scope for international business theories', *Journal of International Entrepreneurship*, **1**, 31–42.

APPENDIX

Table 7A.1   Main characteristics of enterprises interviewed in Florina

	Year of start-up	Year of CBE	Size	Type of activity	Markets served	Form of cooperation
Florina E1	1993	2001	5	Large-sized clothes manufacturer	Greece, Cyprus	Subcontracting
Florina E2	1982		55	Clothes Manufacturer	EU	Subsidiary
Florina E3	1987	1999	50	Sportswear and casual clothing manufacturer	Mainly Balkan countries	Subcontracting/Selling into new markets
Florina E4	1990	2001	90	Casual clothes	Various European countries + FYROM	Subcontracting/Franchise
Florina E5	1987		10	Clothes manufacturer	Germany and Netherlands	Subcontracting
Florina E6	1994	1995	40	Processing and packaging on poultry	Greece, Germany	Subcontracting
Florina E7	1983	1991	10	Manufacturer of fruit juices	Greece	Stopped cooperation/subcontracting
Florina E8	2003	2003	6	Travel agency	Greece, Balkans	Selling into new markets
Florina E9	1993	1996	7	Trading of electric mechanical equipment	Greece, FYROM	Selling into new markets?
Florina E10	1980	1990	15	Foodstuff trading	Greece, Albania FYROM	Stopped cooperation/selling into new markets

Florina E11	1996	2005	40	Furniture production	Greece, FYROM	Subcontracting
Florina E12	1989	1992–2000	3	Coffee manufacturing and trading	Greece	Stopped cooperation/selling into new markets
Florina E13	1985	2005	18	Electric engineering applications (technical and advisory services)	Greece	Subcontracting
Florina E14	1985	2004		Production of jams, pickles, peppers and patés	Greece, Balkans	Supply of products
Florina E15	1980	1982–2004	6	Wood retailing business	Greece	Stopped cooperation/raw materials
Florina E16	1988	1993 (6 months)	3	Car spare parts retailing	Greece	Stopped cooperation/selling into new markets
Florina E17	1981	1985	4	Tyre retailing & recaps for heavy trucks	Greece, FYROM	Selling into new markets
Florina E18	1990	Early 90s–2003	6	Construction material trading	Greece	Stopped cooperation/selling into new markets
Florina E19	1987	2000	55	Meat and delicatessen production	Greece, Balkans	Selling into new markets

Table 7A.2 Main characteristics of enterprises interviewed in Görlitz

	Year of start-up	Year of CBE	Size	Type of activity	Markets served	Form of cooperation
Görlitz E1	1989	2000	46	Manufacturer of fire engines and vehicles for disaster control	Germany but also some exports	Subcontracting
Görlitz E2	1996	2002	5	Manufacturer of hydraulic tubes and components	Germany, Poland	Selling into new markets
Görlitz E3	1996		17	Real estate services	Germany	Stopped cooperation/ selling into new markets
Görlitz E4		2004	36	Orthopaedic products/ services	Germany, Poland	Subsidiary
Görlitz E5	2006	2006	40	Manufacturer of pellets of chipped wood	Germany	Raw materials
Görlitz E6	2000	2000	3	Legal services	Germany, Poland	Born international
Görlitz E7	2002	2003	78	Beer producer	Germany	Stopped cooperation/ selling into new markets
Görlitz E8	1992	1999	25	Engineering services	Germany, Poland	Subsidiary
Görlitz E9			11	Real estate services	Germany, Poland	Born international
Görlitz E10	1999	2003	3	Plumbing services	Germany, Poland	Selling into new markets

Company	Year 1	Year 2	Employees	Activity	Markets	Internationalization
Görlitz E11	1992		750	Manufacturer of stream turbines	Worldwide	Selling into new markets
Görlitz E12	1946	2005	16	Clothes designer and manufacturer	Germany, Poland	Subcontracting
Görlitz E13	1997	2006	5	Trade and maintenance of hearing aids	Germany	Failed attempt
Görlitz E14	1994		15	IT and software development	Germany, Czech Republic, Poland	Subcontracting
Görlitz E15	1991		32	Machines for the ceramic industry	Europe, China and India	Failed attempt
Görlitz E16	1995		5	Customs services	Europe	Born international
Görlitz E17	1990	1997	35	Manufacturer of ropes	Europe, Turkey, South Africa	Selling into new markets
Görlitz E18	1896	1990s	185	Producer of candies	Worldwide	Selling into new markets
Görlitz E19	2003	2003	5	Travel agency	Germany, Poland	Born international
Görlitz E20	1993	1994–2005		Inn	Germany, Poland	Stopped cooperation/supplies

8. The entrepreneurship potential within Swiss regions: a comparison based on cluster analysis

Katharina Becker, Franz Kronthaler and Kerstin Wagner

INTRODUCTION

New businesses are considered to be important for regional economic development and growth (see, for example, Audretsch et al., 2006; Fritsch and Mueller, 2008). New venture creation, however, varies considerably between regions, indicating differences in their endogenous potential and structural characteristics for new business formation. Taking both these factors into account, policy-makers and stakeholders should strive to increase entrepreneurial activity at the national as well as at the regional level, in order to increase economic welfare. In Switzerland, a New Regional Policy (NRP) instrument has been created, with the aim of increasing entrepreneurial activity in peripheral and semi-peripheral regions. One important question, however, is how to support this entrepreneurial activity in such a way that limited resources are used most efficiently, and so that any policy measures taken best fit the prevailing regional structural conditions.

The present study examines the conditions for new venture creation in Swiss regions. The conditions for new venture creation include the resources, structural characteristics and abilities of a region to generate new firms. They are measured by a set of variables derived from theoretical and empirical literature on entrepreneurship. In particular, answers are being sought to two main questions. First, in what way do Swiss regions vary with regard to their potential for venture creation, and by which strengths and weaknesses are they characterized? Secondly, what can be derived from the characteristics of regions for the NRP to strengthen entrepreneurial activity?

Cluster analysis is used to identify homogeneous groups of regions according to their entrepreneurship potential. It merges regions into classes with homogeneous potential. The analysis is carried out at the level of Swiss *mobilité spatiale* regions (MS), which are functional units based on economic interaction and commuting movements. This allows the identification of regions with high and low entrepreneurship potential on the basis of those determinants used, and enables the strengths and weaknesses of Swiss regions to be discussed with regard to their potential for new venture creation. This is particularly important with respect to the formulation of policy recommendations, because entrepreneurial determinants are a strong indicator of real entrepreneurial activity in regions. In order to foster entrepreneurial activity one should consider these determinants as they strongly indicate the likelihood of optimal conditions for new venture creation.

There are numerous studies dealing with new business formation and the related impact on regional economic growth. From the early 1990s, when firm formation data at the regional level became available, empirical studies have dealt with regional variation in new firm formation rates, with the identification of explanatory determinants at the regional level (Reynolds et al., 1994; Audretsch and Fritsch, 1994). Subsequent studies also distinguish between demand and supply side orientated determinants for entrepreneurship (for an overview see Verheul et al., 2002). While the demand side stresses market influences and the need for new products and services, the supply side focuses on the human and social capital of the population of a region or nation. Regional economics literature provides further evidence supporting the relevance of agglomeration economies, in particular urbanization and localization economies. Numerous studies have highlighted the positive effects of agglomeration on the formation of new ventures, regional innovation activities and growth (e.g. Acs et al., 2008; Glaeser et al., 1992). Our study reviews this theoretical and empirical literature to identify the factors that determine entrepreneurial activity in regions. It extends the literature by using the established factors to compare regions with one another, by employing cluster analysis as an approach to determine regional differences. Furthermore, it builds on current research at the regional level which uses and maps single individual pieces of data on entrepreneurial attitudes (Bosma and Schutjens, 2009).

The remainder of this chapter is organized as follows. In the next section, we discuss the literature on determinants which influence entrepreneurial activity, their type of impact on start-up rates and the selection of the indicators. The third section describes the data set and methodology. The fourth section discusses the results. The concluding section summarizes the results and discusses selected policy recommendations.

FACTORS ACCOUNTING FOR REGIONAL ENTREPRENEURIAL ACTIVITY

Theoretical and empirical literature on entrepreneurship suggests that numerous determinants have an impact on start-up activities. In particular these are: (1) factors of the demand side for entrepreneurship; (2) factors of the supply side for entrepreneurship; and (3) urbanization and localization effects.[1]

Demand Side for Entrepreneurship

The demand side for entrepreneurship refers to opportunities to create a venture, influenced by the market demand for new goods and services (Verheul et al., 2002). In particular, an increase in demand and in technological and structural transformation goes hand in hand with changes in consumer preferences and leads to opportunities for venture creation. Economic development and structural change comes along with individualized, diversified consumer preferences for new, specialized and differentiated goods and services. It offers numerous entrepreneurial opportunities for new entrepreneurs in market niches, as new firms serve local markets first (Armington and Acs, 2002). The structural shift from manufacturing towards services is considered to have a positive impact on firm formation. The service sector is characterized by low start-up requirements and a small size structure, and the number of firms increases with higher per capita income. These characteristics make new venture creation more likely, due to smaller start-up costs and lower market entry barriers (e.g. Fritsch, 1997). Subsequently, a smaller business density of manufacturing firms also has a positive impact on the number of new firms being created (Reynolds et al., 1995).

A further demand side factor is the size structure of a region's industry. Small firms are more capable of responding to changing market needs for new and specialized products and services due to a more flexible approach and adaptability (Loveman et al., 1991). Additionally, small-scale activity fosters regional competition and contributes to higher start-up rates (Fotopoulos and Spence, 1999), while the role of scale economies has become less important for innovative industries and technological advancement in many sectors (Acs and Audretsch, 1987).

A negative relationship exists between the number of employees within a firm and the probability that an employee will start his or her own business. The reason is that small firms better serve as role models; but also more favourable conditions in large firms restrain employees from quitting their jobs and becoming self-employed (Storey, 1994; Wagner, 2004).

Supply Side for Entrepreneurship

The supply side for entrepreneurship deals with the endogenous potential of the regional population to create new firms. It includes factors such as the size and structure of the population, employment structure, age structure, human capital and share of immigrants (Verheul et al., 2002).

The population density in a region shows a high correlation with a number of factors such as business infrastructure, market proximity, wage level, educated workforce and access to innovative products (e.g. from universities), and quality of communication infrastructure. As a result, this variable can be regarded as a catch-all variable for a variety of regional characteristics (Fritsch and Mueller, 2008). The creation of new business activities in highly populated regions signals attractiveness to other businesses because of cooperation opportunities and spillover effects (Audretsch and Fritsch, 1994).

Also, employment structure is relevant as a further factor for entrepreneurial activity. The literature indicates that a high number of self-employed persons tend to increase entrepreneurial activity in regions. Start-up activity is self-reinforcing because existing entrepreneurs provide role models and information for regional stakeholders and potential entrepreneurs (Minniti, 2005; Mueller, 2006). Furthermore, those who are or were already self-employed (serial entrepreneurs) are predestined for further start-up activities (Westhead and Wright, 1998; Thurik et al., 2009).

New venture creation is influences not only by the employment structure, but also by the age structure of a region's population. The Global Entrepreneurship Monitor (GEM) shows that especially people between 35 and 44 years of age, in other words mid-career, show the highest propensity to become self-employed (Reynolds et al. 2002). Further studies report that many entrepreneurs start a new venture in their mid-thirties and are typically between 25 and 40 years old (Storey, 1994; Evans and Leighton, 1989). Also, the level of entrepreneurial activities is declining as the age of the population increases. Subsequently, nations with a higher number of persons in the 25–44 year age group demonstrably have more start-up activities than others (Reynolds et al., 1999). Furthermore, studies show that even if there are more opportunities to become self-employed for older than for younger persons, older employees are less willing to become self-employed (Van Praag and van Ophem, 1995).

Additionally, the level of education, experience and background can all influence entrepreneurial success (Brüderl et al., 1998). A positive relationship exists between the duration of professional education and training and the probability of starting a company, indicating a higher ability to recognize business opportunities. Hinz (1998) concludes that individuals with a graduate degree are more inclined towards entrepreneurship and likely to start a company, particularly in knowledge-intensive industries, although the relationship is not linear. Entrepreneurs tend to be people with a more hands-on educational background (vocational school, technical college, etc.) than an academic background.

The number of immigrants in a region plays an important role with regard to firm birth rates. First, it has indirect effects due to consequences of the age structure of a regional population because foreign families are usually younger and have more children. Second, studies have found a significant and positive effect of immigrants on new firm formation (Reynolds et al., 1995), distinguishing between two groups of immigrants. The first consists of immigrants who lack skills, resources and networks; however, they still tend to be more predisposed to self-employment than non-immigrants. The second group consists of extremely well-educated and skilled immigrants. They are highly engaged in technology start-up activities and in particular can be found in leading export and innovative regions (Saxenian, 1999). Both groups enrich a region with new ideas and cultures, create new business opportunities, and are risk-takers (Lee et al., 2004).

A last supply factor could be the relationship between unemployment and self-employment, although this link is ambiguous and still not conclusive (Parker, 2004; Bergmann and Sternberg, 2007). Serving as a supply-side factor, unemployment reduces the opportunity of paid employment and offers the option of becoming self-employed, particularly when there is a shortage of alternative job opportunities. Nevertheless, high unemployment rates lower the demand for products and services that firms offer. Subsequently, the income and also the available capital for entrepreneurs are reduced, and the risk of bankruptcy increases, indicating a negative relationship between self-employment and starting a venture. Empirical results tend to reflect the method applied and do not represent a significant quantifiable result. While cross-section studies mainly show a negative relationship between unemployment and entry rates, most of the time-series studies demonstrate positive effects of unemployment rates on new firm formation rates (see Parker, 2004 for an overview).

Urbanization and Localization Economies

Urbanization and localization economies both belong to the broader concept of agglomeration economies, which dates back to Marshall

(1920). The main argument is that firms benefit from spatial concentration, which leads to advantages due to market size, spillovers, synergies and labour market effects. Good access to markets enables firms to achieve relatively higher rents, so that the concentration of firms increases with market size. This forms a large workforce pool, enabling technological spillovers by means of transfer of technology and knowledge, and can intensify networking of enterprises. The difference between urbanization and localization economies is that the former arise for spatially concentrated firms irrespective of their industry. The latter refers to benefits for firms spatially concentrated within the same industry (Hoover, 1948).

With regard to entrepreneurship and urbanization economies there is empirical evidence that urbanization economies have a positive impact on the new firm formation rate (Armington and Acs, 2002; Reynolds et al., 1994). Urbanization economies provide access to highly educated people and a large workforce in general, infrastructure, research institutions and universities, customers, capital, suppliers, markets and demand for products and services. Jacobs (1969) argued that an open and diverse city attracts talented people, stimulating creativity and innovation, which are necessary preconditions for entrepreneurship. Thus, urbanized and densely populated regions are attractive regions in which to start new business activities.

Localization economies show a similar linkage to that of urbanization economies with respect to entrepreneurship. They stress the relevance of knowledge spillover within the same industry. Knowledge spillover supports firms in reducing uncertainty which is particularly associated with innovation activities. Furthermore, existing industries foster competition and force new firms to implement their new products on the market. Because of the lower costs with regard to gaining knowledge of the business environment, start-ups are attracted by regions where certain industries already exist (Audretsch et al., 2008).

Overall, our study is based on this theoretical and empirical literature when selecting the relevant variables with regard to the entrepreneurship potential of regions. The selected variables are: industry structure, firm size structure, population density, self-employment, human capital and age structure of the population. The selected variables are all structural variables. This selection is not exhaustive, for example there are further links between entrepreneurship and institutional factors or cultural attitudes. However, due to the limited availability of appropriate data at the regional level we have not introduced these concepts.

DATA AND METHODOLOGY

Data and Descriptive Statistics

Our analysis aims to cluster regions according to their entrepreneurial potential on the spatial level of 106 Swiss MS regions (*mobilité spatiale*). MS regions are functional units based on economic interaction and commuting movements of the labour workforce. They account for differentiation on a more disaggregated level than the level of the 26 cantons in Switzerland, particularly those which are larger and contain different agglomeration categories. When selecting variables to describe the relevant factors for entrepreneurial activity, one has to take into account that the availability of statistical data is limited. Table 8.1 and the following description give a short overview of the variables selected.

The indicator 'population density' represents both the demand and supply side for entrepreneurship as well as urbanization economies. Population density is highly correlated with a number of factors such as purchasing power,[2] business infrastructure, market proximity, access to innovative products and quality of communication infrastructure and stands for specialized and individualized consumer preferences. A high population density indicates high regional start-up rates. The variable can be regarded as a 'catch-all indicator'. It is defined as the number of population by square kilometres.

Density of business services is an indicator of the demand side and urbanization economies. It can be considered as a proxy for structural change and economic progress towards a service economy. The service sector shows a high rate of new venture creation due to low entry barriers, defined as the ratio of the number of firms in the service sector divided by 1000 inhabitants.

Besides the density of the business sector, the density of the manufacturing sector is also used as an indicator for the demand side. However, the linkage of this indicator to entrepreneurial activity is ambiguous. First, a high manufacturing density indicates a low economic level of development, and it can be assumed that it influences entrepreneurial activity negatively. Secondly, it can be considered as an indicator for localization economies if a regional concentration of specific industries exists. If so, a high industry share indicates a high potential for new venture creation. As two interpretations are possible, this indicator has to be used carefully. It is defined as the ratio of the number of firms in the manufacturing sector divided by 1000 inhabitants.

The share of small firms may be viewed as a determinant of the demand side as well as an indicator of the supply side. First, it can be

Table 8.1   Indicators used in the study

Factors based on theory	Indicator name	Indicator	Influence of indicators on firm formation rate	Source
Demand/ supply side/ agglomeration economies	Population density	Number of inhabitants 2007 per km^2	Positive	Swiss Federal Statistical Office, ESPOP 2007[a]
Demand side/ agglomeration economies	Density of business services	Number of firms of the business services per 1000 inhabitants (2005)	Positive	Swiss Federal Statistical Office, UDEMO 2005,[b] ESPOP 2005
Demand side/ agglomeration economies	Density of manu- facturing sector	Number of firms of the manufacturing sector per 1000 (2005) inhabitants	Negative (in special cases positive)	Swiss Federal Statistical Office, UDEMO 2005, ESPOP 2005
Demand side/ supply side	Share of small firms	Number of small firms (until 49 employees) per 1000 inhabitants (2005)	Positive	Swiss Federal Statistical Office, UDEMO 2005, ESPOP 2005
Supply side/ agglomeration economies	Labour force	Labour force per number of inhabitants (2000)	Positive	Swiss Federal Statistical Office, VZ 2000[c] ESPOP 2000
Supply side/ agglomeration economies	Graduate degree	Number of persons with graduate degree per number of inhabitants (2000)	Positive	Swiss Federal Statistical Office, VZ 2000, ESPOP 2000
Supply side	Diversity Index	Number of foreign born persons per number of inhabitants (2006)	Positive	Swiss Federal Statistical Office, ESPOP 2006

Table 8.1   (continued)

Factors based on theory	Indicator name	Indicator	Influence of indicators on firm formation rate	Source
Supply side	Young people of 25–40 years	Number of 25–40-year-olds per number of inhabitants (2000)	Positive	Swiss Federal Statistical Office, VZ 2000, ESPOP 2000
Supply side	Self-employed persons	Number of self-employed persons (incl. family members) per number of inhabitants (2000)	Positive	Swiss Federal Statistical Office, VZ 2000, ESPOP 2000
Validation variable	Start-up rate	Average number of new firms per 1000 workers (1996-2006)		Swiss Federal Statistical Office, UDEMO 2005

Sources:
a. ESPOP: Annual Population Statistics (*Statistik des jährlichen Bevölkerungsstandes*).
b. UDEMO: Federal Establishment Census (*Unternehmensdemografie*).
c. VZ: Federal Population Census (*Volkszählung*).

considered as a further indicator regarding structural change and flexible specialization. Secondly, small firms serve as role models for other potential entrepreneurs. Hence, a high share of small firms is supposed to have a positive impact on new firm formation. It is measured by the proportion of the number of small firms relative to the total population of a region.

Labour force is selected as an indicator for the supply side of entrepreneurship as well as an indicator of urbanization economies. It can be considered as an indicator for the availability of new entrepreneurs and future employees for new and young firms. It is defined as the ratio of available work force per inhabitants.

A further indicator for the supply side is the number of persons with a graduate degree. It is used as a proxy for high qualification since there is a positive relationship between education and entrepreneurial activity. It includes not only university degrees but also an applied educational background. This background plays an important role in the probability of

Table 8.2   Summary statistics of variables used in cluster analysis

Indicator name	Mean	Standard deviation	Minimum	Maximum
Population density	374.93	676.74	7.87	5006.14
Density of business services	9.85	4.50	3.83	37.40
Density of manufacturing sector	10.98	2.17	6.89	15.64
Share of small firms	40.32	7.92	29.11	74.34
Labour force	53.34	3.92	44.86	69.91
Graduate degree	6.43	3.15	2.11	17.05
Diversity index	17.39	6.86	3.40	37.32
Young people of 25–40 years	24.42	1.89	19.67	32.68
Self-employed persons	7.85	1.84	4.95	13.34

starting a company. Besides graduates with a university degree, graduates from *Höhere Fachschulen*, which are more vocational schools, have also been included. It is defined as the number of inhabitants with a graduate degree compared to the total number of inhabitants.

The share of immigrants in a region is expressed by the diversity index. It is the proportion of foreign-born persons in a region relative to the total number of inhabitants. A high value indicates a large potential for venture creation because both well and low qualified foreigners have a high probability of creating a venture.

Young highly qualified people are used as a further indicator of the supply side. Many entrepreneurs start their new venture typically between the ages of 25 and 40. Hence, the share of this age group in relation to the total number of inhabitants is selected.

A final indicator of the supply side is the number of self-employed persons. On the one hand, self-employed persons act as role models for potential entrepreneurs. On the other hand, self-employed persons are likely to be serial entrepreneurs. This indicator is defined as the number of self-employed persons per number of the regional population.

Table 8.2 gives a brief summary of variables used in cluster analysis and their characteristics.

In addition to the aforementioned indicators, which are included in cluster analysis, the number of new businesses is also considered. This variable serves as a validation variable to verify the results of cluster analysis. This data only comprises information about newly founded independent firms; subsidiaries are not registered. Start-up rates are calculated based on the labour market approach. They are defined as the number of start-ups per 1000 of a region's workforce.[3] This data varies considerably between the regions. On average, over all regions, the start-up rate is 2.5 new businesses per 1000 workers per year, with a standard deviation of 1.2. The region with the highest start-up rate experiences 10.3 new businesses per 1000 workers in a year, whereas the region with the lowest start-up rate sees only 0.9 new businesses. The region with the highest start-up rate, however, is clearly an outlier, but a start-up rate of 4 and more is common.

Cluster Analysis

To compare different regions according to their structural potential for new venture creation, and to find out about the strengths and weaknesses of regions with regard to their entrepreneurial activity, cluster analysis is used. The objective of a cluster analysis is to form homogeneous groups of objects which are described by a variety of characteristics (see, for example, Hair et al., 2006; Backhaus et al., 2008). Here cluster analysis is used to form several homogeneous groups of Swiss labour market regions, the MS regions, according to their individual structural potential and for comparative purposes. The method of cluster analysis is an established instrument in regional economics which allows complexity to be reduced and relevant regions and measures for regional policy to be identified (Eckey et al., 2002). For example cluster analysis is used by the German Sachverständigenrat zur Begutachtung der Gesamtwirtschaftlichen Entwicklung (1999) to find out about regional disparities in East Germany, and by Kronthaler (2005) to compare the economic capability of East German regions with West German regions.

In the calculation of the clusters, first Ward's minimum-variance method is used. This technique belongs to the group of hierarchical agglomerative methods in which every object is represented by an individual cluster at the beginning of the algorithm. The clusters are then successively joined together in groups until only a single cluster remains. The objective of Ward's method is to join two clusters at each step, such that the *variance* for the joined clusters is minimized. In comparison to other hierarchical fusion algorithms, which use minimization of the *distance* between clusters as the fusion criterion, several simulation studies have shown that the Ward technique appears to be superior to alternative approaches and forms very homogeneous clusters (Everitt et al., 2001; Backhaus et al., 2008). However, since clusters which are merged using Ward's method cannot be separated again in subsequent steps, it has been suggested that the results from the Ward technique should be corrected in an additional step, for example by using an optimizing clustering algorithm, which allows for a reassignment of regions (see, for example, Hair et al., 2006; Everitt et al., 2001).

A first issue when applying cluster analysis is whether or not the variables used are highly correlated, since such variables tend to dominate the cluster analysis and may distort the results (Backhaus et al., 2008). In the literature it is recommended that variables with a correlation coefficient $r > 0.8$ (Schmidt, 1995) or $r > 0.9$ (Backhaus et al., 2008) should be excluded. Calculation of the correlation coefficients shows that none of the variables are correlated to this extent. Another problem is the possible different weighting of the variables due to differing unit scales. To avoid this, variables are standardized by a z-transformation (Bacher, 1996).

As mentioned above, the Ward algorithm stops when there is only one cluster left. To determine the optimal number of clusters, we employ the agglomeration schedule and the measure of homogeneity, ETA^2.

The agglomeration schedule (see Appendix Table 8A.1) reveals increases in the distances at each step of the fusion process. As an informal test, high increases in these distance levels are checked, because a high increase suggests an optimal number of clusters. Jumps in the distance levels are apparent from cluster number 25 to 24, 21 to 20, 14 to 13, 10 to 9, 9 to 8, 7 to 6, and 5 to 4. Therefore several cluster solutions are possible and it has to be decided which cluster solution is preferable. Considering the jumps more precisely, one can judge that the increases from 10 to 9 and 9 to 8 are the substantial ones, so we proceed with the 10-cluster solution. This is in line with the objective of cluster analysis to reduce complexity and to facilitate interpretation of the cluster solution. Furthermore, it is in line with the second criterion, the measure of homogeneity of the cluster solution, ETA^2. This measure describes the share of the variance which occurs between clusters. With the 10-cluster solution, ETA^2 is about 70 per cent, meaning that most of the variance is between clusters.[4] Finally, with the help of a non-hierarchical clustering algorithm (k-means), the selected cluster solution is optimized using the cluster seeds resulting from the Ward algorithm. In six iteration steps, 14 regions have been reassigned, improving the original solution.

To interpret the individual clusters, the F-values, t-values and mean values of the variables are used. The F-value provides information about the homogeneity of the individual groups. It is the quotient of the variance of a variable within the cluster and the variance of the variable in the population:

$$F_j^C = \frac{Var_j^C}{Var_j}. \tag{8.1}$$

The smaller this quotient is, the more homogeneous is the cluster. F-values smaller than 1 indicate homogeneous clusters (the variance of the variable *j* within the cluster is smaller than the variance of the variable *j* within the population).

The t-value is used to characterize each cluster. It is the difference between the cluster mean value of the variable *j* and the mean value of the variable *j* of the population divided by the standard deviation:

$$t_j^C = \frac{\overline{X}_j^C - \overline{X}_j}{\sqrt{Var_j}}. \tag{8.2}$$

Negative (positive) t-values therefore indicate that the variable *j* is lower (higher) than the mean of the population. In addition to the t-value, the mean value of the variable is used in the interpretation because it provides information about the variables in their original scale.

RESULTS

According to the discussion of the results of the cluster analysis, we were able to identify 10 clusters with different entrepreneurial potentials. Table 8.3 shows the characteristic profile of the clusters with the strengths and weaknesses of the respective clusters as well as the validation variable start-up rates. It can be observed that in these clusters where strengths outweigh the weaknesses, start-up rates are high, and vice versa. This means that clusters with a high (low) potential have in fact high (low) venture creation rates. For example, cluster A has high t-values in nearly all variables, which is in accordance with the relatively high start-up rate. As in this study start-up rates act as a validation variable, this means that cluster analysis performed well in identifying clusters with high, medium and low potentials for venture creation.

Each cluster is briefly described in terms of demand-side factors, supply-side factors, urbanization and localization economies, and how they differ from each other.

Cluster A consists of two of the main agglomerations of Switzerland, namely Zurich and Basel. As such, it is naturally well endowed with both demand and supply-side factors, as well as urbanization and localization economies for specific industries. In particular, nearly all variables indicate a high entrepreneurial potential with the exception of the variable relating to self-employed persons. With 6.3 per cent of self-employed persons the proportion is relatively low compared to other clusters, thus

Table 8.3   Characteristic profile of the clusters

		Population density	Labour force	Diversity Index	Young people of 25 to 40 years	Self-employed persons	Graduate degree	Share of small firms	Density of manu-facturing sector	Density of business services	Validation variable: Start-up rate 1999–2006
ROR	Mean value	374.94	53.43	17.39	24.42	7.85	6.43	40.32	10.98	9.85	2.52
Cluster A (N = 2)	Mean value	4543.01	57.48	29.55	28.76	6.29	14.25	50.77	7.00	21.93	4.08
	t-value	6.13	1.03	1.77	2.28	−0.84	2.47	1.31	−1.83	2.68	1.37
	F-value	0.47	1.88	0.01	4.27	0.03	0.41	0.70	0.00	1.10	0.15
Cluster B (N = 16)	Mean value	888.94	56.02	24.67	26.01	6.32	11.67	37.88	8.12	12.60	3.05
	t-value	0.76	0.66	1.06	0.84	−0.83	1.66	−0.31	−1.31	0.61	0.47
	F-value	0.48	0.46	0.85	0.58	0.30	0.85	0.11	0.18	0.28	0.21
Cluster C (N = 24)	Mean value	346.07	55.58	18.44	24.64	7.28	6.15	38.71	10.63	10.61	2.55
	t-value	−0.04	0.55	0.15	0.11	−0.31	−0.09	−0.20	−0.16	0.17	0.03
	F-value	0.07	0.24	0.29	0.20	0.17	0.15	0.26	0.25	0.16	0.15
Cluster D (N = 19)	Mean value	146.18	53.48	11.39	24.43	8.21	4.93	34.36	10.81	6.93	1.95
	t-value	−0.34	−0.01	−0.87	−0.00	0.20	−0.48	−0.75	−0.08	−0.65	−0.50
	F-value	0.01	0.28	0.24	0.24	0.21	012	0.22	0.23	0.06	0.09
Cluster E (N = 13)	Mean value	123.58	50.32	17.58	22.82	7.17	4.30	38.82	13.31	6.56	2.06
	t-value	−0.37	−0.79	0.03	−0.84	−0.37	−0.67	−0.19	1.07	−0.73	−0.40
	F-value	0.03	0.48	0.36	0.33	0.16	0.07	0.26	0.18	0.15	0.20

Table 8.3 (continued)

		Population density	Labour force	Diversity Index	Young people of 25 to 40 years	Self-employed persons	Graduate degree	Share of small firms	Density of manufacturing sector	Density of business services	Validation variable: Start-up rate 1999–2006
Cluster F (N = 12)	Mean value	63.21	51.47	9.04	22.75	11.01	3.59	40.81	13.21	7.61	1.73
	t-value	-0.46	-0.50	-1.21	-0.88	1.71	-0.90	0.06	1.03	-0.50	-0.69
	F-value	0.01	0.30	0.25	0.26	0.48	0.09	0.51	0.39	0.20	0.33
Cluster G (N = 3)	Mean value	165.35	62.51	18.71	27.77	9.91	5.72	60.19	13.65	15.23	3.48
	t-value	-0.31	2.30	0.19	1.76	1.12	-0.22	2.50	1.23	1.20	0.84
	F-value	0.09	1.93	0.19	0.52	0.84	0.06	0.15	0.06	0.98	3.04
Cluster H (N = 1)	Mean value	527.00	58.34	20.91	28.12	7.10	10.55	74.34	11.22	37.40	10.35
	t-value	0.22	1.25	0.51	1.95	-0.41	1.30	4.28	0.11	6.10	6.83
	F-value	0.00	0.00	0.00	0.00	0.00	0.00	0.00	0.00	0.00	0.00
Cluster I (N = 12)	Mean value	159.07	49.20	21.81	24.43	6.64	6.72	41.98	9.70	9.35	2.88
	t-value	-0.32	-1.08	0.64	0.00	-0.66	0.09	0.21	-0.59	-0.11	0.32
	F-value	0.04	0.14	0.67	0.35	0.24	025	0.52	0.10	0.49	0.82
Cluster J (N = 4)	Mean value	13.56	48.59	13.66	21.34	11.52	4.47	57.73	14.75	10.09	2.15
	t-value	-0.53	-1.23	-0.54	-1.62	2.00	-0.62	2.19	1.74	0.05	-0.32
	F-value	0.00	0.33	0.22	0.29	0.46	0.13	0.46	0.09	0.01	0.18

indicating some weaknesses in one of the proxies for the supply side of entrepreneurship. One of the causes of the relatively low share of self-employed persons is certainly the fact that huge industries (banking in Zurich and chemistry in Basel) are located in this cluster. Overall, the high level of entrepreneurial potential in this cluster is shown by the relatively high start-up rate, with nearly 5 new firms per 1000 workers in one year.

Cluster B is a cluster that is also comprised of some of the main agglomerations of Switzerland, such as Berne, Fribourg, Geneva, Neuchâtel, Lausanne, as well as the greater Zurich area. Hence for cluster B the same assumptions are valid as for cluster A. Nearly all variables for the demand side, supply side and urbanization and localization economies show high entrepreneurial potential. Exceptions again include the number of self-employed persons, with a share of 6.3 per cent, and the number of small firms with 37.9 small firms, per 1000 workers.

Cluster C contains 24 regions such as St Gallen, Chur, Davos and the Zurich lake area. It includes not only agglomerations and urban regions, but also semi-peripheral regions.[5] Overall, the potential for new venture creation is lower than in clusters A and B, but it is still middle to high. It has start-up rates of 2.5 per cent per 1000 labour force, which is slightly above the Swiss average start-up rate. Strengths lie in a high number of young and diversified people as well as in a high density of business services. Cluster C, in particular, features a high level of given labour force, with 55.6 per cent. Weaknesses can be seen, however, in a relatively low level of self-employed persons and small firms. To summarize, Cluster C shows all three categories of factors (supply and demand side, agglomeration economies) with a mixed picture of high and low levels of entrepreneurial potential.

Cluster D mainly consists of semi-peripheral and peripheral regions, which are mainly located in mountainous areas such as the upper Berne areas. They share some similar characteristics to cluster C. Nevertheless, there are differences with regard to specific variables, such as a low diversity index, with 11.4 per cent of the total number of inhabitants, and a low density of business services compared to cluster C. Overall, the potential for venture creation with regard to the underlying variables seems to be quite weak. Furthermore, weaknesses lie in a low population density and a lack of young people and graduates. Nevertheless, cluster D has a relatively high number of self-employed (8.2 per cent) compared to the first three clusters A, B and C.

Belonging to the clusters with the lowest entrepreneurial potential, cluster E has at least an average diversity index, while all other variables are clearly below average. The start-up rate is 2.1 per cent and therefore close to the average. With 13.3 per cent, cluster E has one of the highest shares of manufacturing firms.

Cluster F contains rural areas including Toggenburg, Einsiedeln, Emmental and Appenzell. As in the case of the clusters above, the characteristics of all three categories (demand and supply side and agglomeration economies) can be found in this cluster. The entrepreneurial potential is significantly below the average in comparison to the other clusters. An exception is the number of self-employed persons per number of inhabitants, which is very high for Swiss regions.

Cluster G only consists of three regions, including the Upper Engadine. These are semi-peripheral and peripheral regions with a relatively high potential for new venture creation. Strengths can be identified in most of the variables except for population density and the number of graduates. Young people number 27.8 per cent (supply side). The four variables referring to the proportion of young people, self-employed persons, small firms and the density of business services have very high values. They belong to both the demand and the supply side influences.

Cluster H can be considered as an outlier, consisting only of the region Zug, which is a small canton. It has a high potential regarding nearly all variables which is in line with an extraordinarily high start-up rate of 10.4 per cent per 1000 labour force, as indicated by our validation variable. In addition, the values for the shares of small firms, with 74 per 1000 inhabitants, and of graduated people, with 10.6 per cent of the regional population, are extraordinarily high.

Cluster I comprises 12 regions, all located in the southern valleys of Switzerland, such as Lugano, Bellinzona and Martigny. The diversity index, the number of young and graduated people and the share of small firms are all above average and all relate to supply-side factors.

In cluster J, with region such as the Lower Engadine, extreme differences exist regarding the levels of entrepreneurial potential. On the one hand, there are very high numbers of self-employed persons (11.5 per cent of inhabitants) and shares of small firms (58 firms per 1000 inhabitants). On the other hand, there is a lack of regional labour force, young people and of young people and graduates.

The spatial distribution of the clusters is shown in Figure 8.1. Considering the spatial dimension of the clusters, it can be seen that clusters A and B mainly consist of regions that are classified as agglomerations or urban regions in Switzerland.[6] Cluster C also comprises urban regions, but includes semi-peripheral regions as well. Another urban cluster is cluster H, which only contains the region Zug. All the other clusters (D, E, F, G, I, J) mostly consist of semi-peripheral and peripheral regions. With regard to this, one important result is that some semi-peripheral regions

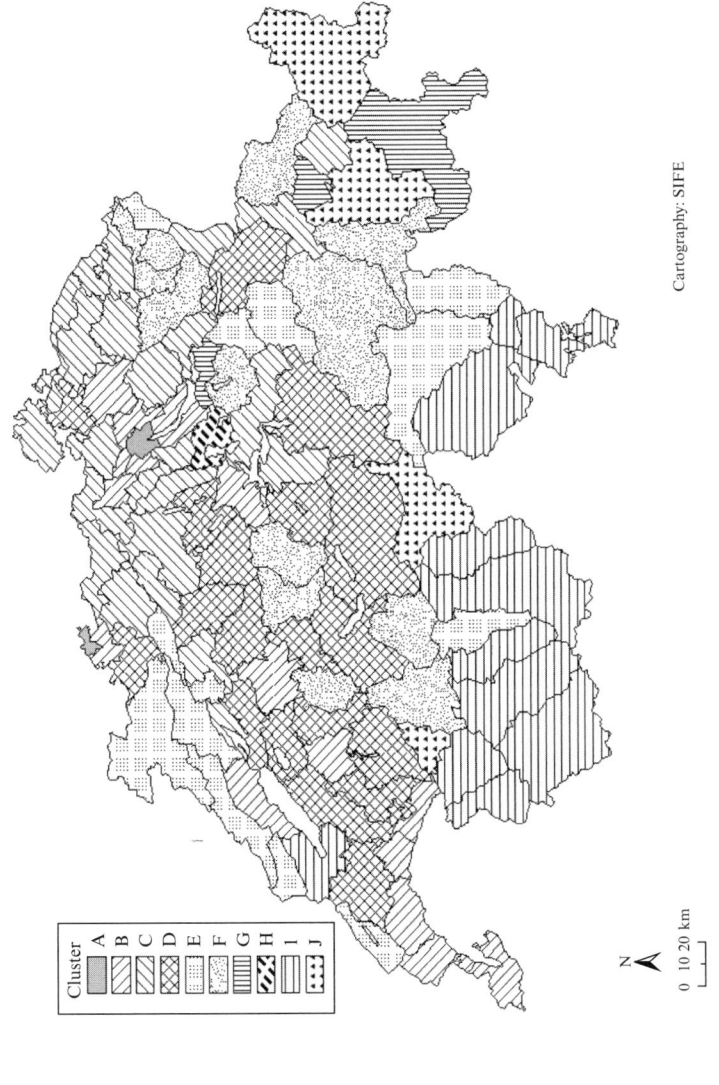

Cartography: SIFE

Sources: BFS, Themakart 2008, Esri 2008.

Figure 8.1   Spatial distribution of clusters

are within the same cluster, including urban regions, and therefore show a similar potential.

CONCLUSIONS AND POLICY RECOMMENDATIONS

The results of the cluster analysis, based on established factors in the literature, suggest that those regions outlined are unique and distinct with regard to their potential for venture creation. With these results it is possible to discuss different strategies for fostering entrepreneurial activity for the respective regions.

Cluster analysis has shown that, in general, agglomeration and urban regions, such as clusters A and B, have high entrepreneurial potential compared to all other Swiss regions. These findings are internally consistent as they have high values regarding the supply side, the demand side and the agglomeration economies, as well as high start-up rates. In spite of that, there seems to be a weakness shown by the low value in the number of self-employed people, who provide role models for venture creation. Furthermore, the value of the share of small firms is low in cluster B, indicating a lack of role models as well. However, this has to be interpreted in relationship to the already high start-up rate, meaning that role models already exist to some extent.

As illustrated in the description of the results, cluster H can be considered as an outlier consisting only of the region Zug, which is a small canton. It has a high potential regarding nearly all variables. Additionally, this region focuses on a low taxation rate[7] to attract venture creation and new businesses. Furthermore it is close to Zurich. All three points help to explain the extraordinarily high start-up rate indicated by our validation variable. Overall, there seems to be no need for action for clusters A, B and H. This is in line with the Swiss NRP, which does not target agglomeration and urban regions.

More important are the results with regard to semi-peripheral and peripheral regions, which lie within the targeting area of regional policy. Some of these regions have a relatively high potential for venture creation but with some weaknesses (clusters C and G). Given that resources are limited within the NRP, it can be discussed whether it would be a good strategy to focus on these regions. Fostering these regions might support the formation of regional focal points in the long run, which can act as a nucleus for the surrounding area. However, this would also mean that already weak regions are neglected.

Cluster C is the most interesting cluster with regard to regional policy in Switzerland. It includes semi-peripheral regions with relatively high potential; the profile shows explicit strengths and weaknesses (see section 'results'). With regard to this, two overall strategies are available. One would be to focus on already existing strengths; the other would be to compensate for existing weaknesses. Since strengths outweigh existing weaknesses, it might be a valid strategy to concentrate on existing weaknesses. On the one hand there are only a few existing weaknesses and, furthermore, such weaknesses lie in particular in the lack of role models for entrepreneurship, which can be straightforwardly/easily compensated through education. By using this strategy, these regions could strengthen their ability to transfer their already existing entrepreneurship potential into economic value by sustaining entrepreneurship education. Especially for these types of regions, universities of applied sciences can help to compensate for existing weaknesses. They play a major role for three reasons: First, they could provide role models through entrepreneurship education; second, they strengthen the regional knowledge and human capital base of the population; third, they support existing regional small and medium-sized firms and entrepreneurs with regard to their individual needs for innovation and research activities. However, if there is no higher education institution located, another option could be to implement entrepreneurial support and educational activities in the curricula of secondary schools and at the vocational training level.

Considering all regions within the target area of the NRP, the results can be used to identify the strengths and weaknesses of single regions and, if necessary, to extend the analysis with the help of case studies. Based on this, policy-makers should be able to formulate well-founded strategies.

In clusters D, E, F, I and J the situation is completely different. These peripheral and semi-peripheral regions only have a few strengths compared to the predominant existing weaknesses. Applying the same reasoning, it might be more appropriate for these regions to focus on their existing strengths, because compensating for weaknesses would involve significantly more effort, on the basis of the law of diminishing returns. With regard to these regions, it seems to be the case that many have an existing small-firm base and a relatively high number of entrepreneurs. In combination, this indicates that there might be some industry concentration consisting of small firms, for example in the agricultural sector, the craft sector and in tourism, together with plenty of entrepreneurial role models. In the framework of localization economies this indicates an especially high potential for venture creation in a specific industry. Therefore strategies could be implemented to support the existing industrial sectors and to form industrial clusters. Moreover, the tourism industry might be a good focal point in some of these regions. At the same time, the results first need to be deepened by further case studies.

In conclusion, the results provide means for benchmarking regions, that is regions can find out about their specific characteristics in comparison to other regions and clusters. Furthermore, the results can assist NRP decision-makers to evaluate projects to establish whether or not they are in line with regional policy strategy. Additionally, the results could serve as a basis for case studies to validate and extend the knowledge of specific regions, particularly in the case of clusters that include diverse regions. A further caveat of the study is the non-availability of data on a highly disaggregated regional level. From earlier studies it is known that both individual and regional variables affect the decision to become self-employed. A better match of databases on both levels should therefore be regarded as a major challenge for future research in this field.

NOTES

1. A similar classification is used in the literature; see for example Bosma et al. (2008), Verheul et al. (2002).
2. In fact population density is highly correlated with regional GDP per capita.
3. The start-up rate according to the labour market approach may be regarded as the propensity of a member of the regional workforce to start their own business. New ventures are usually located close to the residence or the former workplace of the founder (Stam, 2007). Thus, the number of firm founders who choose the location of their firm primarily on the basis of regional characteristics is very limited.
4. More formal criteria to decide about cluster solution, is the use of Mojena test statistics I and II (Bacher, 1996). However, both tests normally provide different results and are not really reliable. Hence, we do not consider the test results, which both indicate different solutions.
5. Semi-peripheral regions are defined as regions which do not belong to Swiss agglomeration and urban regions but are classified as a middle–large town.
6. The classification in agglomeration, urban and peripheral regions is based on the definition of the Swiss New Regional Policy.
7. A low taxation rate is considered in the entrepreneurial literature as a positive environmental factor for venture creation, too. Unfortunately there are no data available at the regional level, so we were not able to include these data in our study.

REFERENCES

Acs,.Z., N. Bosma and R.Sternberg (2008), 'The entrepreneurial advantage of world cities. Evidence from Global Entrepreneurship Monitor data', EIM scales paper, 2008–10.
Acs, Z.J. and D.B. Audretsch (1987), 'Innovation, market structure, and firm size', *Review of Economics and Statistics*, **69**(4), 567–74.

Armington, C. and Z. Acs (2002), 'The determinants of regional variation in new firm variation', *Regional Studies*, **36**(1), 33–45.

Audretsch, D.B. and M. Fritsch (1994), 'The geography of firm births in Germany', *Regional Studies*, **28**(4), 359–65.

Audretsch, D.B., A.G. Brett and P.P. McDougall (2008), 'Clusters, knowledge spillovers and new venture performance: an empirical examination', *Journal of Business Venturing*, **23**, 405–22.

Audretsch, D.B., M.C. Keilbach and E.E. Lehmann (2006), *Entrepreneurship and Growth*, New York: Oxford University Press.

Bacher, J. (1996), *Clusteranalyse*, 2nd edn, Munich/Vienna: Oldenbourg.

Backhaus, K., B. Erichson, W. Plinke and R. Weiber (2008), *Multivariate Analysemethoden*, 12th edn, Berlin: Springer.

Bergmann, H. and R. Sternberg (2007), 'The changing face of entrepreneurship in Germany', *Small Business Economics*, **28**, 205–21.

Bosma, N. and V. Schutjens (2009), 'Mapping entrepreneurial activity and entrepreneurial attitudes in European regions', *International Journal of Entrepreneurship and Small Business*, **7**(2), 191–13.

Bosma, N., A. van Stel and K. Suddle (2008), 'The geography of new firm formation: evidence from independent start-ups and new subsidiaries in the Netherlands', *International Entrepreneurship Management Journal*, **4**, 129–46.

Brüderl, J., P. Preisendörfer and R. Ziegler (1998), *Der Erfolg neugegründeter Betriebe*, 2nd edn, Berlin: Duncker and Humblot.

Dunn, T. and D. Holtz-Eakin (2000), 'Financial capital, human capital and the transition to self-employment: evidence from intergenerational links', *Journal of Labor Economics*, **18**(2), 282–305.

Eckey, H.-F., R. Kosfeld and M. Rengers (2002), *Multivariate Statistik*, Wiesbaden: Gabler.

Evans, D.S. and L.S. Leighton (1989), 'The determinants of changes in US self-employment, 1968–1987', *Small Business Economics*, **1**, 111–19.

Everitt, B.S., S. Landau and L. Morven (2001), *Cluster Analysis*, 4th edn, London: Arnold.

Fotopoulos, G. and N. Spence (1999), 'Spatial variations in net entry rates of establishments in Greek manufacturing industries: an application of the shift-Share ANOVA model', *Environment and Planning*, **31**(11), 1731–55.

Fritsch, M. (1997), 'New firms and regional employment change', *Small Business Economics*, **9**, 437–48.

Fritsch, M. (2008), 'How does new business formation affect regional development? Introduction to the special issue', *Small Business Economics*, **30**, 1–14.

Fritsch, M. and P. Mueller (2004), 'Effects of new business formation on regional development over time', *Regional Studies*, **38**(8), 961–75.

Fritsch, M. and P. Mueller (2008), 'The effect of new business formation on regional development over time: the case of Germany', *Small Business Economics*, **30**, 15–29.

Glaeser, E.L. H.D. Kallal, J.A. Scheinkman and A. Shleifer (1992), 'Growth in cities', *Journal of Political Economy*, **100**(6), 1126–52.

Hair, J.F., W.C. Black, B.J. Babin, R.E. Anderson and R.L. Tatham, (2006), *Multivariate Data Analysis*, 6th edn, Upper Saddle River, NJ: Pearson/Prentice Hall.

Hinz, T. (1998), *Betriebsgründungen in Ostdeutschland*, Berlin: edition sigma.

202   *Entrepreneurship, growth and economic development*

Hoover, E.M. (1948), *The Location of Economic Activity*, New York: McGraw-Hill.

Jacobs, J. (1969), *The Economy of Cities*, New York: Random House.

Kronthaler, F. (2005), 'Economic capability of East German regions: results from a cluster analysis', *Regional Studies*, **39**(6), 741–52.

Lee, S., R. Florida and Z.J. Acs (2004), 'Creativity and entrepreneurship: a regional analysis of new firm formation', *Regional Studies*, **38**(8), 879–91.

Loveman, G.W., M.J. Piore and W. Sengenberger (1991), 'The evolving role of small business', in K.G. Abraham and R.B. McKersie (eds), *New Developments in the Labor Market*, Cambridge: MIT Press, pp. 121–50.

Marshall, A. (1920), *Principles of Economics*, London: Macmillan.

Minniti, M. (2005), 'Entrepreneurship and network externalities', *Journal of Economic Behavior and Organization,* **57**(1), 1–27.

Mueller, P. (2006), 'Entrepreneurship in the region: breeding ground for nascent entrepreneurs?' *small business economics*, **27**, 41–58.

Parker, S.C. (2004), *The Economics of Self-Employment and Entrepreneurship*, New York: Cambridge University Press.

Reynolds, P.D., M. Hay and S.M. Camp (1999), *Global Entrepreneurship Monitor*, Babson Park, MA: Babson College and London Business School.

Reynolds, P.D., B. Miller and W.R. Maki (1995), 'Explaining regional variation in business births and deaths: US 1976–88', *Small Business Economics*, **7**, 389–407.

Reynolds, P.D., D.J. Storey and P. Westhead (1994), 'Cross-national comparisons of the variation in new firm formation rates', *regional studies*, **28**(4), 443–56.

Reynolds, P.D., W.D. Bygrave, E. Autio, L.W. Cox and M. Hay (2002), 'Global entrepreneurship monitor', executive report, available at http://www.gemconsortium.com, accessed 12 May 2009.

Sachverständigenrat zur Begutachtung der gesamtwirtschaftlichen Entwicklung (1999), *Wirtschaftspolitik unter Reformdruck – Jahresgutachten 1999/2000*, Stuttgart: Metzler-Poeschel.

Saxenian, A. (1999), *Silicon Valley's New Immigrant Entrepreneurs*, San Francisco: Public Policy Institute of California.

Schmidt, B. (1995), *Kreistypisierung und Zentralörtliche Gliederung mit Statistischen Verfahren*, Regensburg: eurotrans-Verlag.

Stam, E. (2007), 'why butterflies don't leave: locational behaviour of entrepreneurial firms', *Economic Geography*, **83**(1), 27–50.

Storey, D.J. (1994), *Understanding the Small Business Sector*, London: Routledge.

Swiss Federal Statistical Office (BfS) (2000), *Federal Population Census*, Special data interpretation.

Swiss Federal Statistical Office (BfS) (2000, 2006, 2007), *Annual Population Statistics*, Special data interpretation.

Swiss Federal Statistical Office (BfS) (2005), *Federal Establishment Census*, Special data interpretation.

Thurik, Roy, Jolanda Hessels, Isabel Grilo and Peter van der Zwan (2009), 'Entrepreneurial exit and entrepreneurial engagement', *Scales Research Reports* H200910, EIM Business and Policy Research.

Van Praag, C.M. and H. van Ophem (1995), 'Determinants of willingness and opportunity to start as an entrepreneur', *Kyklos, International Review for Social Sciences*, **48**(4), 513–40.

Van Stel, A. and D.J. Storey (2004), 'The link between firm births and job creation: is there a upas tree effect?', *Regional Studies*, **38**, 893–909.

Verheul, I., A.R.M. Wennekers, D.B. Audretsch and A.R. Thurik (2002), 'An eclectic theory of entrepreneurship', in D.B. Audretsch, A.R. Thurik, I. Verheul and A.R.M. Wennekers (eds), *Entrepreneurship: Determinants and Policy in a European–US Comparison*, Dordrecht: Kluwer, pp. 11–81.

Wagner, J. (2004), 'Are young and small firms hot-houses for nascent entrepreneurship? Evidence from German micro data', *Applied Economics Quarterly*, **50**(4), 379–91.

Wagner, J. and R. Sternberg (2004), 'Start-up activities, individual characteristics, and the regional milieu: lessons for entrepreneurship support policies from German micro data', *Annals of Regional Science*, **38**(2), 219–40.

Westhead, P. and M. Wright (1998), 'Novice, portfolio, and serial founders: are they different?', *journal of business venturing*, **13**(3), 173–204.

APPENDIX

Table 8A.1   *Agglomerations schedule (Ward technique, last 35 steps)*

Number of cluster	Cluster combined		Sum of squares	Distance	Increase in distance	ETA^2 (%)
35	4	35	82.744	6.060	0.115	91.24
34	20	28	85.804	6.120	0.060	90.92
33	14	37	89.016	6.424	0.304	90.58
32	40	96	92.380	6.728	0.304	90.22
31	80	82	96.069	7.379	0.651	89.83
30	67	89	99.777	7.415	0.036	89.44
29	21	22	103.521	7.489	0.074	89.05
28	23	69	107.390	7.736	0.247	88.64
27	39	86	111.522	8.264	0.528	88.20
26	24	27	115.823	8.602	0.338	87.74
25	5	8	120.204	8.763	0.161	87.28
24	9	20	125.399	10.389	1.625	86.73
23	14	79	131.551	12.304	1.916	86.08
22	4	62	137.716	12.329	0.025	85.43
21	40	81	144.103	12.775	0.445	84.75
20	2	5	152.216	16.227	3.452	83.89
19	4	13	160.694	16.955	0.728	83.00
18	21	23	169.647	17.907	0.952	82.05
17	6	39	180.103	20.911	3.004	80.94
16	33	63	191.945	23.683	2.772	79.69
15	40	80	204.305	24.721	1.038	78.38
14	2	6	216.796	24.981	0.261	77.06
13	4	24	231.260	28.928	3.947	75.53
12	17	21	246.863	31.207	2.279	73.88
11	2	84	263.763	33.801	2.594	72.09
10	1	47	281.334	35.141	1.340	70.23
9	17	67	301.510	40.351	5.210	68.09
8	33	38	327.522	52.024	11.673	65.34
7	4	9	353.973	52.902	0.878	62.54
6	14	17	388.363	68.781	15.878	58.90
5	4	40	423.265	69.802	1.021	55.21
4	1	2	495.382	144.235	74.433	47.58
3	1	33	585.340	179.915	35.680	38.06
2	4	14	691.327	211.974	32.058	26.84
1	1	4	945.000	507.347	295.373	0.00

9. A theoretical model of competitiveness and its application in the Hungarian SME sector

László Szerb and József Ulbert

INTRODUCTION

While competitiveness is a popular research topic amongst scholars of economics and business, our knowledge is still limited on the exact meaning, content and factors of competitiveness (Chaudhuri and Ray, 1997; Man et al., 2002). Moving away from the traditional Ricardian idea of comparative advantages, Michael Porter has developed the most widely acknowledged approach (Porter, 1990; 1998). While Porter emphasizes the importance of firms in competitiveness as opposed to countries or regions, he pays less attention to firm-level factors. According to Porter, the government can play an important role by means of effective industry and anti-trust policies, stimulating demand and specialized factor creation. A further development of the original Porter diamond model is the World Economic Forum's (WEF) index, which defines competitiveness as the mix of institutions, policies and factors that influence the level of productivity of a country (Porter and Schwab, 2008).

At the same time, recent Nobel laureate Paul Krugman claims that competitiveness is empirically unfounded, the concept of international competition is wrong, and consequently national economic policy focusing on competitiveness can be harmful (Krugman, 1994). There are similar doubts about the proper interpretation of competitiveness at regional levels. While it is generally agreed that regional competitiveness depends on the combined competitive advantage of firms and the comparative advantage of a regional economy (Budd and Hirmis, 2004), the relative importance of the institutional and firm-level factors is basically unknown. Sporadic, one-aspect analyses underline the dominance of firm-level characteristics (e.g. Sternberg and Arndt, 2001), but comprehensive multidimensional research is still rare (with Man et al., 2002 and Slevin and Covin, 1995 as exceptions).

There are two approaches to assessing the firm-level competitiveness within an industry. First, Porter's Five Forces model emphasizes the characteristics of competitiveness in an industry: the degree of existing firm rivalry; the threat of substitutes; the power of buyers; the power of suppliers; and the threats of new entry (Porter, 1998). The firm can position itself broadly in terms of the strategies of cost leadership, product differentiation and focus. By understanding the industry trends, leading managers can formulate efficient strategy to gain competitive advantage over other businesses. While the Porter model identifies the most important factors of competitiveness, it cannot explain the individual firm-level differences in competitiveness within the same industry.

A second set of approaches examines the characteristics of the firms themselves. There are several traditional theories besides Porter's (Ambastha and Momaya, 2004), such as structure–conduct–performance (SCP) and the resource-based view (RBV) (Barney, 1991). A common characteristic of these theories is the decisive importance given 'to the firm's internal rather than to its external conditions for understanding its competitive market position' (Foss and Knudsen, 1996, p 13). The present study builds our arguments based on RBV.

A further issue of firm-level competitiveness is associated with firm size. Most analyses focus on large, sometimes multinational firms or clusters (Lengyel, 2001; Porter, 1990; 1998; Rugman and Verbeke, 2001), while there is a lack of small business-related competitiveness studies. In contrast to Porter and his followers, who maintain that competitiveness should only be examined in those sectors where a country has certain competitive advantage, we suggest and emphasize a more general investigation that refers to all the sectors in the economy and includes smaller size businesses too. Moreover, if we accept that small firms are not scaled-down versions of large firms but they differ in structure, style of management, and other important characteristics, then examining competitiveness in the small and medium-sized business sector (SME) requires special methodology (Dean et al., 1998; Man et al., 2002; Malecki and Tootle, 1996).

Context: The Hungarian Business Sector

While the national and regional-level competitiveness is well researched (Lengyel, 2000; 2001; 2006; Török, 1999), there is a lack of firm-level investigation in Hungary. The most significant research on the competitiveness of Hungary's medium and large firms was completed by Attila Chikán's research group at Corvinus University of Budapest (Chikán and Czakó, 2009). The results of the latest 2004–2006 survey are contradictory.

While the performance of the Hungarian businesses is closely related to the most important factors of competitiveness (strategy, HRM, adaption capability, information management, and so on), the differentiation of the Hungarian businesses continues. Large, foreign–owned firms can compete globally but lag in innovation, information management, production-organization management and HRM techniques, amongst others (Chikán and Czakó, 2009). It also worth noting that due to the negative changes in the macroeconomic environment, Hungary has continuously fallen in the Global Competitiveness Index during the 2004–2008 period. Hungary is now only just ahead of Romania and Bulgaria in the European Union ranking of GCI competitiveness (Porter and Schwab, 2008).

There are some other sporadic, small sample researches focusing on Hungarian SMEs. Kadocsa (2006) identified a few management and organizational methods that positively affected the competitiveness of the Hungarian SMEs. Márkus et al. (2008) focused on identifying the factors of competitiveness, and on providing a useful analytical framework for analysing competitiveness in a small business framework. While the statistical–econometric methodology proved to be useful to group/cluster the businesses, the small number of the variables and the sample of only 100 did not make it possible to evaluate the competitiveness of Hungarian SMEs.

Summing up, while the competitiveness literature includes a large number of articles and books, there is still a lack of firm-level and small business focus studies. Even less is known about the competitiveness of Hungary's SMEs. Therefore a comprehensive, theoretically based, empirically tested analysis of the Hungarian SMEs could provide valuable insight on the problems facing Hungarian SMEs.

The basic aim of this chapter is to develop a conceptual model capable of determining and examining the competitiveness of small businesses. While most competitiveness research tries to focus on identifying the key factors of competitiveness, we view competitiveness from a system perspective. In this respect, the combination of the different elements is more important than a single factor. We focus on showing how the different elements of competitiveness can be recognized and combined by applying a unique methodology, called the penalty for bottleneck (PFB). The calculation of the competitiveness points of the firms in an individual basis is a distinctive approach in the competitiveness research. A small research survey in the Hungarian SME sector serves to present the empirical applicability of the conceptual model and the PFB methodology.

The chapter is structured in the following way. The second section provides the theoretical basis and presents the conceptual model that is adjusted to fit the small business framework. The third section discusses the practical application of the theory and the method of individual level competitiveness point calculation. The fourth section includes the description of the data set and describes the empirical methodology. The recently created penalty for bottleneck (PFB) method makes it possible to address the configuration of the factors of competitiveness. The research findings and a short discussion are in the fifth section. Correlation coefficients are applied to show the connection between the competition points and the different measures of competition. The sixth section provides an application of the model for analysing the competitiveness of the Hungarian businesses. The cluster analysis technique serves to identify dominant competitive strategies over the factors of competitiveness and the performance of the businesses. A further relevance of the methodology is to provide a tailor-made recommendation to individual businesses regarding the enhancement of the competitiveness by improving the weakest link in the system. The chapter concludes in the final section.

THEORETICAL SET-UP AND THE CONCEPTUAL MODEL

As our basic aim is to derive a unique competitiveness index we need to identify the factors that lead to competitiveness of SMEs (Chaudhuri and Ray, 1997). While there is an agreement amongst leading scholars that basically firms–not nations and regions–compete (Porter, 1990), most competitiveness concepts model firm competitive behaviour within the framework of national or local environment (Nelson, 1992). This approach assumes that the macroeconomic or industry-specific characteristics, institutions and policies affect the performance of the firms in a given geographical entity, industry, cluster region or nation. The application of regional, national and aggregated firm data is also typical in this *top-down* approach. Though this methodology can be useful to analyse institutional development, it does not help us to understand the behaviour of an individual firm or the variations of different firm characteristics in the same industry. This approach misses not only a vital microeconomic firm-level aspect of competitiveness but also tends to view aggregate variables in an inappropriate way (see Krugman, 1994 critique). Consequently, we consider the *bottom-up* approach as a more useful way to understand the differences in firm-level competitiveness.

Contrary to the frequently applied Porter models that emphasize the role of industry-specific factors and cluster-forces, we rely on the RBV theory. Barney (1991) identifies four characteristics of these unique resources that lead to sustainability: (1) valuable basically means that the resource should be effective and efficient; (2) rarity takes into account the specificity of the resource; (3) imperfect inability refers to the difficulty to reproduce the resource; and (4) substitutability involves the availability of an alternative resource. A resource, which can be interpreted as an asset, competency, organizational processes, information, knowledge or capability, is considered to be unique if it is valuable, rare, difficult to imitate and has no close substitute. Moreover, distinctive resources lead to sustained competitiveness and superior returns (Rugman and Verbeke, 2001). The knowledge-based view of the firm identifies knowledge as the single most significant resource of the firm because it is relatively rare, difficult to imitate, and socially complex (Grant, 1996).

Since most competitiveness theories and empirical studies focus on large firms, the conceptual model should reflect that small businesses are not scaled-down versions of large firms but they differ in organization, style of management and the way of competition (Man et al., 2002). For example, of Porter's three strategic choices of cost leadership, differentiation and focus, only the last one is appropriate to most small business (Porter, 1998). Despite increasing globalization, small firms compete mainly in the local, domestic markets or market niches. Analysing the internet offered new opportunities; Tetteh and Burn (2001) claim that small firms have to apply entirely different strategies and management techniques than large firms. Leadership and management differences in the small firm–large firm set-up are reinforced by Gray and Mabey (2005). Innovation is also a frequently mentioned factor where small businesses behave differently (Malecki and Tootle, 1996; Verhees and Meulenberg, 2004; Utterback and Suárez, 1993). SMEs frequently experience a lack of proper internal resources, which are particularly vital in terms of human resources and innovation (Bridge et al., 2003; Storey, 1994). As a consequence, networking, outside collaboration, cooperation as well as efficient internal knowledge-sharing methodologies are the core of effective competition for SMEs (Dyer and Singh, 1998; Eisenhardt and Schoonhoven, 1996 Håkansson and Snehota, 1989; Perry, 1999).

Inspired by the strategic management, the small business and the RBV literature, we define firm-level competitiveness as competencies available in physical and human resources/capabilities, networking, innovational and administrative routine processes that allow a firm to compete effectively with other firms and serve customers with valued goods/services. Internal resources, capabilities and processes together form the basic competencies of businesses that should fit the customers' need (demand conditions) and that should be appropriate for the competitive pressure of the firms within the industry as well as the threat of substitutes (supply conditions) (Grant, 1991; Lengnick-Hall, 1992; Man et al., 2002; McGahan, 1999; Peteraf, 1993; Ray et al., 2004). Although the external institutional factors of competition can be important, we focus on the internal factors.

Besides the identification of the factors of competitiveness, it is equally important to combine these elements (Dess et al., 1993). The configuration theory, introduced by Dennis Miller, argues that the elements of a system cannot fully be understood in isolation, so the investigation of the system as a whole is inevitable (Miller, 1986). While it is easy to copy a single element, the competitive advantage lies 'in the power of the orchestrating theme and the degree of complementarity it engenders among the elements' (Miller and Whitney, 1999, p. 13). Miller describes three potential applications of the configuration: concepts, typologies/taxonomies and organizations (Miller, 1996). From our perspective, the third approach is the most relevant when configuration is interpreted as a quality or property that varies among organizations. In this case configuration is the 'degree to which an organization's elements are orchestrated and connected by a single theme' (Miller, 1996). Unlike Miller, whose core focus is strategy, our 'single theme' is competitiveness. The supportive 'organization's elements' are the physical resources, human resources, innovation, networking, administrative routines, supply and demand conditions. Comprehensive, higher 'degree' configuration means a greater a number or wider range of elements.

While pure theoretical models are not constrained by data and variable availability, this is not valid in the cases of empirical investigations. Therefore, the suggested conceptual model in Figure 9.1, which is based on the definition of competitiveness and the configuration of the elements reflects the limitations of the data set.

As depicted in Figure 9.1, five of the seven pillars constitute the core competencies of businesses: physical and human resources or capabilities on the one hand, and innovation, networking and administrative routine processes on the other hand. Core competencies enable businesses to be competitive; however, competencies should be adjusted to the other two pillars: to customers (demand conditions) and to competitors (supply conditions). Competitiveness can be measured basically by relative performances of profitability and efficiency. Other measures, such as growth and exports, are also frequently applied success criteria of competitiveness. Since we do not have profitability or efficiency data (bracketed terms), the level of competitiveness can be quantified by growth and export willingness. The description of the variables can be found in the Appendix.

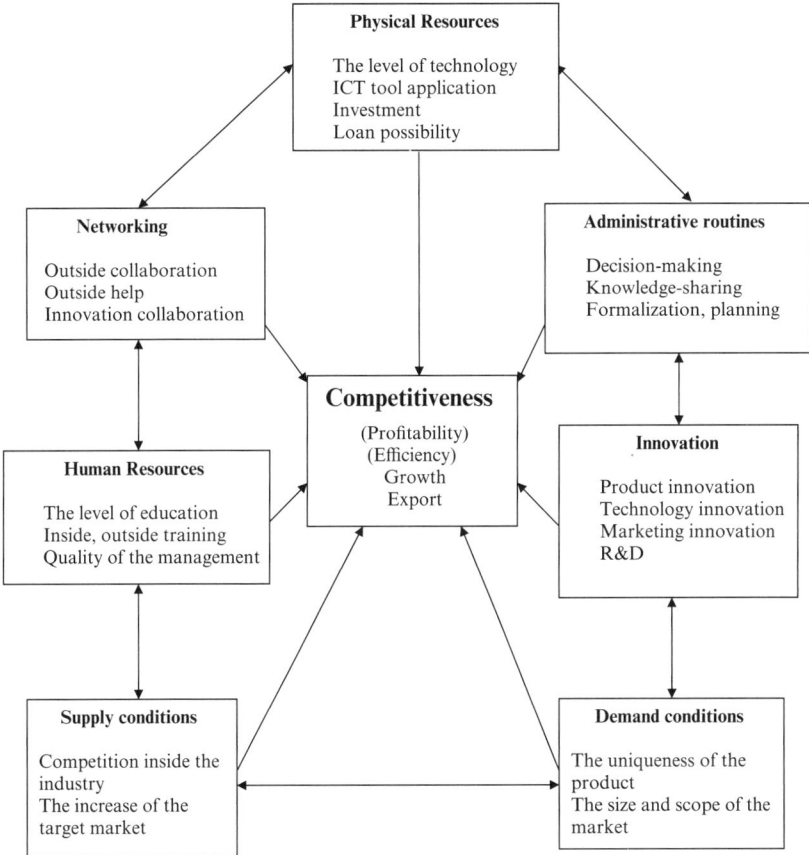

Figure 9.1   The conceptual model of SME competitiveness

FROM THEORY TO PRACTICAL COMPETITIVENESS MEASUREMENT

In the previous section we have built a multidimensional model claiming that there are seven main interrelated pillars of competitiveness. However, we have not discussed the practical combination of the seven pillars and the method of a single competitiveness index calculation.

Here, our starting point is the configuration theory that considers the complementarity of the pillars of competitiveness (Miller, 1996). The interaction and the fit of the seven pillars are vital. In the sense of Miller, it is not the stand-alone but the combined effect of these factors that is the key to the overall level of competitiveness. For the practical combination of the factors there are several possibilities, from factor analysis, via cluster analysis, to simple methodologies such as addition and just calculating the average values. A disadvantage of these mathematical-statistical methods is the lack of theoretical foundation. Without identifying the crucial elements of competitiveness there is no reliable, single measure of competitiveness. Moreover, the best way to improve competitiveness basically remains unknown.

Therefore, a new theory-based methodology should be developed. The main question is which factors or pillars play the determining role in the competitive performance of an individual firm? A widely held view is that the key element of competitiveness, is the concept of core competencies. According to this view, firms should focus on their most important strengths, so-called core competencies, and outsource all the others (Prahalad and Hamel, 1990; Quinn and Hilmer, 1994). At first glance, the configuration theory seems to contradict this view. However, core competencies are interpreted in terms of diversification of the businesses or the value chain, and configurations are the combinations of the inside strategy elements to gain competitive advantages. Of course, outsourcing of the less important activities has important consequences in narrowing the strategy repertoire. Miller and Chen (1996) warn against negative consequences: simplification can diminish certain capabilities and damage long-run competitiveness of the business which is especially vital under uncertain environmental conditions. The notion of balance regarding the different elements of the strategy is provided by the balanced scorecard, which shows the formulation of a single strategy for a specific business unit, and not for the whole business (Kaplan and Norton, 1996).

Turning the above logic to competitiveness, there are two lessons we can learn. First, the two concepts of core competitiveness and the balance of the elements are distinct. In this chapter we are not trying to identify core competitiveness. Instead, we are dealing with the general factors of competitiveness that are appropriate for all businesses. Second, similar to strategy formulation, the balance different elements of competitiveness should be maintained.

Up to now we have not addressed the main question: which one is the most determinant pillar of competitiveness? To answer this question we rely on the literature dealing with the private provision of public goods. According to Hirschleifer (1983) there are three potential solutions: the total amount, the best shot and the weakest link rule. In the first case the total amount, in the second case the maximum amount, and in the third case the minimum amount determines the provision of public good. The same principle can be applied to define the determinant factors of competitiveness with three potential solutions:

- The competitiveness points can be calculated by summing the seven pillars;
- The competitiveness points depend on the best pillar value;
- The competitiveness points depend on the worst pillar value.

To choose between the three versions, we rely on two concepts: the theory of the weakest link (TWL) and the theory of constraints (TOC). A central tenet of both these theories is that the performance of the system depends on the worst performing element in the structure. The TOC claims that the improvement of the system can only be achieved if the constraint, the weakest element, is removed or improved (Goldratt, 1994). The notion of TWL is frequent in the fields of engineering, production and operation management. For example, the popular Six Sigma management theory holds that the production process can be improved by removing the causes of mistakes: in other words, the weakest link in the system (Nave, 2002; Stamatis, 2004). According to the TWL, there is only a limiting case where each elements of the system can compensate for all the others at a constant rate. The weakest element can be compensated by others with increasing difficulty (Tol and Yohe, 2007).

Relying on the TWL and the TOC theories, we define the weakest pillar of the business as the most determinant factor of competitiveness. The imbalance of the seven pillars, that is, the differences in the performances, causes a loss in the performance of the whole system. The competitiveness of the business depends on the weakest pillar and the magnitude of the loss depends on the size of the weakest link, called the bottleneck.

This notion of bottleneck is important for business policy and strategy purposes. The conceptual model suggests that physical resources, human resources, innovation, networking, administrative routines, supply and demand conditions interact; if they are out of balance, competitiveness is inhibited. The seven pillars should be adjusted in a way that takes this notion of balance into account. The value of each pillar is penalized by linking it to the score of the pillar with the weakest performance in that firm. This simulates the notion of a bottleneck; if the weakest pillar were improved, the overall competitiveness would show a significant improvement. The methodology is called the *penalty for bottleneck* (PFB) and originates from Acs and Szerb (2009).

DATA DESCRIPTION AND METHODOLOGY

The aim of the data collection was to examine the basic factors of establishment and growth in the Hungarian SME sector. Besides collecting the basic data, the survey included nine blocks and 53 question groups covering all major functional areas of the business, from strategy through innovation, knowledge management, HRM, finance, risk management and marketing. While the survey was conducted in April–June 2008, the time period examined was 2004–2007. Based on the conceptual model, we used 24 question groups including 109 questions altogether to analyse the competitiveness of the businesses. While the survey included several types of questions, we applied mainly those that had only two alternatives (yes or no). Since we were aiming to measure real and conscious commitments, the 'do not know' answers were considered as a 'no'. In the cases of question groups, 4–6 point Likert scale variables were created. Since the original questionnaire did not aim to examine the different question groups together, we did not pay attention to making the scale uniform, unfortunately. In many cases, the application of a more sophisticated scale (5–7) was limited by the shortage of strategic choices of the smaller-sized businesses. The number of created variables, reflecting Figure 9.1, was 21 altogether.

The survey was conducted in April–June 2008 by a professional vendor company, Szociográf Market and Survey Research Co. After an initial telephone call asking for approval, a face-to-face interview was carried out with one of the SME owners who were part of the top management, in the case when the firm had less than 20 employees, and one of the top executives – not necessaily having ownership in the business–in the case of larger firms.

The initial sample was based on an Opten company database that includes all the present and former businesses registered in the Business Registry.[1] The aim was to collect a total sample size of 700. Firms were randomly selected, but stratification was applied to make sure there were enough businesses in each size category, region and industry sector. The size distribution of the sample compared to the total number of businesses reported by the Hungarian Statistical Office (HSO) is presented in Table 9.1. Stratification caused a smaller sample in the 2–9 employee category and a larger sample in all the other three categories than is implied by the representativeness principle. We also show the response rates in the different categories.

Since the initial response rate of below 40 per cent was lower than expected, we increased the number of firms invited to participate in the survey to 1628. A total of 702 businesses, each with at least two employees, participated in the survey and completed the questionnaire. After discounting surveys containing missing data or inconsistent answers, the

Table 9.1   *The distribution of the sample based on the number of employees in 2007 as compared to the total number of the same size businesses in 2006*

Number of employees 2007	Tota l number/ percent of businesses in 2006*		Initial sample		Final sample		Response rate (%)
	Freq- uency	Percent	Freq- uency	Percent	Freq- uency	Percent	
2–9	193092	84.5	963	58.3	373	53.7	38.6
10–49	29388	12.9	538	32.6	230	33.1	42.9
50–249	5010	2.2	127	7.7	75	10.8	59.1
Over 250	924	0.4	25	1.5	17	2.4	38.0
Total	228490	100.0	1628	100.0	695	100.0	41.4

Note: * Based on the HSO report (2008).

sample size for further analysis was reduced to 678 small businesses and 17 large firms, with a response rate of 42 per cent.

In the following we present the practical calculations for the individual competitiveness points. Here, we apply a four-step method as follows:

1. *Normalization.* In order to have the same scale for each variables, we normalized to a 0–1 scale for each of the 21 variables.
2. *The calculation of the pillar values.* The particular pillar value was calculated as the arithmetic averages of the constituting variables.
3. *The calculation of the penalty for bottleneck (PFB) points from the seven pillars.* The following problem is how to combine the seven pillars. Here we follow exactly Acs and Szerb's (2009). methodology. Technically, the bottleneck is achieved for each pillar by adding one plus the natural logarithm of the difference between that pillar's firm score and the score for the weakest pillar for that firm to the score for the weakest pillar for that firm. Thus improving the score of the weakest pillar will have a greater effect on the competitiveness than improving the score of the stronger pillar. For example, assume the normalized score of a particular pillar in a firm is 0.60, and the lowest value of the pillar is 0.40. The difference is 0.20. The natural logarithm of 1.2 is equal to 0.18. Therefore the final adjusted value of the pillar is 0.40 + 0.18 = 0.58. Larger differences between the pillar values implies a higher penalty.[2] The PFB methodology is consistent with the Miller (1986) configuration theory emphasizing the combined interplay of the pillars.

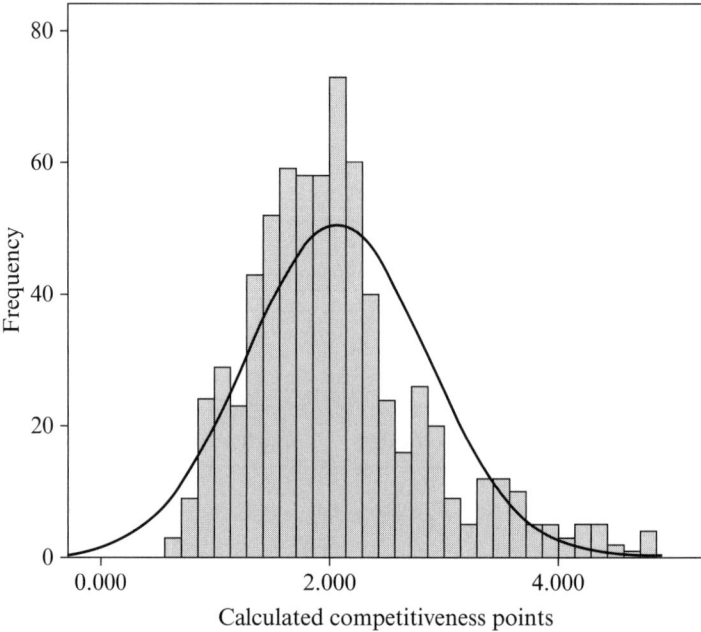

Note: Mean = 2.07081; Std Dev. = 0.782783; N = 695.

Figure 9.2   Histogram of the competitiveness points of the sample businesses

4.   *The calculation of the overall competitiveness point of the individual firms.* The overall competitiveness point of an individual firm is simply the sum of the seven PFB-adjusted pillar values. For example, the PFB-adjusted pillar values are 0.50, 0.72, 0.45, 0.55, 0.38, 0.78 and 0.63. The overall competitiveness point for that particular business is: 0.50 + 0.72 + 0.45 + 0.55 + 0.38 + 0.78 + 0.63 = 4.01. The maximum point is seven, when the business is the best in all categories. The histogram of the calculated competitiveness points of the 695 businesses with 2.07 mean and 0.78 standard deviations can be seen in Figure 9.2.

RESEARCH FINDINGS AND DISCUSSION

First, the calculated competitiveness points for each business are examined in relation to the competitiveness performance measures and to some basic demographic characteristics of the business. Both the normalized and the PFB-adjusted pillar values are reported. The simple average competition points perform slightly, but insignificantly better than the PFB-adjusted values if we compare and evaluate the connection between competitiveness points and performances. The question is logical: why should we prefer the application of the PFB-adjusted method of calculation? The reasoning refers to the policy suggestion regarding how to improve the competitiveness of the business. Since the PFB adjustment considers the weakest link in the pillars, the enhancement of that particular pillar has a positive effect on all the other pillar values. Therefore the enhancement of the bottleneck is vital to improve the overall competitiveness of the businesses.

Table 9.2 shows that the highest correlation coefficient can be found between the planned increase of sales and the competitiveness points, followed by the planned increase of employment and the percentage of exports. The actual growth rate of sales shows only a lower level of correlation with the factor of competitiveness; sometimes the sign of the correlation is negative (e.g. physical resources) and/or the correction is weak and insignificant (e.g. administrative routines). This implies that present competitiveness is a better predictor of future sales than actual sales. All seven pillars but one correlate positively with all the measures of competitiveness; only the human resource pillar is insignificant. Taking into account the weakest link –that is, adjusting for bottleneck–the human resources pillar becomes significant. Altogether, human resources explains the expected growth of the business, and exports only weakly. This finding is consistent with other human resources (HR) studies showing a moderate development of HR strategies in the Hungarian SME sector (Karoliny et al., 2009; Richbell et.al., 2009). Supply conditions (competitive pressure) and innovation processes show the highest correlation with competitiveness performance measures.

Size, as can be expected, is also positively related to competitiveness (coefficient = 0.37); hence, larger businesses are more competitive. To a lesser extent, the same is true for the age of firms: older businesses are more competitive (coefficient = 0.10). There are various reasons for these findings. Larger businesses benefit from economies of scale and scope (Chandler, 1962). Moreover, larger and older businesses are more likely to survive (Evans, 1987). The higher survival rate can be due to the learning effect, in other words older businesses are more experienced than younger firms. Moreover, efficient – more competitive – businesses learn faster and survive while slowly learning, while inefficient businesses disappear (Jovanovic, 1982). However, some opposite effects can also be expected: according to Barnett (1997) larger size businesses can survive even if their competitiveness is low.

Table 9.2 *The correlation values of the competitiveness points and the measures/characteristics of the business, normalized and PFB-adjusted*

	2	3	4	5	6	7	8	9	10	11	12	13	14	15	16	17	18	19	20	21
1 Increase of net sales 2004–2007	**0.19**	0.01	0.00	−0.03	0.05	−0.01	−0.07	0.00	0.01	−0.01	0.00	0.06	0.00	−0.05	0.01	0.01	0.00	0.02	0.01	0.00
2 Increase of employment 2004–2007	*0.00*	*0.09*	**0.22**	*−0.03*	**0.11**	*0.09*	*−0.02*	*−0.02*	*0.07*	**0.11**	*0.00*	**0.12**	**0.11**	*0.01*	*0.00*	*0.07*	**0.11**	**0.02**	*0.10*	*0.09*
3 Planned sales increase		1.00	**0.52**	**0.13**	**0.35**	**0.20**	**0.29**	0.07	**0.32**	**0.25**	**0.27**	**0.38**	**0.25**	**0.32**	**0.12**	**0.32**	**0.28**	**0.31**	**0.42**	**0.43**
4 Planned employment increase			1.00	**0.20**	**0.37**	**0.23**	**0.23**	0.06	**0.19**	**0.30**	**0.24**	**0.40**	**0.27**	**0.26**	**0.10**	**0.20**	**0.30**	**0.27**	**0.39**	**0.40**
5 Percentage of sales exported				1.00	**0.12**	**0.22**	**0.28**	0.00	**0.19**	**0.20**	**0.19**	**0.14**	**0.24**	**0.29**	0.04	**0.19**	**0.21**	**0.21**	**0.28**	**0.28**
6 Supply condition, normalized values					1.00	**0.21**	**0.16**	**0.10**	**0.17**	**0.23**	**0.17**	**0.98**	**0.24**	**0.20**	**0.13**	**0.18**	**0.25**	**0.21**	**0.47**	**0.50**
7 Demand conditions, normalized values						1.00	**0.25**	0.04	**0.28**	**0.21**	**0.21**	**0.23**	**0.98**	**0.28**	0.07	**0.28**	**0.23**	**0.24**	**0.47**	**0.52**

8	Physical resources, normalized values	1.00	0.19	0.44	0.31	0.44	0.21	0.32	0.98	0.25	0.44	0.35	0.48	0.63	0.65
9	Human resources, normalized values		1.00	0.17	0.13	0.17	0.13	*0.08*	0.22	0.99	0.18	0.15	0.20	0.42	0.43
10	Innovation, normalized values			1.00	0.46	0.30	0.29	0.44	0.56	0.28	1.00	0.53	0.43	0.77	0.69
11	Networking, normalized values				1.00	0.29	0.29	0.30	0.37	0.20	0.47	0.99	0.36	0.67	0.67
12	Administrative routines, normalized values					1.00	0.20	0.26	0.45	0.21	0.31	0.31	0.98	0.59	0.64
13	Supply condition, PFP adjusted						1.00	0.29	0.27	0.18	0.31	0.32	0.26	0.57	0.57
14	Demand conditions, PFB adjusted							1.00	0.38	0.14	0.44	0.33	0.32	0.60	0.62

Table 9.2 (continued)

	2	3	4	5	6	7	8	9	10	11	12	13	14	15	16	17	18	19	20	21
15 Physical resources, PFP adjusted														1.00	**0.29**	**0.57**	**0.42**	**0.53**	**0.73**	**0.72**
16 Human resources, PFP adjusted															1.00	**0.29**	**0.23**	**0.26**	**0.51**	**0.51**
17 Innovation, PFP adjusted																1.00	**0.54**	**0.45**	**0.79**	**0.70**
18 Networking, PFB adjusted																	1.00	**0.40**	**0.73**	**0.71**
19 Inside routines, PFB																		1.00	**0.70**	**0.72**
20 Calculated competition point, PFB adjusted																			1.00	**0.98**
21 Calculated competition point, normalized																				1.00

Notes: Figures in bold are **significant P = 0.01 level**. Figures in italics are *significant at P = 0.05 level.*

We have asked the businesses to provide an individual (subjective) view about their competitive advantages over other businesses. In all 13 categories the respondents were asked to evaluate whether the particular item is their competitive advantage (value = 1) or not (value = 0), only moderately competitive (value = 2) or strongly competitive (value = 3). The correlation matrix between the individual (subjective) view about competitive advantages and the actual findings about the value of the seven pillars is provided in Table 9.3.

According to Table 9.3, most of the connection between the subjective and the actual variables of competition is moderately strong but highly significant. The correlation in every category is the highest in terms of the competition points.

In general, the innovation measures of competitiveness – unique product, advanced technology, and continuous innovation – have the highest correlation coefficients with competitiveness. This finding reinforces the claims that innovation is one of or the single most important factor of competitiveness (Clark and Guy, 1998; Porter, 1998). Product management, leadership, outstanding subcontractors, and outstanding human resources correlate moderately strongly (0.28–0.33) with competitiveness points. This finding to supports our previous discussion about the moderate role of human factors in the small business set up (Karoliny et al., 2009; Richbell et al., 2009). Outstanding location and low-cost production surprisingly, have the lowest correlation with the competitiveness points. While low-cost production is a vital factor of competitiveness (Peteraf, 1993 Porter, 1998; Prahalad and Hamel, 1990) this is not valid in the case of the smaller businesses. For example, Pelham (1999) found that a low-cost strategy does not have a significant influence on performance, and Narver and Slater (1990) argue in favour of the differentiation, as opposed to a low-cost strategy.

While the subjective and the actual categories of competitiveness are not exactly the same, it can be expected that the correlation is higher between similar categories. For example, unique products should correlate highly with demand, supply conditions and innovation, or outstanding HR with human resources. This expectation is only partially valid, according to Table 9.3. It is worth noting that the correlation coefficients between networking and the subjective measures of competitiveness are relatively high, implying that the effective use of outside resources is a vital aspect of small business competitiveness.

Table 9.3   *The correlation coefficient between the individual (subjective)*
view about competitiveness and the seven normalized,
non-adjusted values of the seven pillars

Individual view about competitiveness	Competition points	Supply condition	Demand conditions	Physical resources	Human resources	Innovation	Networking	Admin. routines
Unique products	**0.41**	**0.34**	**0.33**	**0.22**	**0.13**	**0.25**	**0.27**	**0.22**
Advanced technology	**0.42**	**0.31**	**0.27**	**0.21**	**0.21**	**0.23**	**0.34**	**0.22**
Advanced ICT tool	**0.33**	**0.24**	**0.15**	**0.13**	**0.21**	**0.14**	**0.35**	**0.16**
Continuous innovation	**0.38**	**0.24**	**0.23**	**0.19**	**0.17**	**0.18**	**0.35**	**0.23**
Low-cost product	**0.14**	**0.11**	0.02	*0.08*	0.03	*0.09*	**0.15**	**0.05**
Individual marketing	**0.24**	**0.16**	**0.10**	**0.13**	**0.18**	**0.09**	**0.23**	**0.15**
Quick response to customers demand	**0.26**	**0.06**	**0.14**	**0.22**	**0.22**	**0.19**	0.07	**0.18**
Outstanding product management	**0.36**	**0.20**	**0.18**	**0.26**	**0.17**	**0.17**	**0.30**	**0.25**
Outstanding leadership	**0.30**	**0.17**	**0.14**	**0.21**	**0.21**	**0.10**	**0.19**	**0.26**
Outstanding HR	**0.28**	**0.19**	*0.09*	**0.22**	**0.18**	**0.13**	**0.18**	**0.18**
Outstanding location	**0.22**	*0.08*	0.05	**0.16**	**0.11**	**0.11**	**0.20**	**0.14**
Strategic partners	**0.30**	**0.18**	**0.14**	**0.21**	**0.11**	**0.17**	**0.27**	**0.18**
Outstanding sub-contractors	**0.32**	**0.16**	**0.12**	**0.32**	**0.11**	**0.22**	**0.16**	**0.24**

Notes: Figure in bold are **significant at P = 0.01 level**. Figure in italics are *significant at P = 0.05 level.*

THE APPLICATION OF THE METHODOLOGY: CLUSTER AND INDIVIDUAL LEVEL ANALYSIS OF THE HUNGARIAN SMES

In this section, we provide a further practical application of our model and the results. The calculation of the competitiveness points enables a ranking of firms' competitiveness. Since these points contain condensed and reduced information about the competitiveness of the individual business, they only have a limited value. Therefore analysis should be based on all seven pillar values of the businesses. Moreover, the normalized values rather than the PFB-adjusted values offer a more appropriate method for the analysis because they refer to the original values. In the following we provide two practically useful applications of the model and the results: (1) the dominant combinations of the pillars; and (2) a strategy suggestion regarding the improvement of the competitiveness on an individual firm basis.

Cluster Analysis

In the following we analyse the basic competition strategies of the firms in terms of the seven pillars using a cluster analysis technique. The combination of the pillars provides an inside view about the components of the dominant competitive strategies of the businesses. The three measures of competitive performances (planned increase of sales, employment and percentage of exports) are also included as explanatory variables of cluster membership. At the same time, competition point, the size of the business and the age of the business values are also calculated and reported; however, they are not part of the cluster analysis. Table 9.4 reports the results.

Table 9.4 implies huge differences in the SME sector. Overall competition points of the clusters range from 1.27 to 3.49 average from the lowest to the highest values. The individual competition points range from 0.61 to 4.84. Since the highest value is 7, even the best business reaches only 69 per cent of the potential competitiveness.

Out of the seven clusters, the 23 Cluster 7 firms perform the best: they rank first in two pillars, and second in another four pillars. Their relatively weak point is human resources. The average competitiveness point is 3.49, the highest with relatively well-balanced performances over the seven pillars. As a consequence, not only the competition points but all the competition measures – planned sales increase, planned employment increase and export – are the highest in this group. These businesses are the largest, the oldest and export most out of all seven

Table 9.4   The clusters of firms in terms of the seven pillars of competitiveness

Clusters	1	2	3	4	5	6	7	Average
Planned sales increase	0.256	0.146	0.441	0.522	0.227	0.258	0.558	0.287
Planned employment increase	0.262	0.161	0.271	0.466	0.174	0.235	0.646	0.252
Percentage of sales exported	0.077	0.040	0.177	0.074	0.064	0.840	0.902	0.183
Supply conditions	0.454	0.274	0.513	0.577	0.318	0.398	0.543	0.398
Demand conditions	0.434	0.370	0.638	0.551	0.438	0.515	0.631	0.471
Physical resources	0.296	0.244	0.526	0.390	0.379	0.401	0.522	0.354
Human resources	0.316	0.202	0.416	0.317	0.430	0.273	0.385	0.315
Innovation	0.071	0.019	0.563	0.054	0.054	0.096	0.412	0.119
Networking	0.552	0.112	0.513	0.277	0.224	0.273	0.686	0.298
Administrative routines	0.397	0.251	0.638	0.552	0.563	0.482	0.691	0.464
Competition points	2.140	1.271	3.469	2.235	1.999	2.057	3.491	2.071
Size	2.396	1.874	3.215	2.735	2.814	3.016	3.870	2.637
Age	2.571	2.358	2.708	2.265	2.400	2.547	2.609	2.483
Number of businesses	91	151	65	68	140	64	23	602
Percentage of businesses	15.12	25.08	10.80	11.30	23.26	10.63	3.82	

clusters. These firms definitely compete in international markets. The main problem is their low number: only 3.82 per cent of all firms belong to this category.

Based on the competition point values, Cluster 3, with 65 businesses, performs second. Excellent demand conditions, good physical resources, high innovation and well-balanced performance in all seven pillars. Their competitive performance is a little below that of Cluster 7. While they plan to increase their sales considerably, the planned increase of employment is barely above average. The export activity of the businesses is low, so they produce and compete mainly in the domestic market.

Sixty-eight businesses belong to Cluster 4, with 2.235 competition points, slightly above the overall average. The performance of these businesses in terms of expected sales and employment growth seems to be better than Cluster 3, despite their lower points of competitiveness. The individual analysis of the seven pillar values demonstrates considerable differences. Of the seven pillars, the only area where Cluster 4 businesses are better than Cluster 3 businesses out is supply conditions, meaning that they sell relatively unique products/services in a not too highly competitive environment. However, the low level of innovation activity does not reflect this uniqueness. Maybe the excellent supply position is the result of previous innovation activity. Examining the other demographic characteristics, these businesses are the youngest and their size is about average. Another alternative explanation for the good performance is the well-positioned start-up strategy that has had a longer-lasting effect on the performance of the business.

Ninety-one smaller-than-average businesses belong to Cluster 1, which ranks number 4 in terms of the competition points. These firms' strong point is the in excellent networking, but innovation is out of any acceptable range. While supply conditions are relatively good, demand conditions are not favourable, implying that they should be improved, by increasing their customer base. The planned increase of sales and employment is about average.

Cluster 6 businesses' overall performance in terms of planned increase of sales and employment and competitiveness points are very similar to Cluster 1 businesses. The most important difference is in internationalization: while Cluster 1 businesses produce almost exclusively for domestic markets, Cluster 6 businesses show high export activity. The comparison of the seven pillar points shows an unbalanced performance: Above average demand conditions, physical resources and administrative routines, about average supply and networking activity, and below-average innovation and human resources.

The competitiveness of Cluster 5 businesses is slightly below average, as are their expected sales and employment growth. Low exporting, and relatively poor supply and demand conditions characterize these ventures. The level of human resources is excellent, physical resources and administrative routines are above average, but networking and, mainly, innovation are below average, providing an uneven level among the seven pillars of competitiveness.

Cluster 2 businesses, the largest group, with 151 businesses (25 per cent of the sample), is at the bottom of competitiveness with a very low 1.271 points. This group seems to be the absolute loser in the competition race. Harsh competition, inadequate demand, few physical and human resources and a lack of administrative routines, innovation, or networking all contribute to the low competitiveness points. Cluster 2's performance rates the lowest in every category, suggesting that improvements in all seven pillars are necessary for future survival. Regarding the future growth of sales and employment, these firms expect a decline or a very low increase, at best. In addition, these ventures are the smallest; this may explain their limited competitiveness position.

Table 9.5   The individual investigation of four businesses in terms of the seven pillars and the competitiveness points

	Supply	Demand	Physical resour-ces	Human resour-ces	Inno-vation	Network	Admini strative routines	Competi-tiveness
Business 177	0.500	0.933	0.554	*0.436*	0.542	0.917	0.667	4.330
Business 82	0.500	0.889	0.413	*0.301*	0.521	0.694	0.611	3.658
Business 67	0.250	0.556	0.392	0.433	*0.000*	0.389	0.556	2.126
Business 628	0.000	0.300	0.100	*0.000*	*0.000*	0.333	0.472	1.032
33% percentile	0.250	0.309	0.134	0.083	0.083	0.167	0.250	1.890
67% percentile	0.500	0.550	0.350	0.340	0.417	0.417	0.491	2.809

Individual Analysis

While the previous cluster analysis is useful for policy-makers, the individual investigation provides information for business managers and owners. We conduct the investigation in terms of the pillars of competitiveness and check the relative performance of the particular business in all the seven pillars. Table 9.5 provides a visual aid to show the relative position of the business as compared to the position of 33 per cent (lowest third) and 67 per cent (highest third) of the businesses. The shading demonstrates the relative position of the particular business in each pillar, ranked from highest to lowest and split into top (light grey, favourable), middle (middle grey, neutral) and bottom (dark grey, unfavourable). In addition, the pillar value with the lowest performance is in *italics*. The importance of this is to show the pillar that should be improved first even if the business performs relatively well in each pillar. Because of the PFB methodology, the improvement of the lowest pillar boosts the PFB-adjusted values of all the other pillars; hence, it increases the competitiveness of the business considerably. In Table 9.5 we selected four businesses as typical examples.

As we can see, business 177 has relatively high competitiveness points of 4.330. This business is amongst the best 33 per cent of all businesses in all but one of the seven pillars. Despite the business being amongst the middle percentile in supply, this business could enhance its competitiveness by improving the level of human resources which has the lowest value of all seven pillars (indicated by italics). An improvement of human resources by 0.1 would lead to an increase in the competitiveness points by 0.162 to 4.492.

The overall competitiveness of business 82 is relatively high, at 3.658 points; however, its performance is very uneven. This firm has the best points for demand, but low points in human resources. The policy suggestion to business 82 is clear: improve human resources. By improving human resources by 0.1, the competitiveness point would increase to 3.872, by 0.214. Increasing physical resources by 0.1 would lead only to a 0.086 increase in the overall points of competitiveness.

Business 67 has an average 2.126 competitiveness points. The performance of this business over the seven pillars is very uneven, ranging from 0.000 (innovation) to 0.556 (demand and administrative routines). The business performs relatively well in human resources and networking. However, besides innovation, supply conditions is also in the dark grey zone. By expanding its innovation by 0.1, the business could improve its competitiveness by 0.262 to 2.388.

Business 628 has a very low competitiveness point, 1.032. Most of its pillar values are in the dark grey zone; supply, human resources and innovation are the worst, with 0.000 points. Demand and physical resources are better than innovation but still in the dark grey zone. Networking and administrative routines are average. By improving supply, innovation or human resources by 0.1, its competition points would increase by only 0.112. The reason for this relatively small increase is that in this case the other two pillars become the bottleneck. The best way to improve the competitiveness of the business would be to increase supply, innovation and human resources all at the same time. A 0.033 increase in innovation and administrative routines would increase the competitiveness from 1.032 to 1.159, by 0.127.

Similar analysis can be done in any businesses in the data set. Moreover, it is possible to make an even more detailed investigation by including the variables in the analysis.

SUMMARY AND CONCLUSION

In this chapter we presented a potential way to examine the competitiveness of small businesses. Since most firm-level competitiveness models aim to investigate large, mainly multinational firms, we created a new conceptual model that fits better to the small business set-up. The conceptual model contains 21 individual variables and seven pillars. The RBV and Dennis Miller's configuration theory served as a basis to construct the seven pillar model of competitiveness. A potential drawback is that this conceptual model still prefers larger size businesses. Since most small firms do not have any administrative routines, sell primarily in narrow niche markets and have very low innovation capabilities, it can be expected that most micro businesses would have a low level of competitiveness. Moreover, the availability of the variables limits the empirical application of the model.

The calculation of the competition points is based on a unique methodology called the penalty for bottleneck (PFB). The PFB argument is based on the theories of constraint and weakest link. Bottlenecks are defined as the lowest value factor out of the seven pillars of competitiveness. Each pillar value is related to the weakest pillar, and penalized for differences.

A stratified representative sample of 695 Hungarian businesses served as a basis for the empirical investigation. The competition points correlate significantly with the selected three measures of competitiveness: planned increase of sales, employment and export. The seven pillar calculated points correlate significantly with the subjective view points of competitiveness reported by the entrepreneurs. The strongest correlations are with the innovation measures, while human resources and outstanding leadership show a moderate connection, and outstanding position and low-cost position are found to have low correlation points with the competitiveness points.

The competitiveness points of the individual firms range from 0.61 to 4.84, implying that even the best firm reaches only 69 per cent of the potential points. The average value is 2.07, about 30 per cent of the maximum available value of 7. The results highlight that innovation is the weakest point on average in the businesses examined, followed by networking and human resources. Public policy-makers aiming to improve the competitiveness of Hungarian SMEs should pay more attention to improving these factors.

The cluster analysis shows large differences amongst the seven groups of businesses in terms of competitiveness in the Hungarian SME sector. In addition, the clusters represent the dominant competitive strategies of the Hungarian SMEs. While the top group constitutes only 3.82 per cent of the businesses, around 25 per cent of the ventures have an average of 1.27 competitiveness points, which represents only 18 per cent of the potential seven points. The performance of the clusters over the seven pillars of competitiveness is generally unbalanced. Even the best group lacks the proper level of human resources. Only two groups, 12.7 per cent of the whole sample, consider innovation as a major part of their competitiveness.

The methodology is appropriate for use in providing tailor-made policy-strategy recommendation to individual firms. The demonstration of the four businesses with different levels of competitiveness shows examples of the identification of the weak points of a business. Consulting service companies could also use this methodology if they have a relatively large, homogeneous database that contains competition connected variables.

ACKNOWLEDGEMENTS

We are grateful for the valuable comments and help provided by Siri Terjesen, the two autonomous referees, and the participants of the RENT conference held in Budapest, 21–23 October 2009. We thank the OTKA Research Foundation, theme number NK 69283, for supporting this research financially

NOTES

1. More information can be found in the following Opten website: http://www.opten.hu/ismerteto/cegtar-translation-en.html.
2. While, generally speaking, it could happen that a increase in one pillar can cause a decrease in another pillar, it is not the case here, because the different pillars of competitiveness are positively correlated to each other (see later).

REFERENCES

Ács, Z.J. and L. Szerb (2009), 'The global entrepreneurship index (GEINDEX)', *Foundations and Trends in Entrepreneurship*, **5**(5), 341–435.
Ambastha, A. and K. Momaya (2004), 'Competitiveness of firms: review of theory, frameworks and models', *Singapore Management Review*, **26**(1), 45–61.
Barnett, W.P. (1997), 'The dynamics of competitive intensity', *Administrative Science Quarterly*, **42**, 128–60.
Barney, J. (1991), 'Firm resources and sustained competitive advantage', *Journal of Management*, **17**(1), 99–120.
Bridge, S., K. O'Neill and S. Cromie (2003), *Understanding Enterprise, Entrepreneurship, and Small Business*, Basingstoke: Macmillan Press.
Budd, L. and A. Hirmis (2004), 'Conceptual framework for regional competitiveness', *Regional Studies*, **38**(9), 1015–28.
Chandler, A.D. (1962), *Strategy and Structure: Chapters in the History of the American Industrial Enterprise*, Cambridge, MA: MIT Press.
Chaudhuri, S. and S. Ray (1997), 'The competitiveness conundrum: literature review and reflections', *Economic, and Political Weekly*, **32**(48), 83–91.
Chikán, A. and Á. Czakó (2009), *Versenyben a Világgal*, Budapest Akadémiai: Kiadó.
Clark, J. and K. Guy (1998), 'Innovation and competitiveness: a review', *Technology Analysis & Strategic Management*, **10**(3), 363–95.
Dean, T.J., R.L. Brown and C.E. Bamford (1998), 'differences in large and small firm responses to environmental context: strategic implications from a comparative analysis of business formations', *Strategic Management Journal*, **19**(8), 709–28.
Dess, G.G., S. Newport and A.A. Rasheed (1993), 'Configuration research in strategic management: key issues and suggestions', *Journal of Management*, **19**(4), 775–96.

Dyer, J.H. and H. Singh (1998), 'The Relational View: Cooperative Strategy and Sources of Interorganizational Competitive Advantage', *The Academy of Management Review*, **23**(4), 660–79.

Eisenhardt, K.M. and C.B. Schoonhoven (1996), 'Resource-based view of strategic alliance formation: strategic and social effects in entrepreneurial firms', *organization Science*, **7**(2), 136–50.

Evans, D.S. (1987), 'The relationship between firm growth, size, and age: estimates for 100 manufacturing industries', *Journal of Industrial Economics*, **35**(4), 567–81.

Foss, N.J. and C. Knudsen (1996), *Towards a Competence Theory of The firm*, London: Routledge.

Goldratt, E.M. (1994), *The Goal: A Process of Ongoing Improvement*, 2nd edn, Great Barrington, MA: North River Press.

Grant, R.M. (1991), 'Toward the resource-based theory of competitive advantage: implications for strategy formulation', *California Management Review*, **33**(3), 114–35.

Grant, R.M. (1996), 'Toward a knowledge-based theory of the firm', *strategic management journal*, **17**, 109–22.

Gray, C. and C. Mabey (2005), 'Management Development: Key Differences between Small and Large Businesses in Europe,' *International Small Business Journal*, **23**(5), 467–85.

Håkansson, H. and I. Snehota (1989), 'No business is an island: the network concept of business strategy', *Scandinavian Journal of Management*, **5**, 187–200.

Hirschleifer J. (1983), 'From weakest-link to best-shot: The voluntary provision of public goods', *Public Choice*, **41**(3), 371–86.

Jovanovic, B. (1982), 'Selection and the evolution of industry', *Econometrica*, **50**(3), 649–70.

Kadocsa, G. (2006), 'Research of competitiveness factors of SME', *Acta Polytechnica Hungarica*, **3**(4), 71–84.

Kaplan, R.S. and D.P. Norton (1996), 'Linking the balanced scorecard to strategy', *California Management Review*, **39**(1), 53–79.

Karoliny, Z., F. Farkas and J. Poór (2009), 'In focus: Hungarian and Eastern European characteristics of human resource management: an international comparative survey', *Journal for East European Management* Studies, **1**, 9–47.

Krugman, P. (1994), 'Competitiveness: a dangerous obsession', *Foreign Affairs*, **73**(2), 28–44.

Lengnick-Hall, C.A. (1992), 'Innovation and competitive advantage: what we know and what we need to learn', *Journal of Management*, **18**(2), 399–429.

Lengyel, I. (2000), 'A regionális versenyképességről', *Közgazdasági Szemle*, **47**(12), 962–87.

Lengyel, I. (2006), 'A regionális versenyképesség értelmezése és piramismodellje', *Területi Statisztika*, **2**, 148–66.

Lengyel, I. (2001), 'Iparági és regionális klaszterek. Tipizálásuk, térbeliségük és fejlesztésük főbb kérdései', *Vezetéstudomány*, **32**(10), 19–43.

McGahan, A.M. (1999), 'Competition, strategy and business performance', *California Management Review*, **41**(3), 74–101.

Malecki, E.J. and D.M. Tootle (1996), 'The role of networks in small firm competitiveness', *International Journal of Technology Management*, **11**(1–2), 43–57.

Man, T.W.Y., T. Lau and K.F. Chan (2002), 'The competitiveness of small and medium enterprises a conceptualization with focus on entrepreneurial competencies', *Journal of Business Venturing*, **17**, 123–42.

Márkus, G., Z. Potó, Z. Zsibók, J. Soó, R. Schmuck and A. Duczon (2008), 'A mikroszintű regionális versenyképesség mérése', *Vállalkozás és innováció*, **2**(1), 30–53.

Miller, D. (1986), 'Configurations of strategy and structure: towards a synthesis', *Strategic Management Journal*, **7**, 233–49.

Miller, D. (1996), 'Configurations revisited, *Strategic Management Journal*, **17**(7), 505–12.

Miller, D. and M. Chen (1996), 'The simplicity of competitive repertoires: an empirical analysis', *Strategic Management Journal*, **17**(6), 419–39.

Miller, D. and J.O. Whitney (1999), 'Beyond Strategy: configuration as a pillar of competitive Advantage', *Business Horizons*, **42**(3), 5–17.

Narver, J.C. and S.F. Slater (1990), 'The effect of a market orientation on business profitability', *Journal of Marketing*, **54**, 20–35.

Nave, D. (2002), 'How to compare six Sigma, Lean and the Theory of Constraints', *Quality Progress*, **35**(3), 73–8.

Nelson, R. (1992), 'Recent writing on competitiveness: boxing the compass', *California Management Review*, **34** (2), 127–37.

Pelham, A.M. (1999), 'Influence of environment, strategy, and market orientation on performance in small manufacturing firms', *Journal of Business Research*, **45**(1), 33–46.

Perry, M. (1999), *Small Firms and Network Economies*, London: Routledge.

Peteraf, M.A. (1993), 'The cornerstones of competitive advantage: a resource-based view', *Strategic Management Journal*, **14**(3), 173–91.

Porter, M.E. (1990), *The Competitive Advantage of Nations*, New York: The Free Press.

Porter, M.E. (1998), *On Competition*, Boston, MA: Harvard Business School.

Porter, M.E. and K. Schwab (2008), *The Global Competitiveness Report 2008–2009*, Geneva: World Economic Forum.

Prahalad, C.K. and G. Hamel (1990), 'The core competence of the corporation', *Harvard Business Review*, **68**, 79–91.

Quinn, J. and F. Hilmer (1994), 'Strategic outsourcing', *Sloan Management Review*, **35**(4), 43–55.

Ray, G., J.B. Barney and W. Muhanna (2004), 'Capabilities, business processes, and competitive advantage: choosing the dependent variable in empirical studies', *Strategic Management Journal*, **25**, 23–37.

Richbell, S., L. Szerb and Z. Vitai (2009), 'HRM in the Hungarian SME sector', *Employee Relations*, **32**(3), 262–80.

Rugman, A.M. and A. Verbeke (2001), 'Location, competitiveness, and the multinational enterprise', in A.M. Rugman and T.L. Brewer (eds), *The Oxford Handbook of International Business*, Oxford: Oxford University Press, pp. 146–80.

Slevin, D.P. and J.G. Covin (1995), 'Entrepreneurship as firm behaviour', in J.A. Kataz and R.H. Brochaus Sr (eds), *Advances Entrepreneurship, Firm Emergence, and Growth*, vol.2, Greenwich, CT: JAI Press, pp. 175–224.

Slevin D.P. and J.G. Covin (2005), 'New ventures and total competitiveness: a conceptual model, empirical results, and case study examples', in *Frontiers of Entrepreneurship Research 1995*, Babson Park, MA: Center for Entrepreneurial Studies, Babson College, Chapter 35.

Stamatis, D.H. (2004), *Six Sigma Fundamentals: A Complete Guide to the System, Methods, and Tools*, New York: Productivity Press.
Sternberg, R. and O. Arndt (2001), 'The firm or the region: what determines the innovation behavior of European firms?', *Economic Geography*, **77**(4), 364–82.
Storey, D. (1994), *Understanding the Small Business Sector*, London: Routledge.
Tetteh, E. and J. Burn (2001), 'Global strategies for SME-business: applying the SMALL framework', *Logistics Information Management*, **14**(1–2), 171–180.
Tol, R.S.J. and G.W. Yohe (2007), 'The weakest link hypothesis for adaptive capacity: an empirical test', *Global Environmental Change*, **17**(2), 218–27.
Török, Á. (1999), 'Verseny a versenyképességért?', Working paper, MEH, Budapest.
Utterback, J.M. and F.F. Suárez (1993), 'Innovation, competition, and industry structure', *Research Policy*, **23**(1), 1–21.
Verhees, F. and M.T.G. Meulenberg (2004), 'Market orientation, innovativeness, product innovation, and performance in small firms', *Journal of Small Business Management*, **42**(2), 134–54.

APPENDIX

Table 9A.1   Applied variables: description

Pillars/variables	Description
Supply conditions	
Competition inside the industry	The intensity of the competition in a 3-point Likert scale: 1: many competitors, 2: a few competitors, 3: no competitors
The increase of the target market	The future increase of the market in a 4-point Likert scale from: 1: considerable shrinkage to 4: considerable increase
Demand conditions	
The uniqueness of the product	The number of customers considering the main product of the business is new in a 3-point Likert scale: 1: nobody, 2: a few 3: everybody
The size of the market	The geographical extent of the selling area in Hungary in 6-point scale from: 1: one place, one plant to 6: county-wide
The scope of the market	The type of plant location in a 5-point scale from: 1: place with number of inhabitants below 2000 to 6: Budapest
Physical resources	
The level of technology	The level of applied technology in a 6-point scale from: 1: well below industry average to 6: world new tech
ICT tool application	The intensity of the info-communication tool application in a 5-point scale from: 1: applies 1–2 ICT tools to 5: applies 9–10 ICT tools
Investment	The size of investment in 2004–2007 in 5 categories from: 1: 0HUF to 5: over 100 million HUF
Loan possibility	The willingness of the business to rely on outside resources in a 4-point scale from: 1: no outside finance, 2: short-term loan, 3: long-term loan, 4: long-term loan + outside capital
Human resources	
The level of education	The importance of the human resource: a combination of the share and the number of the employees having tertiary education degree
Inside, outside training	The share of employees participating in inside or outside training in 2004–2007 in a 5-point scale from: 1: nobody to 5: over 75% of employees
Quality of the management	A combined measure of the management capabilities of the main decision-maker in a 5-point scale

Table 9A.1   (continued)

Pillars/variables	Description
Innovation	
Product innovation	Product innovation in 2004–2007 in 4 categories: 1: no innovation, 2: renewed product, 3: new product at the firm level, 4: new in the country
Technology innovation	Technology innovation in 2004–2007 in 4 categories: 1: no innovation, 2: renewed tech, 3: new tech at the firm level, 4: new in the country
Marketing innovation	The magnitude of marketing innovation in 2004–2007
Research and Development (R&D)	Intensity of R&D money and collaboration in 5-point scale in 2004–2007: 1: no R&D to 5: R&D with more than 1 million HUF or R&D collaboration with other
Networking	
Outside collaboration	Intensity of outside collaboration in 2004–2007 in a 4-point scale from: 1: no collaboration to 4: over 4 types of collaboration
Outside help	The average of outside help evaluated in 10 categories in a 5-point Likert scale
Innovation collaboration	The intensity of outside innovation collaboration in 2004–2007 in a 4-point scale from: 1: no collaboration to 4: regular collaboration
Administrative routines	
Decision making	The type of decision-making in the firm in 5-point scale from: 1: one-man-show to 5: collective decision-making with outside help
Knowledge sharing	The intensity of knowledge sharing in the business in 4-point scale from: 1: no knowledge sharing to 4: regular meeting/various tools
Formalization, planning	The formalization of the administrative routines in 4-point scale in describing working duties, organizational description, business planning, strategy planning

10. The emergence of a knowledge-intensive industry: a study of the RFID industry

David Finn and Colm O'Gorman

INTRODUCTION

The generation of new knowledge-based innovations is important not just to firms but also to regions and states (Drucker, 1993; Schumpeter, 1934). New growth theory argues that innovative activity is a key determinant of growth (Romer, 1990; Krugman, 1995). Regions that have successfully 'spawned' the commercialization of new technologies have enjoyed significant economic benefits (Audretsch and Lehmann, 2005). Therefore the question of how innovation leads to the emergence of new industries is an important one.

Understanding the processes by which new industries emerge is of interest to scholars of entrepreneurship (Schumpeter, 1934; Romanelli and Schoonhoven, 2001), of economic growth (Audretsch, 1995; Porter, 1998), and of organizational studies (Aldrich, 1999; Hannan and Freeman, 1977). From a public policy practitioner perspective, identifying the factors that explain the emergence of high-tech and knowledge-intensive industry sectors is of particular interest. In many regions there are extensive policy efforts and investments to encourage new knowledge-based economic activity. These efforts often include policies and programmes to encourage and support the commercialization of technologies through the creation of new firms.

The theoretical motivation of this research was to understand how new knowledge-intensive industries emerge and in particular the processes by which individuals create commercially successful innovations. While extant research highlights the role of entrepreneurial firms and knowledge spillovers during the early stages of some industries, a fundamental question on knowledge spillover that has received relatively little empirical attention in the literature concerns the factors that initiate or trigger the process of knowledge spillover.

We present an inductive study of the emergence of the radio frequency identification (RFID) industry, and more specifically the development of a syringe-implantable glass encapsulated transponder for animal identification. We study the actions of inventors and entrepreneurs during the early stages of industry emergence, focusing on the processes of knowledge spillovers and entrepreneurial entry. We argue that a core generative process to the emergence of a new industry is knowledge spillover. The discovery, evaluation and exploitation of opportunities by individuals were the result of knowledge spillovers that resulted from extensive social interactions. We argue that the discontentment, often triggered by negative forces, acted as a catalyst to human agency, in particular, the decision to pass on knowledge to another party. Discontented individuals diffused knowledge to entrepreneurs or sought to exploit their knowledge through entrepreneurship.

LITERATURE REVIEW

Industry emergence is typically described either in terms of innovations created and exploited by existing firms or by new firms. Innovation can occur within established organizations, reflecting a process of adaptation and transformation over time (Chandler, 1990; Child, 1997). Innovative insights occur when individuals are within existing organizations, as organizations are a store of knowledge (March, 1991). As innovation is important to organizational survival, organizations might be expected to seek to commercialize such innovations. However, there are a number of reasons why this might not occur. First, the economic outcomes of innovation are unpredictable, and the process of seeking to innovate can damage a firm's short-term performance (March, 1991).

Second, organizations are often characterized by 'inertia' (Weick, 1995). Powerful forces from within organizations and from the external environment may promote stability in organizational strategy and structure. For example, managers may promote consistency in strategy as a means of defining the organization's purpose and thereby increasing customer loyalty and aiding in the attraction of resources to the firm. Third, the population ecology perspective argues that selection forces may positively 'favour' organizational forms that are characterized by structures that are difficult to change, leading organizations to under-invest in innovation (Hannan and Freeman, 1978). Fourth, the cognitive and behavioural biases that lead to failure avoidance may result in managers avoiding projects with uncertain outcomes (McGrath, 1999).

An alternative explanation of industry emergence emphasizes that innovation, and hence the emergence of new industries, occurs through the creation and entry of new organizations (Hannan and Freeman, 1977; Aldrich, 1999). Extant evidence suggests that many new industries are characterized by high levels of entrepreneurial activity during the early phases of development (Aldrich, 1999). Audretsch and Fritsch (2000) have argued that the mechanisms through which innovations occur differ across time and space, referring to specific times when new firms, as opposed to incumbent firms, have the advantage. During these times, referred to as 'entrepreneurial regimes', the knowledge generated in some organizations 'spills over', as individuals seek to commercialize their innovations through the creation of a new firm.

Acs and Audretsch (1988, 1990) have shown that small entrepreneurial firms are the driving force of innovative activity in certain industries, despite a lack of formal R&D activities. While incumbent firms in related industries might be expected to be best placed to exploit emerging opportunities and technologies, Klepper (2002) has shown that in some industries it is *de novo* entrants that are most successful. The early entrants to a new market matter because they impact on the subsequent industry structure and location of an industry (Klepper and Simons, 2000; Rindova and Fombrun, 2001).

Why are individuals important during the early stages of a new industry? Innovation, by its nature, starts with individuals (Loasby, 2001). Loasby (2001) argues that innovation requires an individual to perceive a situation as a problem and to respond to this problem in terms of 'imagining' solutions. The perceptions of problems and the imaging of a solution is a situation-specific event. Individuals typically draw on information that is local and perceptual in nature, what Boisot (1998) refers to as 'uncertain, weak, and fuzzy' information. In seeking to develop this unstructured information into new products, the challenges facing the individual, according to Boisot (1998), are the need to understand causal relationships among underlying data and the need to identify the range of applications to which the information applies. This process of creating and exploiting knowledge involves the codification and diffusion of knowledge, and therefore, over time the knowledge is more available to others.

While extant literature argues that individual entrepreneurs can be important during the early stages of a new industry, it is still unclear why and how individuals seek to commercialize innovations through new ventures. Individuals seeking to commercialize new innovations through new firm creation face significant obstacles. This observation that the innovator faces many challenges is not new as nearly 500 years ago, Niccolò Machiavelli wrote in *The Prince* (1513) that 'there is nothing more difficult to plan, more doubtful of success, nor more dangerous to manage than the creation of a new order of things'. An emerging industry based on a technological innovation represents the emergence of a new order. It is a context defined by technological uncertainty; by the absence of established market mechanisms (Loasby, 2000); and by the absence of institutional supports for the emerging organizational forms (Aldrich and Fiol, 1994). So in addition to the general entrepreneurial challenge of mobilizing resources in response to a perceived market opportunity, entrepreneurs during the early stages of a new industry may need to engage in activities that build market mechanisms, develop organizational, intra-industry, inter-industry and institutional legitimacy, as well as develop the new technology (Aldrich and Fiol, 1994, p. 649).

In seeking to commercialize new knowledge, individuals face a dilemma of whether they should seek to protect new knowledge or share the knowledge. A strategic imperative among inventors and early entrants is to protect their intellectual property (IP), through processes such as patenting. In addition to providing market protection, IP can help technology firms attract external venture capital. However, in contexts where there are no established market mechanisms, the new entrant faces the challenge of building market mechanisms and developing organizational, intra-industry, inter-industry and institutional legitimacy (Aldrich and Fiol, 1994). This may require the entrepreneur to share knowledge and to attract other entrepreneurs and firms to the opportunity. For example, in trying to establish legitimacy for a new organization, entrepreneurs may need to improve the perception by potential customers and financiers (Tornikoski and Newbert, 2007). In building technological expertise, entrepreneurs frequently engage in labour poaching in high-tech industries (Alsleben, 2005). For scientists, the process of science-based innovation is characterized by a norm of openness and incentives to publish, leading to the codification and potential diffusion of knowledge (Sorenson and Singh, 2007). The actions of the lead inventors and entrepreneurs can build legitimacy for an emerging technology, the entrepreneur's firm and for the new industry. They also alert other entrepreneurs and firms to the opportunities in the industry.

In this inductive study we explored the actions of inventors and entrepreneurs during the very early stages of industry emergence, focusing on the processes of knowledge spillovers and entrepreneurial entry. We seek to identify the generative mechanisms that describe and explain the evolution of a knowledge-based industry in terms of the knowledge and actions of the lead inventors and entrepreneurs in the industry. As such we seek to extend existing explanations of industry emergence by exploring the processes by which knowledge spillovers occurred between (i) inventors and entrepreneurs and (ii) between early and subsequent entrants.

RESEARCH METHOD

Our research approach was to start with an empirical description of the RFID industry. In collecting data we focused on two potential generative mechanisms. First, we described the emergence of the industry in terms of the evolution of RFID technology, and more particularly, the evolution of a syringe-implantable identification transponder. Second, we described the industry in terms of the evolution of entrepreneurial firms that were involved in developing and exploiting RFID technology. As such, we developed a detailed case study that described the evolution of the industry from the perspective of the actions of individual entrepreneurs and inventors, including their patent activity.

We drew on published history of the RFID technology (discussed below); extensive interviews with 19 founding entrepreneurs, inventors and investors that made up the RFID industry in the time frame of our study; and secondary published material about these individuals and the firms they started, including published data on litigation between some of the parties we interviewed, and the application and publication of RFID patents relating to the syringe-implantable glass encapsulated transponder for animal identification.

What is RFID?

RFID-enabled devices are used for the identification of objects, animals, goods and products in transit, and people. In the form of a credit card or key fob, they can be used to store electronic cash for payment and ticketing applications. Radio Frequency Identification (RFID) is a term that describes any identification system wherein an electronic device (tag) uses radio frequency (RF), capacitive or magnetic field variations to communicate with an interrogator (reader). The core elements of an RFID tag are a microchip holding identification data, and a means to encode RF with that data, connected to an antenna and packaged in a housing adapted to an application. A copy of Vern Taylor's 1986 patent application, a core development in the technology, containing a graphic of a transponder and his description of its functionality, is presented in Figure 10.1.

The core focus of our study is the development and exploitation of *knowledge* relating to the design and production of animal identification systems, and the *spillover of knowledge* between inventors and firms. *Knowledge* in the context of the RFID industry is scientific and technical expertise and skills acquired through work experience and/or education; the accumulation of process and product innovation and the assimilation of information to create new innovation; the theoretical and practical

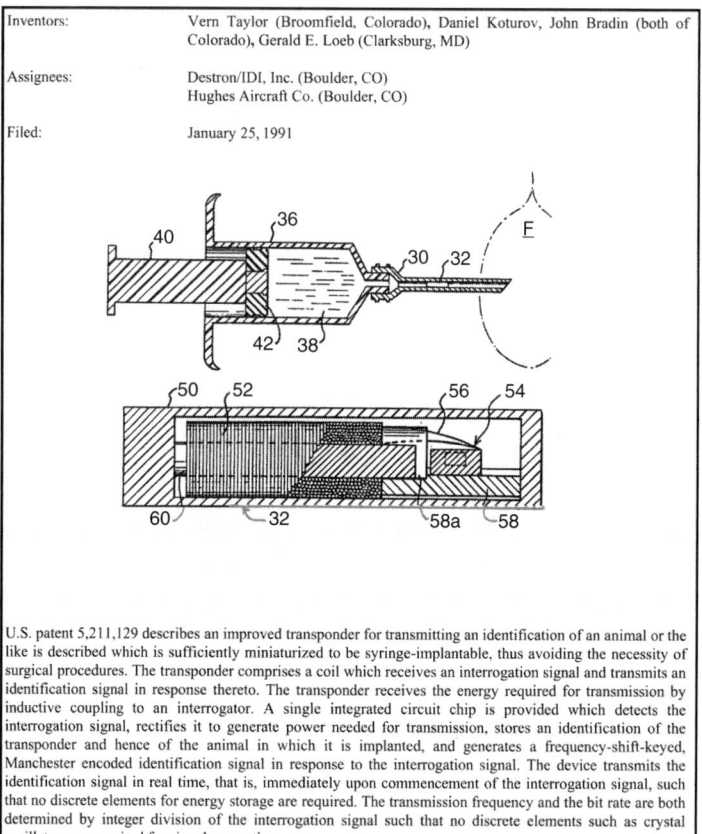

Inventors:	Vern Taylor (Broomfield, Colorado), Daniel Koturov, John Bradin (both of Colorado), Gerald E. Loeb (Clarksburg, MD)
Assignees:	Destron/IDI, Inc. (Boulder, CO) Hughes Aircraft Co. (Boulder, CO)
Filed:	January 25, 1991

U.S. patent 5,211,129 describes an improved transponder for transmitting an identification of an animal or the like is described which is sufficiently miniaturized to be syringe-implantable, thus avoiding the necessity of surgical procedures. The transponder comprises a coil which receives an interrogation signal and transmits an identification signal in response thereto. The transponder receives the energy required for transmission by inductive coupling to an interrogator. A single integrated circuit chip is provided which detects the interrogation signal, rectifies it to generate power needed for transmission, stores an identification of the transponder and hence of the animal in which it is implanted, and generates a frequency-shift-keyed, Manchester encoded identification signal in response to the interrogation signal. The device transmits the identification signal in real time, that is, immediately upon commencement of the interrogation signal, such that no discrete elements for energy storage are required. The transmission frequency and the bit rate are both determined by integer division of the interrogation signal such that no discrete elements such as crystal oscillators are required for signal generation.

Figure 10.1   A syringe-implantable identification transponder

understanding of the market and how it operates; a human understanding of collaborators with the ability to motivate or manipulate them to perform a particular task, and knowing where to find information, ideas and concepts on a subject matter. *Knowledge spillover* is the unidirectional or bidirectional spread of knowledge to members or potential members of a community. The community includes entrepreneurs, scientists, professionals, customers and suppliers.

Why the RFID Industry?

The Radio Frequency Identification (RFID) industry, which is focused on the electronic identification of animals, appeared, a priori, to be an attractive industry for our purposes for three reasons. First, the industry was characterized both by new technological innovations, as evidenced by extensive patent activity, and by efforts by inventors and entrepreneurs to commercially exploit such innovations through new venture creation. The RFID industry is a 'new wave' of innovation, leading to the 'creative destruction' of previous identification methods in a number of market segments, including identification of animals through plastic tags attached to animals ears, and the emergence of new markets, such as the electronic identification of companion animals (pets). The technology was also applied in other market segments such as electronic tolling on roads, electronic tracking of railroad stock, and in the 'access control' market, in terms of electronic locks and access systems. By 1997, the world market for RFID systems (tags, readers, software and services) exceeded US$540 million in supplier revenues, with global shipment of RFID tags amounting to 111 200 000 units (according to a technology market researcher firm, Venture Development Corporation). In 1997, 20 firms controlled over 89 per cent of the global RFID system shipments, though no one company controlled more than 15 per cent of the market. In one sense, a priori, we had access to what looked like a classic Schumpeterian (Mark I) story of inventors and entrepreneurs starting new firms to exploit new technologies and new knowledge, with the 'creative destruction' of prior technologies and the emergence of several new markets.

Second, the age and scope of the industry suggested to us that we would be able to develop a comprehensive description of the early emergence of this industry. While the technological inventions and innovations have a long history, industry experts describe the 1970s and 1980s as the timeframe from which the current RFID industry emerged. We believed that many of the original inventors and founders would still be available for interview (though as we learnt, some are more than 80 years old, and some have passed away). From our perspective the industry was neither too recent nor too old. In terms of scope, the technologies underpinning this industry, and the initial perceived commercial applications, that is animal tagging, were relatively narrow, giving us confidence that we would be able to capture and understand the dynamics of the early stages of industry emergence.

Third, the lead author had direct experience of this sector, having developed and commercially exploited RFID technology during the 1990s. An appreciation of the underlying technology enabled us to gain access to the interviewees and to establish credibility with them so that they would share their story.

Sample, Data Collection and Data Recording

Our sampling strategy was to identify and interview all those that were involved in the early development of the RFID industry. Our focus was to write up a chronological record of events, identifying how the collective activities of these individuals and firms resulted in the birth of the RFID industry. This apparently simple task turned out to be more difficult than anticipated when we realized that the current documented history of the RFID industry was insufficient and incomplete for our purposes. The standard reference work on the RFID industry is 'Shrouds of time: the history of RFID', by Dr Jeremy Landt, published by The Association for Automatic Identification and Data Capture Technologies (AIM) in October, 2001. Although the article provides an excellent insight into the emergence of the RFID industry from a technical standpoint, it is incomplete in areas such as the timing of certain inventions, and, reflecting the focus on technology, some of the key people who created the industry as we know it today, are not mentioned.

From the global trade association (AIM) for RFID, technical journals and web searches for RFID companies, we identified a group of entrepreneurs and inventors in the United States and Europe who appeared to have spearheaded the development, production and marketing of low and high frequency transponders. These included individuals from four locations, the US (principally in Albuquerque, New Mexico; California; Denver, Colorado; and New York), Switzerland, Germany and Sweden. Data collection began in October 2006, when the lead author went to Boulder in Colorado, USA. Data collection continued for an 18 month period from October 2006, including extensive travel to interview others involved in the development of RFID.

Our interviews were unstructured as our objective was to describe the setting, the people and the events relating to the RFID industry. We began with a narrative retrospective description of the life stories of the entrepreneurs and their firms, relying on historical recall. Reflecting the effort on our part to get access to the interviewees (typically travel time was one or two days), and the technical knowledge of the lead author, the interviews were typically substantive engagements, lasting on average 3 to 4 hours. Interview notes were written up and sent to the interviewee for correction and clarification.

The interview data was then written as detailed case histories of the individual and, where appropriate, the technology or the firm they were involved in developing. The process was to write these case histories, and then to substantiate the histories by cross-referencing the interview story with other stories and histories from other interviewees, by checking with experts and informants who had worked for interviewees, by checking with the interviewees themselves, and by checking the stories against published secondary data in the form of patent applications to pin down the timing of RFID innovations, judgments from litigation cases concerning patent infringement, legal agreements between rival companies, shareholder agreements, business plans, memorandums, purchase orders, nondisclosure agreements, travel itineraries, contractual agreements between companies and their employees and from more general secondary data such as newspaper clippings and photo material. The result was 450 pages, approximately 90 000 words, of text describing the emergence of the RFID industry via a series of stories of individuals, innovations and new firms.

A second phase of data collection was an analysis of patent data. The inventive steps undertaken by the scientists and engineers in the industry were tracked over time by examining the content of patent applications filed at the US Patent Office and the publication of novel ideas in technical journals. Prior to June 1995, there were only non-provisional applications, meaning that patent applications prior to June 1995 remained secret until the day of publication. Depending on the number of consultations with the examiner at the US Patent Office concerning patent claims, the duration between application filing and publication could range from 18 months to several years. According to US patent law (35 USC § 102) a person shall be entitled to a patent unless the invention was patented or described in a printed publication in the United States or a foreign country or in public use or sale in the US, more than one year prior to the date of application for patent in the United States. Each individual associated with the filing and prosecution of a patent application has also a duty of candour and good faith in dealing with the US Patent Office, which includes a duty to disclose to the Patent Office all information known to that individual to be material to patentability of any claim in his or her application.

CASE STUDY

Early Research in RFID

Work on RFID systems as we now know them began in earnest in the 1970s. At this stage the tags were based on analogue and VHF radio frequencies. Research laboratories and academic institutions such as Los Alamos Scientific Laboratory (LASL), Northwestern University, and the Microwave Institute Foundation in Sweden were actively working on RFID. It was not until 1984 that scientists from LASL sought to commercialize the emerging RFID technology. Independent of this work, a number of individuals played an important role in the development of RFID technology and the market for RFID products, through the establishment of new firms in the 1970s in the US. Not all development in RFID technology occurred in the US. During the 1970s and 1980s a number of important technical developments occurred in the Netherlands.

However, the breakthrough in developing an implantable identification transponder in animals occurred in New York in the late 1970s. In 1979 the entrepreneur Thaine Clark, inventor Michael Beigel and the vet Edward Tindall formed International Identification Inc. (III) and sought to develop an animal identification system for thoroughbred horses to prevent fraud in horse racing events. The New York Jockey Club expressed an interest in the product. On 6 August 1979, Michael Beigel filed a patent application describing an identification system for verifying the identity of an animal, object or thing. The patent application was granted on 1982 June 1 (US Patent 4,333,072). Prior to this granting, on 12 August 1980 Michael Beigel revealed in a telephone conversation with Vern Taylor (IDI) (Colorado) the idea of subcutaneously implanting a plastic encapsulated transponder underneath the skin of animal using a hypodermic needle. International Identification Inc. (III) closed shortly after filing its patent application due to a lack of funding. However, while the firm closed, the technological developments were exploited by others.

Vern Taylor and the Emergence of IDI

Vern Taylor's firm IDI had a major impact on the emergence of other firms in the RFID sector. The 'story' of Vern Taylor's entry into RFID is that following the theft of one of his horses, or the horse of an 'in-law', in 1971 he started a firm, Equine Services Inc. Equine Services Inc. developed a device that could positively identify horses by scanning their knuckles. Taylor sold his interest in this firm to start IDI in 1980. While Vern Taylor exited IDI within five years, both IDI and Taylor played an important role in the development of RFID technology and its application to animal identification. Table 10.1 presents the development of IDI in terms of the development of management and technical staff, and their subsequent exit, often to start their own firm. This demonstrates the impact that IDI had on other firms in RFID in the Denver Colorado area and beyond. IDI spawned a number of competitors in RFID in animal identification through either direct spin-off of IDI employees or as a result of Vern Taylor alerting other entrepreneurs and firms of the RFID technology and opportunities in the animal identification market (Table 10.2).

Vern Taylor started IDI to develop an electronic tagging system for animal identification. In starting IDI Vern Taylor spoke with Michael

Table 10.1 Entry and exit of management and technical staff at IDI: 1981–1991

Name and role at IDI	Exit date from IDI	Post IDI job/role
1981: Founding team		
Vern Taylor, Chairman of the Board and Chief Executive Officer, founder of IDI	End of 1985	(Forced) departure of the founder, Vern Taylor, from IDI by Dieter Heidrich, Venture Capitalist, Inter Mountain Technology Venture.
Michael L. Taylor, VP of Corporate Development (Vern Taylor's son and ex Equine Services firm)	End of 1985	Vern Taylor starts new firm, Taymar, Inc., in same building, to act as a distributor for IDI for 'large animals', but 'reneges' on agreement and starts to develop RFID 'companion' animal market.
L. Elwood Witherspoon, VP Marketing & Sales (others are involved as directors and in financing the firm)	1993	
1982: Appointment of the initial management team		
Dominick (Nick) Alston, Vice President of Sales (ex-stockbroker)	September, 1984	Four staff, Don Alston, Ben Polzkill, Thomas Milheiser, and Mick Simon start new RFID firm, Telsor Corporation' in Englewood, Colorado focused on industrial applications. (Financed by Gerry Abbots). This exit happens post an attempt by Ben, backed by an investment group (Gerry Abbots) offer US$5million deal to buy out Vern Taylor.
B.W. (Ben) Polzkill, President, Chief Operations Officer (ex United Bank, Denver)	September, 1984	
Thomas Milheiser, Vice President Technical Operations	September, 1984	
Mick Simon	September, 1984	
Frank Simon	1987	

Table 10.1 (continued)

Name and role at IDI	Exit date from IDI	Post IDI job/role
	1983: Formation of the engineering team	
Whitney Patten (ex University of Denver)	1993	Continued as a consultant to National Marine Fishery Services
John Bradin (Technical design)	May, 1987	(an IDI customer) Leaves the RFID industry for a brief period,
Donald J. Urbas (Quality Control Manager, May 1983)		and starts the company UMG in Evergreen, Colorado, supplying readers and implantables for laboratory animals to Bio Medic Data System. In **1988** Don Urbas goes into competition with Destron/IDI producing glass tube transponders and readers for Bio Medic Data Systems.
	1984: Expansion of management team	
Thomas W. Payne (Director of Marketing Services) (Key role in developing access control business IDI)	1991	
Jerry Tuneberg, IC design engineer	1984	
1985: Appointment of new management team following departure of the founder, Vern Taylor		
James (Jim) Seiler, Chief Financial Officer	1987	Jim Seiler leaves and rejoins to become President/CEO in 1989, replacing Charles Cushing
Charles Cushing, President (ex GE and General Instruments)	1987	Charles Cushing fired as president by Dieter Heidrich (investor). Charles starts Racom to produce RF tags. Charles works for Indala (Ted Geiszler-access control). Charles quits in 1993/1994. Indala is sold to Motorola in 1993/94. Charles moves to Thailand in 1995.
Joseph Hitt, VP of Marketing & Sales		
Michael Malmer (replaced Thomas Milheiser as engineering director)	1990	A deal in 1989 by Dayl Yurek (IDI) to sell IDI's access control business to Hughes Aircraft, leading to creation of HID, requires Michael Malmer to move to HID. Resisting move to HID, Michael Malmer moves to Racom in 1990.

Table 10.2 IDI and the firms that it attracted to RFID

Firm	Year of founding/'inventive' step	Location	Entrepreneurs/Inventors	Application & Technology	Innovation
Identification Devices, Inc. (IDI), USA	1980	Denver, Colorado, US	Vern Taylor Dominick Alston, Ben Polzkill and Thomas Milheiser	Electronic identification of thoroughbred race horses, tracking salmon migration patterns and integrating RFID into automatic animal feed systems	In 1985, IDI developed the first commercial glass-encapsulated transponder operating on the principle of inductively coupling at a frequency of 400 KHz, which was to have a major impact on the animal identification industry.
Firms that compete with IDI					
Taymar	1986	Denver, Colorado, US	Vern Taylor	Animal identification using glass-encapsulated inductive coupling transponders	
Audemars/Datamars SA, Switzerland	1986	Lugano, Switzerland	Flavio Audemars	Companion animal identification using glass-encapsulated inductive coupling transponders	Production of passive radio frequency identification (RFID) devices using accumulated experience manufacturing stepping motors for the watch industry.
Avid Identification Systems, Inc. USA	1987	Norco, California, US	Douglas Hull	Identification of exotic birds & micro-chipping pet animals using an implantable glass-encapsulated transponder	Databases were established storing the identification code of each animal implanted with a glass-encapsulated transponder. Lost animals brought to animal care professionals could be identified and returned to their owner.

Table 10.2 (continued)

Firm	Year of founding/ 'inventive' step	Location	Entrepreneurs/ Inventors	Application & Technology	Innovation
Bio Medic Data Systems Inc., USA	1987	Maywood, New Jersey, US	Neil Campbell	Identification of laboratory animals using an implantable glass-encapsulated transponder	To circumvent the IDI syringe implantable tranponder patent (US 5,211,129), glass rods were purchased with one side sealed like a glass tube and the other side than filled with biocompatible glue.
UMG Inc., USA	1988	Evergreen, Colorado, US	Donald J. Urbas	Identification of laboratory animals using injectable glass tube transponder	Don replicated the IDI glass-encapsulated transponder and reader for laboratory animals.
Sokymat SA, Switzerland	1988	Châtel-Saint Denis, Switzerland	Åke Gustafson	Glass-encapsulated transponders for animal identification and immobilizer devices	In 1991, Sokymat automated the production of glass-encapsulated transponders using a technique of flyer winding and directly connecting the ultra fine wire ends of a microcoil to gold bumps on an RFID chip.
Trovan Ltd, Great Britain/ Euro ID Usling GmbH, Germany/EID Inc., USA	1989	Santa Barbara, California and Euskirchen, Germany	Josef Mašin and Ulrich Usling	Electronic identification of livestock using glass-encapsulated transponders	In 1989, Philip Troyk invented a dual antenna, low frequency glass-encapsulated transponder using PSK modulation.

Beigel (12 August 1980) and the following summer, in 1981, Michael Beigel's co-founder, Thaine Clark, met with Taylor in Denver to discuss the electronic identification of horses. Taylor also engaged a local firm, EMA (Electromagnetic Applications) to do a feasibility study of using microwaves for identification purposes. EMA-contracted Tom Milheiser to conduct the study. Milheiser later joined Vern Taylor (after his non competition agreement with EMA expired) and developed Taylor's technology. Milheiser developed a transponder, which was patented in 1984 and cited Beigel as prior art. During the early developments of IDI, Vern Taylor actively publicized the technical developments at IDI. For example, on 7 January 1985 a newspaper (Denver, Colorado) article reported on technological developments at IDI, highlighting technical achievements, markets and applications of RFID. Vern Taylor also made contact with Dr Ralph Knowles, the Chief Staff Veterinarian for equine diseases at the National Headquarters of the United States Department of Agriculture (USDA) in Washington, DC. Vern was focused on methods of identification and in numerous telephone conversations he would 'pick Ralph's brain'. He then persuaded Knowles to work for IDI.

On 28 July 1985 an external consultant to IDI, Dr Gerald Loeb (from Maryland, USA), recommended an encapsulation package made of glass to replace plastic to protect the transponder electronics from animal body fluids. This allowed Vern Taylor (IDI) to file a patent application incorporating the knowledge he gained from his discussion with Michael Beigel, but specifying glass, as proposed by Dr Gerald Loeb, as the encapsulation medium to house the transponder electronics. This was filed on 25 February 1986. The patent application was granted and published on 18 May 1993 (US Patent 5,211,129).

However, towards the end of 1985, Vern Taylor was forced by investors to leave IDI. He started another firm (see below). Prior to the start-up of IDI by Vern Taylor in 1980, another RFID firm was started in Denver, Colorado. In 1978 Gary Carroll founded BI, Inc. to develop, manufacture and sell electronic feeding and control systems to the dairy market. Don Pauley was the engineer at BI. The firm went public in 1983 as a provider of a 'home incarceration' product. Carroll's background was as a design engineer with Wang Laboratories in Massachusetts. Vern Taylor approached Carroll, but because of time constraints, Carroll did not work with Taylor or IDI. Later in the mid-1980s, after selling BI, Carroll started GnuCo Technology Group in Denver, and worked on RFID projects for AVID, HID, Motorola Indala, and Racom Systems.

The first company to replicate the technology developed by IDI in Westminster, Colorado was the coil vendor company Audemars from Lugano, Switzerland (founded in the nineteenth century). In October 1984

Flavio Audemars met with Vern Taylor in Denver, introduced by his US distributor. Audemars had extensive experience in winding microcoils for the watch industry, and the manufacturing process was ideal for producing transponders (also his experience was in using the much cheaper copper wire rather than the aluminium wire that had been used in the US). Audemars developed coils for IDI, but the expected sales to IDI failed to materialize (only about one tenth of the promised 1 million coils were ordered). Given the large investment Audemars had made, he decided in 1986 to go into competition with IDI. In 1986 Flavio Audemars put a development team together, to develop a chip, with Texas Instruments in Italy. Audemars later established a joint venture entity with an Italian firm, Datalogic, who were involved in the production of bar-code readers. The new firm, Datamars, started in 1988 with Parvis Hassen Zade as managing director.

The second company to replicate the technology was the franchise distributor of IDI transponders for exotic birds, namely American Veterinary Identification Devices, Inc. (AVID) in Norco, California. The founder, Dr Hannis L. Stoddard III, purchased Michael Beigel's (1986) patent through a middleman. In 1987, Douglas Hull partnered with Hannis, and Michael Beigel (formerly of International Identification Inc.) was engaged to develop an RFID system which circumvented existing prior art cited in RFID patents. AVID also contracted Gary Carroll and Don Pauley of BI Inc. to develop an RFID reader. In December 1987 Douglas Hull from AVID visited IDI's manufacturing subcontractor in Thailand for transponders and readers. On 31 August 1988, AVID (California, USA) filed design patents on the features of an RFID reader (Des. 318,658) and transponder (Des. 321,069), similar in design to those of Destron/IDI. Douglas Hull left Avid in 1997 and moved to Thailand, establishing a company in competition with AVID.

The third company to compete with IDI in 1986 was Vern Taylor's company, Taymar, Inc., working out of the same premises as IDI in Westminster, Colorado. With his buy-out package from IDI, Vern attempted to relaunch his visionary dream by putting together a new team to develop a glass-encapsulated transponder. In 1987, Vern Taylor acquired the right, title and interest in a 1972 US patent by Thomas Kriofsky and Leon Kaplan. This was to allow him to circumvent Thomas Milheiser's patent.

In 1988 the fourth company to copy the engineering developments of IDI was Don Urbas, who started the company Urbas Manley Group (UMG) in Evergreen, Colorado. Their immediate customer was Bio Medic Data Systems (BMDS), managed by Neil Campbell. IDI had been working with Bio Medic Data Systems to develop identification technology for laboratory rats. Effectively, Urbas was the 'conduit' that transferred transponder and reader technology to BMDS. In 1986, as an employee of IDI, Urbas had visited Audemars in Switzerland.

Prior to this, Neil Campbell of BMDS had actively sought a way of identifying laboratory animals. In the mid-1980s he studied articles form the LASL labs, and through this he came across an article about IDI. He met Vern Taylor in 1984, and engaged IDI to develop a system. BMDS received the first readers and transponders in 1987. On 6 October 1986 Neil Campbell (BMDS) (Maywood, New Jersey, USA), a customer of IDI who identified the leakage problem of using plastic encapsulated transponders for laboratory animal identification, filed a patent application on the invention of an 'implanting apparatus' which can be 'injected subcutaneously into a laboratory animal' and 'comprising a glass capsule having therein an electronic transponder'. The patent application was granted and published on 24 December 1991. It was BMDS that pushed and persuaded IDI of the technical problems of their plastic transponder and the need to find an alternative package to protect the internal electronics. IDI had resisted a 'glass' package as plastic was considered the preferred choice in the livestock market, for safety concerns.

The fifth company to emerge from the enthusiastic entrepreneurial spirit of Vern Taylor was Trovan. In 1987, the German entrepreneur Ulrich Usling met Vern Taylor, who was at the time trying to sell the distribution rights for animal RFID products for Europe, though at this stage Taylor's firm, Taymar, could not produce the tags. This meeting happened as a result of a friend of Usling reading an advert about electronic horse identification. Usling introduced Josef Mašín, a wealthy businessman from California, to the idea of electronically identifying animals. From this Trovan was formed in 1987, with Euro ID, controlled by Usling, owning distribution in Europe and the Middle East, and EID, controlled by Mašín, owning distribution in the Americas and the rest of the world. When Taylor failed to produce a working product, Mašín went to the consultants, including Gerald Loeb, one of the original inventors of Vern Taylor's 1986 patent, who introduced him to Philip Troyk, a scientist working in Illinois. Troyk, with an ex-student of his, Glenn de Michele, developed an RFID chip and reader for Trovan. Mašín also engaged a separate team of engineers who worked for Raytheon though they concluded that a long-range transponder was not feasible. Trovan used AEG (a division of Daimler) in Germany to manufacture the transponders, which in turn used Sokymat, from Switzerland, to wind the coils. Loeb developed the glass encapsulation process for the transponder used by AEG.

Sokymat was the sixth company to enter the glass-encapsulated transponder market. Sokymat was a micro-coil winder for the watch industry located near Vevey, Switzerland. Sokymat became a supplier of assembled coils in unsealed glass tubes to Destron/IDI in 1988. Sokymat, managed by the inventor Åke Gustafson (formerly involved with the development of the Tetra Pak milk carton), went on to produce transponders for Trovan (Josef Mašín) in 1989. Gustafson solved many technical problems for the production of tags and became the leading manufacture of glass-encapsulated transponders. This firm also attracted other firms to the industry, including the Swedish firm Metget. Sokymat was subsequently sued for patent infringement by Trovan.

Following the merger between Destron and IDI, two staff, Roger Scarr and Herbert Marshall, left Destron/IDI in 1988, having obtained the distribution rights for Destron's animal identification technology in Canada, to found Anitech Enterprises. They implemented a national programme of pet microchip identification and recovery services in Canada.

In 1993 the loss-making IDI/Destron was taken over by the small company Fearing from Minnesota, to become Destron Fearing. Fearing was a small plastic tag manufacturer for livestock. The owner, Randy Geissler, feared that electronic tags would replace plastic tags. Geissler hired an engineer to solve technical problems with IDI/Destron's products. When he realized that farmers did not see any economic benefit, Geissler switched to the animal companion market, and joined forces with Schering Plough, who would distribute and market, while Deston Fearing would create an installed base of readers.

On 18 May, 1993 the original IDI patent (5,211,129) was granted and published. Destron/IDI litigated against Trovan for patent infringement (Boulder, Colorado). During the court proceedings between Destron Fearing and Trovan, in 1995, the enforceability and boundaries of the IDI patent claims were discussed in detail, directing inventors and entrepreneurs of rival firms to ways of avoiding infringement of IDI's patent rights. Also at this time Michael Beigel wrote, in reference to Vern Taylor's 1986 patent, 'it is clear from the records we have on hand at this time that the results of III (International Identification Inc.) work were misappropriated by Vern Taylor when he started IDI'.

On 30 June, 1995, with knowledge of the content and patent claims of the original IDI patent (5,211,129), Neil Campbell of BMDS (Colorado, USA) and Donald Urbas, an ex-employee of IDI, developed the novel idea of having one end of the glass encapsulation open like a test tube, but sealed with a bio-compatible cap to prevent migration in animal tissue. On 11 October, 1996, AVID (California, USA) filed a similar patent on the idea of leaving one end of the glass encapsulation open, but sealed with epoxy.

In 2000 Deston Fearing was purchased (for stock), valuing the firm at US$85 million. The firm was renamed and went public in 2002, valued at US$130m.

FINDINGS AND ANALYSIS

Knowledge Spillovers in the RFID Industry

Our description suggests that there was extensive knowledge creation, codification of knowledge and knowledge spillover during the early stages of the RFID industry. The initial entrants in the industry were typically small innovative firms, operating with limited funds, trying to develop and commercialize a product that did not yet have market acceptance. Typically knowledge spillovers were between these firms. As individuals and firms developed the technology, the information became more codified. This occurred through the development with suppliers of the components required to manufacture a transponder and through the patenting of specific inventions. Some firms developed application-specific integrated circuits (ASICs) with design houses and semiconductor companies, a process that involved their tacit knowledge of RFID technology being codified in the layout of the customized silicon chips. In patenting their innovations, individuals and firms described their inventive steps in their patent claims. It transpires that this allowed rivals firms to circumvent and improve upon these patents.

The main sources of knowledge creation, codification of knowledge, and knowledge spillover, were individual inventors and entrepreneurs. Individual inventors and entrepreneurs made significant contributions to the development of the technology, to the patents central to the RFID technology, and to the development of new markets. Knowledge spillover appeared to be a core generative mechanism in the emergence of the RFID industry in the 1980s. The emergence of the RFID industry was the result of knowledge spillovers. The processes by which knowledge spillover occurred in the RFID industry, as we observed from our data, were as follows.

First, the knowledge created within the innovative companies diffused with the departure of employees. In many firms, financial stress put pressure on the entrepreneurs and on employee morale, often leading to employees leaving to work with rival firms, transferring technical knowledge in the process, or leaving to start their own firms.

Second, knowledge spillover occurred through the actions of entrepreneurs that perceived opportunities in specific markets. Not all entrepreneurs were engineers with a technical knowledge of RFID; some were individuals who perceived an opportunity and assembled people around them to develop the product and to give credibility to their new business. These entrepreneurs sought information about the technology or attracted technical staff from other firms to develop expertise about the technology. Transfer of new ideas and knowledge, that is knowledge spillovers, occurred as entrepreneurs shared information as a way of building credibility and legitimacy with potential investors, staff, suppliers and customers. Typically the entrepreneurs engaged with a wide range of sources, including other entrepreneurs, other inventors, consultants working in the industry, and government agencies. For example, some entrepreneurs turned to the Swiss watch industry for manufacturing ideas on coil winding, miniaturization and encapsulation. In doing so, the entrepreneurs in RFID alerted entrepreneurs in the watch industry to the potential of this technology.

Third, patents, applying mainly to inventions embodied in a process or an apparatus, facilitated knowledge disclosure through the publication of patent applications. However, knowledge spillover occurred prior to the publication of patents, as entrepreneurs and inventors shared knowledge and as staff moved from one firm to another. Related to patents, the litigation process transformed written information in the form of patents into knowledge by defining the enforceability and boundaries of patent claims during court proceedings for everyone to access.

The knowledge spillover processes described above of new venture creation, employee mobility, and interactions with suppliers and customers do not explain the actions of inventors and entrepreneurs. By coding and analysing the interview data we identified a re-occurring pattern that allowed us to define categories and to identify three dimensions that explain the pathway which led to knowledge spillover. Our analysis identified three factors, which we labelled *discontentment*, *human agency* and *social interaction*, which describe and explain the generation and propagation of knowledge during the emergence of the industry.

Discontentment

Many of the individuals we interviewed were characterized by discontentment. At the individual level, discontentment and a desire for change were key drivers of both knowledge spillover and of the entrepreneurial process. Discontentment was triggered by forces internal to the firm and by uncontrollable factors such as dramatic life changes and changes in market conditions and competitor threats. The emotion of discontentment with current circumstances was also the result of 'positive' factors such as a desire for self-realization, a need for achievement, a desire for independence, and exposure to a market opportunity. But perhaps the most poignant triggers of negative thoughts and mixed emotions leading to discontentment in our interviews were accounts of how jealousy and envy, as well as the pursuit of money, wealth, power and publicity, created discontentment.

Internal factors cited by the interviewees as triggers of individual or collective discontentment included a lack of recognition, a threat of unemployment, a departure of close colleagues, unfair treatment, a lack of management direction and/or attention, a change in strategic direction, internal restructuring, cost-cutting initiatives, innovation stagnation, new management, financial stress, a lack of communication, customer complaints, deterioration of the firm's image, a change in the firm's culture, perceived arrogance and internal politics.

This leads us to argue that discontentment, which stems from negative and positive forces, compels individuals to share knowledge, to search for opportunities or to assist others starting new ventures. Discontentment was both a trigger to knowledge-sharing and to venture creation. Therefore we argue that during the emergence of the RFID industry, a feeling of discontentment, originating from negative or positive circumstances, was the precursor to individuals sharing knowledge or to exploiting knowledge through new venture creation.

Human Agency

To counteract the feeling of discontentment, the individuals we interviewed acted. This action, what we term human agency, led to knowledge spillover, and was central to the entrepreneurial activity in the emerging RFID sector. We identified multiple ways in which individuals responded to discontentment, but central to them was the process of exploiting their existing knowledge, sometimes through the deliberate sharing of knowledge, the development or procurement of knowledge, or the provocation of others so that they would share knowledge.

For example, we observed 'discontentment provocation', a process by which individuals or entrepreneurs 'moulded' discontentment in a direction they deemed desirable for their entrepreneurial venture. By inciting discontentment in others, they induced or influenced them to alter their behaviour or to act in a manner detrimental to their employer. Typically, discontentment was the outcome and in many cases individuals left their employer to join the 'inciting' entrepreneur's venture. An individual's discontentment can also spread to others. In some of the interviews we learnt of unethical business conduct relating to the acquisition of knowledge.

This included documented cases of the stealing of ideas and intellectual property, bribery, deceitfulness and theft.

We refer to the capacity to make a conscious or unconscious decision and to enact it, and in particular, the decision to pass on information and knowledge, explicit or tacit, to another party, as a form of human agency. In one sense, some of the forms of human agency we identified in the data represent the opportunity discovery, opportunity evaluation, and opportunity exploitation by the individuals we interviewed. As such, they are the 'footprints' to the diffusion of knowledge. During the emergence of the RFID industry, knowledge spillover was a consequence of the human agency, or action, of discontented individuals.

Social Interaction

The final dimension emerging from the data is the extent of social interaction between the individuals involved in the industry. Social interaction was the mechanism through which knowledge diffused from individuals to firms and to the wider industry community. Entrepreneurs influenced and motivated their collaborators through personal contact. Activities such as marketing, communication, information disclosure, litigation and technological advancements were all events involving human action.

Social interactions were core to the discovery of opportunities. Frequently entrepreneurs were the stimulus for other entrepreneurs to exploit opportunities; acting like a 'magnet' they attracted others to the same opportunity. Serendipitous events, involving social interactions, also led to the discovery of opportunities. Social interactions included both specific events and the interactions between individuals or groups of individuals with casual acquaintances, occupational colleagues, organizational members or community members. In the case of specific events we observed a process in which emotion or information was conveyed, which in turn gave rise to new ideas, concepts and practices. In the case of interactive processes between individuals or groups, individuals modified their actions and reactions reciprocally, exchanging, sharing and interpreting information and knowledge. Social interaction at the level of individuals was the mechanism that led to the diffusion of knowledge. During the emergence of the RFID industry, the discovery, evaluation and exploitation of opportunities was the result of knowledge spillovers that resulted from extensive social interactions.

We now describe the sequence in which the three dimensions of discontentment, human agency and social interaction were the pathway to knowledge spillover in the RFID industry. The discontentment dimension, originating from negative or positive forces, acted as a catalyst to human agency, the decision to act or react. Human agency led to social interaction, resulting in the acquisition, interpretation and/or sharing of knowledge. In summary, we argue that during the early stages of the RFID industry, knowledge spillovers were the result of the human action and social interactions of discontented individuals. Therefore, we argue that the three dimensions of discontentment, human agency and social interaction describe the pathway to knowledge spillover during the emergence of the RFID industry.

DISCUSSION

Do our concepts of discontentment, human agency and social interaction resonate with existing literature?

Triggers to Knowledge Spillovers: Discontentment and Human Agency

What factors initiate or trigger the process of knowledge spillover? In terms of the decision to start a new firm, there is evidence from the entrepreneurship literature of the factors that trigger individuals to start new ventures. For example, Zahra (1991) and Morris et al. (2000) suggest an array of triggers, such as unemployment, job dissatisfaction, the quest for survival, the deliberate search for opportunities, dramatic life changes, boredom, a desire for a fresh start or confrontation with a market opportunity. These factors may be brought on by negative or positive factors in an individual's life. Negative forces are adverse or unfavourable conditions that compel entrepreneurs to seek opportunities to counteract a potential loss, while positive forces foster proactive behaviour. They conclude that by speculating that start-up triggers are associated almost exclusively with developments in the personal life of the entrepreneur (Morris et al., 2000).

Our evidence from the RFID industry suggests that discontentment led not just to individuals or groups of individuals pursuing an entrepreneurial activity, often in competition with their former employer, but that it also resulted in deliberate knowledge-sharing. Discontentment can trigger positive or negative actions. In the case of an entrepreneurial person, discontentment from job dissatisfaction may give rise to that person seeking to exploit a perceived opportunity; or a discontented individual may consciously or unconsciously divulge information and knowledge to a third party, aiding the emergence of a rival firm. We also note that an entrepreneurial person may incite or recognize discontentment in an individual and use it to guide the individual in a particular direction. Discontentment may be contagious.

Discontentment is an emotion. It is not the emotion per se that matters, but rather how individuals act and react to the emotion. Therefore discontentment must be considered in terms of the actions that it results in; the mere emotion does not account for the fact of knowledge spillover. This observation suggests that discontentment and human agency are both concepts that require concomitant consideration in evaluating knowledge spillover.

Knowledge Spillovers and Social Interaction

In the RFID industry, successful entrepreneurs did not act in isolation but operated in a community made up of a population of engaging (e.g. competitors) and interdependent organizations (e.g. customers). Van de Ven (1993) describes the entrepreneurial activity of cooperation and competition in the emergence of a new industry as 'running in packs', meaning that entrepreneurs coordinate with others as they develop and commercialize their innovation. Entrepreneurs form relationships with suppliers and customers as a way of acquiring knowledge, supplementing internal skills and generating new capabilities within the firm to exploit new opportunities (Macpherson et al., 2004).

Crucial to the survival and performance of a new venture pursuing radical innovation is how social network ties (strong and/or weak) support the entrepreneurial processes, that is, the discovery of opportunities, securing resources, and gaining legitimacy. Strong ties are important in securing critical resources and facilitating the exchange of tacit knowledge and trusted feedback on the nature and viability of opportunities. Weak ties (strangers in personal networks) are more beneficial in obtaining socio-political legitimacy (Elfring and Hulsink, 2003), and affect the speed with which information circulates to personal network members (Granovetter, 1973). Through social networks (strong and/or weak), enterprising individuals search or uncover additional information about an opportunity.

During the emergence of the RFID industry, knowledge spillover was conceivably a self-perpetuating process: a continuous human activity combining private and public knowledge with new inputs to facilitate the creation of still more knowledge. Thus, the success of a venture was dependent on the actions of other entrepreneurs throughout the community. The dynamics of new industry creation is influenced by a range of entrepreneurial behaviours in supporting innovation and imitation that ultimately determines the success of a collective process of entrepreneurship (Mezias and Kuperman, 2001).

CONCLUSIONS AND MANAGERIAL IMPLICATIONS

This chapter makes a number of contributions to the question of how innovation leads to the emergence of a new industry. Our findings have important implications for the study of the emergence of new organizations in contexts characterized by technological uncertainty; by the absence of established market mechanisms; and by the absence of institutional supports for emerging organizational forms. Such contexts are important, as many policy-makers seek to stimulate economic growth through investments in science that they expect will lead to the 'birth' of new industries.

We argue that a core generative process to the emergence of a new industry is knowledge spillover. The discovery, evaluation and exploitation of opportunities by individuals were the result of knowledge spillovers that resulted from extensive social interactions. We provide an explanation of the process of knowledge spillover in the context of the technical and market development of a syringe-implantable identification transponder for animal identification. We argue that the emotion of discontentment, often triggered by negative forces, acts as a catalyst to human agency, in particular, the decision to pass on knowledge to another party. Discontented individuals were the knowledge conduits who diffused knowledge to entrepreneurs and their collaborators through social interaction.

The managerial implications of this research are that entrepreneurs in knowledge-driven industries need to think differently about the mechanisms which lead to knowledge spillover and the challenges of managing people and business relationships in an emerging industry. In contexts characterized by high levels of technological, market and organizational uncertainty, a strategic and tactical imperative facing entrepreneurs is to build legitimacy with various internal and external stakeholders. This activity, by its very nature, leads to knowledge spillovers. Such spillovers can be positive for the new firm by, for example, attracting resources, including customers, to the industry, or it may lead to convergence of the technology around a dominant design. Yet, the dilemma facing entrepreneurs is that the very same processes can alert others to the same opportunities, thus increasing competition for the emerging, and often struggling, organization.

For public policy practitioners several aspects of this research offer hope to regions that lag in terms of knowledge creation through investments by government and large firms in science research. First, the actions of *individual* entrepreneurs had significant impacts during the early stages of industry development. Second, inventors both successfully created and successfully commercialized new technology-based products. Third, commercialization was often driven by entrepreneurs seeking to meet a perceived market need. These entrepreneurs were able to assemble the technological knowledge needed for commercialization. Fourth, knowledge spillovers occurred across geographical regions and countries. This suggests that efforts directed at connecting entrepreneurs with those with technical knowledge might be the initial useful ways of increasing the level of innovative-based entrepreneurship.

REFERENCES

Acs, Z. and D. Audretsch (1988), 'Innovation in large and small firms: an empirical analysis', *American Economic Review*, **78**, 678–90.
Acs, Z. and D. Audretsch (1990), *Innovation and Small Firms*, Cambridge, MA: MIT Press.
Aldrich, H.E. (1999), *Organizations Evolving*, London: Sage Publications.
Aldrich, H. and C. Fiol (1994), 'Fools rush in? The institutional context of industry creation', *Academy of Management Review*, **19**, 645–70.
Alsleben, C. (2005), 'The downside of knowledge spillovers: an explanation for the dispersion of high-tech industries', *Journal of Economics*, **84**, 217–48.
Audretsch, D. (1995), *Innovation and Industry Evolution*, Cambridge, MA: MIT Press.
Audretsch, D. and M. Fritsch (2002), 'Growth regimes over time and space', *Regional Studies*, **36**, 113–24.
Audretsch, D. and E. Lehmann (2005), 'Does the knowledge spillover theory of entrepreneurship hold for regions?', *Research Policy*, **34**, 1191–202.
Boisot, M. (1998), *Knowledge Assets: Securing Competitive Advantage in the Information Economy*, London: Oxford University Press.
Chandler, A. (1990), *Scale and Scope: The Dynamics of Industrial Capitalism*, Cambridge, MA: Harvard University Press.
Child, J. (1997), 'Strategic choice in the analysis of action, structure, organizations and environment: retrospect and prospect', *Organization Studies*, **18**, 43–77.
Drucker, P. (1993), *Post-capitalist Society*, New York: HarperCollins.
Elfring, T. and W. Hulsink (2003), 'Networks in entrepreneurship: the case of high-technology firms', *Small Business Economics*, **21**, 409–22.
Granovetter, M. (1973), 'The strength of weak ties', *American Journal of Sociology*, **78**, 1360–80.
Hannan, M. and J. Freeman (1977), 'The population ecology of organizations', *American Journal of Sociology*, **82**, 929–64.
Hannan, M. and J. Freeman (1978), 'Structural inertia and organizational change', *American Sociological Review*, **49**, 149–64.
Klepper, S. (2002), 'The capabilities of new firms and the evolution of the US automobile industry', *Industrial and Corporate Change*, **11**, 645–66.
Klepper, S. and K. Simons (2000), 'Dominance by birthright: entry of prior radio producers and competitive ramifications in the US television receiver industry', *Strategic Management Journal*, **21**, 997–1016.

Krugman, P. (1995), *Development, Geography, and Economic Theory*, Cambridge, MA: MIT Press.

Landt, J. (2001), 'Shrouds of time: the history of RFID', Pittsburg, PA: AIM Inc.

Loasby, B. (2000), 'Market institutions and economic evolution', *Journal of Evolutionary Economics*, **10**, 297–309.

Loasby, B. (2001), 'Cognition, imagination and institutions in demand creation', *Journal of Evolutionary Economics*, **11**, 7–22.

McGrath, R.G. (1999), 'Falling forward: real options reasoning and entrepreneurial failure', *Academy of Management Review*, **24**, 13–30.

Macpherson, A., J. Oswald and M. Zhang (2004), 'Evolution or revolution? Dynamic capabilities in a knowledge-dependent firm', *R&D Management*, **34**, 161–77.

March, J. (1991), 'Exploration and exploitation in organizational learning', *Organization Science*, **2**, 71–87.

Mezias, S. and J. Kuperman (2001), 'The community dynamics of entrepreneurship: the birth of the American film industry, 1895–1929', *Journal of Business Venturing*, **16**, 209–33.

Morris, M., S. Zahra and M. Schindehutte (2000), 'Understanding factors that trigger entrepreneurial behavior in established companies', *Advances in the Study of Entrepreneurship, Innovation, & Economic Growth*, **12**, 133–59.

Porter, M. (1998), *The Competitive Advantage of Nations*, New York: Free Press.

Rindova, P. and C. Fombrun (2001), 'Entrepreneurial action in the creation of the specialty coffee niche', in C. Bird Schoonhoven and E. Romanelli (eds), *The Entrepreneurship Dynamic: Origins of Entrepreneurship and the Evolution of Industries*, Stanford, CA: Stanford University Press, pp. 236–61.

Romanelli, E. and C. Schoonhoven (2001), 'The local origins of new firms', in C. Bird Schoonhoven and E. Romanelli (eds), *The Entrepreneurship Dynamic: Origins of Entrepreneurship and the Evolution of Industries*, Stanford, CA: Stanford University Press, pp.40–67.

Romer, P. (1990), 'Endogenous technical change', *Journal of Political Economy*, **98**, 71–102.

Schumpeter, J. (1934), *The Theory of Economic Development*, Cambridge, MA: Harvard University Press.

Sorenson, O. and J. Singh (2007), 'Science, social networks and spillovers', *Industry & Innovation*, **14**, 219–38.

Tornikoski, E. and S. Newbert (2007), 'Exploring the determinants of organizational emergence: a legitimacy perspective', *Journal of Business Venturing*, **22**, 311–35.

Van De Ven, A. (1993), 'The development of an infrastructure for entrepreneurship', *Journal of Business Venturing*, **8**, 211–30.

Weick, K. (1995), *Sensemaking in Organizations*, Thousand Oaks, CA: SAGE.

Zahra, S. (1991), 'Predictors and financial outcomes of corporate entrepreneurship: An exploratory study', *Journal of Business Venturing*, **6**, 259–85.

11. Toward a hermeneutical methodology for entrepreneurship research in a radical subjectivist paradigm

Christoph Streb and Vishal Gupta

INTRODUCTION

The field of entrepreneurship is experiencing a critical phase in its development (Chiles et al., 2007; Davidsson et al., 2001; Kuratko and Audretsch, 2009). On the one hand, entrepreneurship scholars report increasing frustration with the field's state of affairs (Shane and Venkataraman, 2000; Zahra and Dess, 2001). On the other hand, journal editors devote increasing space to publishing entrepreneurship research (Rauch et al., 2009).

Recent entrepreneurship research draws a rather fragmented picture of the field (Welter and Lasch, 2008). For example, a central question in entrepreneurship research involves understanding the unfolding of entrepreneurial processes over time (van de Ven and Engleman, 2004). Entrepreneurship scholars seek to understand the emergence of entrepreneurial actors (individuals, organizations, regions and societies) and to explain disequilibrating processes such as opportunity creation and exploitation as well as organizational emergence (Chiles et al., 2008). Understanding the entrepreneurial process is critical to entrepreneurial research. Nevertheless, entrepreneurship researchers have woefully neglected this, and the few who have attempted to study such processes have usually used the wrong methodology: variance methods (Chiles et al., 2009). Variance-based methods (e.g., hierarchical regression analysis, structural equation modelling) embed a small set of well-developed variables in a nomological net and use statistical techniques to test predicted relationships between variables (Chiles, 2003; Gartner et al., 1992). Although these methods have advanced scholarly understanding of entrepreneurship (Gartner and Birley, 2002), they may also lead us down paths that may not help answer the key questions concerning entrepreneurship scholars (Sarasvathy, 2003). Thus, other methods that can help explain a sequence of events over time and in context, paying particular attention to its temporal ordering, myriad interactions, and institutional environments, are needed to study these critical issues (Chiles et al., 2008).

In recent years, some entrepreneurship researchers have called for the use of processual methods that rely predominantly on qualitative analyses, and which openly embrace non-linearity, outliers and subjectivity (Chiles et al., 2008; 2010; van de Ven and Engleman, 2004). These processual methods seek to explore how complex social phenomena unfold away from equilibrium (Lachmann, 1976; Shackle, 1966). Furthermore, they are uniquely suitable for empirical research in a field in which the inability to understand entrepreneurship as an inherently complex and subjective phenomenon subject to persistent disequilibrating influences, has become a major obstacle to scholarly progress (Gupta and Gupta, 2009). Entrepreneurship researchers have acknowledged the importance of qualitative process-based methods for some time (Bruyat and Julien, 2001; Gartner and Birley, 2002). Hill and McGowan (2001), for example, reviewed extant research on entrepreneurial (small) firms, provided a useful tutorial, and suggested topics for which researchers could effectively use techniques that can be 'found under the auspices of the wider qualitative paradigm' (p. 5).

Despite scholars' recognition of entrepreneurship studies' usefulness and having provided valuable guidance regarding applying these studies, they have rarely used qualitative studies that embrace the radical subjectivism of the entrepreneurial phenomenon. Indeed, in entrepreneurship journals, methodological reviews almost invariably focus on quantitative, variance-based methodologies, ignoring qualitative research contributions to entrepreneurship (Ucbasaran, Westhead, and Wright, 2001). Chandler and Lyon (2001) reviewed empirical entrepreneurship research published in eight top journals and found that only 18 per cent of the articles used some sort of qualitative technique; they furthermore ascertained that there are no trends towards more qualitative research in these journals.

This chapter aims to advance entrepreneurship research in general by presenting researchers with new methodological approaches for the study of process-intensive, context-rich, temporally oriented entrepreneurial phenomena. We believe our chapter takes an important step in addressing the problem of methodological singularism, that is static, cross-sectional studies (Coviello and Jones, 2004) that have been common in entrepreneurship research for some time.

First, we provide a summary of the radical subjectivist paradigm with regard to research methodology issues. Secondly, we review publications in six top entrepreneurship journals with regard to the applied methodology, in order to specifically focus on those that present a qualitative approach, which is usually associated with a more subjectivist paradigm and recommended as a target by Chiles et al. (2007). It is our intention to discover the extent to which, if at all, a radical subjectivist approach might already be represented in the current literature. Finally, by introducing a hermeneutical research approach, we offer suggestions for qualitative entrepreneurship research that takes the unique multilevel nature of entrepreneurial phenomena into account and is consistent with the radical Austrian paradigm's subjectivist ontological and epistemological assumptions. We offer a new methodological direction and encourage process-related, multilevel and historical research.

RADICAL SUBJECTIVISM AND QUALITATIVE RESEARCH: A BRIEF REVIEW

Entrepreneurship scholars have traditionally studied entrepreneurship as an equilibrium-based phenomenon in which innovative entrepreneurs occasionally disrupt the existing market equilibrium to create disequilibrium (Schumpeter, 1954), while arbitraging entrepreneurs move the market from initial disequilibrium toward equilibrium (Kirzner, 1973). Although these renderings of the entrepreneur may seem diametrically opposed, the Schumpeterian and Kirznerian entrepreneurs are actually complementary (Boehm et al., 2000) – neither has meaning without the other (Cheah, 1990). While most organizational entrepreneurship scholars fully embraced the Austrian economics of Schumpeter and Kirzner, acknowledging these approaches as the field's 'two fundamental premises' (Venkataraman, 1997), some researchers expressed dissatisfaction with the privileging of equilibrium in entrepreneurship researchers. They therefore introduced new theoretical frameworks for the study of entrepreneurship (e.g., Sarason et al., 2006; Sarasvathy, 2001).

It was in such an environment that Chiles, Bluedorn and Gupta (2007) introduced the Lachmannian paradigm in entrepreneurship research. Rooted in the works of the Austrian economist Ludwig Lachmann, a maverick scholar who was a central figure in modern Austrian economics (Boehm et al., 2000; Gloria-Palermo, 1999; Kirzner, 2000; Lavoie, 1994; Lewin, 1997; Vaughn, 1994), Chiles et al. (2007, 2008) proposed a radical new approach. This approach encouraged entrepreneurship scholars to slip the shackles of neoclassical economics and completely eschew the notion of equilibrium in their theorizing. This Lachmannian paradigm – a unique blend of economics, psychology and sociology – provided a coherent framework for organizing a wide range of disparate concepts and topics discussed by scholars interested in a disequilibrium-based view of entrepreneurship (Chiles et al., 2008).

A careful reading of Chiles et al. (2007, 2008) reveals five central tenets of the Lachmannian approach: (1) in a world of radical uncertainty, widespread heterogeneity, and perpetual disequilibrium, entrepreneurs create new opportunities through an imaginative capacity to envision the future and to continuously resource recombination; (2) entrepreneurship occurs in the broader institutional context, which both enables and constrains entrepreneurial activity; (3) cross-level influences operate between entrepreneurial and non-entrepreneurial actors at the micro and macro levels; (4) entrepreneurial processes unfold over time; and (5) entrepreneurship engenders perpetual disequilibrium. Lachmann's work represents a fundamental shift in entrepreneurship research – from Joseph Schumpeter and Israel Kirzner's objectively anchored economic paradigms to a thoroughly subjectivist paradigm based on the radical subjectivist notion of subjective ontology and epistemology. Such a radical paradigm shift is likely to require the field to move towards new methodological directions, encouraging processual, multi-level and historical research.

While conceptual work building on radical subjectivism has started to become popular in the entrepreneurship literature (Dew et al., 2004; Foss and Ishikawa, 2007; Foss et al., 2008; Kor et al., 2007; Loasby, 2007), empirical research on this paradigm is rare. We believe that progress in entrepreneurship's radical subjectivist paradigm has been impeded by the lack of attention to an important topic that has remained relatively underdeveloped in the general entrepreneurship literature: research methodology. Where theoretical frameworks and concepts delineate a field's boundaries and identify the core issues central to academic conversations in the discipline (Amit et al., 1993), methodology provides ways to examine the research questions of interest to scholars in the field (Dean et al., 2007).

In the social sciences, research methodology is concerned with the techniques researchers use to yield knowledge about the social world (Healy and Perry, 2000). At the same time, the methods researchers choose influence the questions they can ask. In a recent study of entrepreneurship research, for example, Brush et al. (2008, p. 263) found that such distinctively entrepreneurial qualities as 'newness, innovation, and creation' were ill served by the quantitative, statistical, and variance methods currently dominating the field (see Chandler and Lyon, 2001). On the other hand, non-traditional methodological approaches often inspire researchers to ask original and productive questions that they do not otherwise ask (Sarasvathy, 2003). Such innovative methods can be a key ingredient in the mix of 'creativity/imagination, experimental and playful approaches, and [. . .] passionate curiosity' that some entrepreneurship scholars believe would rejuvenate the field (Hjorth, 2008, p. 329).

Radical subjectivists eschew traditional variance methods that emphasize novel process methods' prediction regarding exploring and understanding how complex social phenomena unfold away from equilibrium (Lachmann, 1976; Shackle, 1966). Radical subjectivists' objection to prediction reflects their view of time, which is often called 'Lachmann's law': 'As soon as we permit time to elapse, we must permit knowledge to change' (Lachmann, 1977, p. 92). In this context, knowledge includes both interpretations of past experience and expectations of future possibilities (Gloria-Palermo, 1999). This continuous change in knowledge makes accurate prediction of the future not merely difficult, but also largely impossible (Gupta and Gupta, 2009). By emphasizing continuously changing human expectations, scholars are freed to investigate unfolding processes, and highlight the role of time in the entrepreneurial process (Chiles et al., 2008). Radical subjectivists recognize the subjectivity and heterogeneity of time (Bluedorn, 2002). They thus advocate treating time as economic actors actually experience it and recognizing that different actors experience it differently. Radical subjectivists therefore believe that in a world of real time and radical uncertainty, prediction is largely impossible. They thus emphasize understanding and interpreting processes after they occur (Gupta and Gupta, 2009).

Since most extant entrepreneurship research is cross-sectional, and the 'physicist's t' view of time dominates our literature (Bird and West, 1997), radical subjectivists call for a complete overhaul of research methodology in entrepreneurship (Chiles et al., 2010). They recognize that 'rigor does not demand deterministic linear models or statistics describing central tendencies' (Meyer et al., 2005, p. 469). Furthermore, they encourage the field to adopt methods more suitable to the phenomena under study (Bygrave, 1989), such as ethnography, critical analysis, or discourse methods to analyse qualitative accounts (Hoang and Antoncic, 2003; Munir and Phillips, 2005). The radical subjectivist methodology is grounded in their philosophical assumption that realities (plural) emerge from multiple mental concepts grounded in subjective experience and social context (Chiles and Gupta, 2004).

ANALYSIS OF METHODOLOGY IN ENTREPRENEURSHIP PUBLICATIONS

In our sampling and data collection process, we closely oriented ourselves on Brereton et al. (2007) who make a strong plea for a rigorous literature review process. According to these scholars, a systematic literature review process needs to cumulate empirical evidence and apply a variety of techniques in widely different contexts. Basically, such a process consists of three main phases: planning, conducting the review and, finally, the report of the results. Although their suggestions originate from a different discipline, we applied them to ensure a scientific standard, and make our results as comparable as possible.

Consequently, besides creating a basis for qualitative methodology's further mapping of entrepreneurship research under a radical subjectivist paradigm, one of the most important contributions of this chapter will be a rigorous review of existing publications of entrepreneurship research in top journals in the field. To attain reliable results and reflect the most influential and relevant scientific contributions, a critical prerequisite is to first define from which journals we should source a first overall sample of publications (Judge et al., 2007). To achieve the best result possible and in order to reflect the different ranking methodologies, we decided to consult several independent journal rankings, namely the SSCI Impact Factor list, the German VHB JOURQUAL Ranking of 2008, an internal ranking of 'top' and 'very good' journals by the Systems, Organization and Management (SOM) Research Institute of the University of Groningen, seminal work by Brush et al. (2008), results from the German entrepreneurship association FGF e.V. found in Kraus and Gundolf (2008), and the *Financial Times* Top 40 Journal Ranking. This allowed us to identify highly relevant publication outlets by means of a variety of ranking systems and viewpoints, and to generate the maximum possible overlap (Bruton et al., 2008). We subsequently identified the following six top journals: *Entrepreneurship and Regional Development* (ERD), *Entrepreneurship Theory and Practice* (ETP), *International Small Business Journal* (ISBJ), *Journal of Business Venturing* (JBV), *Journal of Small Business Management* (JSBM), *and Small Business Economics* (SBE) (see Table 11.1).

To further limit and specify our sample, we decided to add a temporal parameter in order to focus on the most recent publications. Thus, we limited our search to the period 2000 to 2008. This timeframe allowed us to overlook all current streams of research while simultaneously excluding works already incorporated in more recent contributions. After having decided on these rough basic parameters, we applied the ISI Web of Knowledge Web of Science databank to access all relevant publications with a direct relevance to the topic 'entrepreneurship'. We focused on publications explicitly indicated as articles to ensure a more specific sample. Figure 11.1 provides a screenshot of the detailed search query parameters.

Table 11.1   Journals included in our review and different perceptions of their quality

	SSCI Impact Factors 2008	VHB JOUR-QUAL Ranking	SOM Research Institute	Brush et al. (2008)	*Financial Times* 2007
Entrepreneurship and Regional Development	1.521	X			
Entrepreneurship Theory & Practice	1.526	X	X	X	X
International Small Business Journal	1.729	X		X	
Journal of Business Venturing	2.143	X	X	X	X
Journal of Small Business Management	0.875	X	X		X
Small Business Economics	1.415	X	X	X	

Note: A similar table can be found in Brush et al. (2008).

Consequently, we retrieved an overall sample of 402 articles published between 2000 and 2008 in the top six entrepreneurship journals.

Since the ISI Web of Knowledge Web of Science databank did not allow us to further specify and refine this rather large sample in terms of methodological orientation or underlying paradigms, we acted as raters during a two-stage process of coding each single article in the sample. To ensure this process's accuracy, the articles were independently read by both raters during each stage; thereafter they were manually coded. The results were compared and cross-checked by each of us.

First, we coded each article in terms of quantitative or qualitative methodology. We also checked for articles that had a conceptual or review character and did not contain empirical data researched by either quantitative or qualitative means. This stage provided difficulties as, for example, not each article that collected data by methods conventionally associated with qualitative methodology, such as interviews, also analysed the data by qualitative means. In order to have clarity regarding where to draw the line between quantitative and qualitative methodology, we excluded those articles that undertook a quantitative, statistically based analysis of the collected data. As mentioned above, since conceptual and review articles were also excluded from that original sample, this left us with 72 articles

Figure 11.1   Initial search parameters

269

clearly identified as qualitative in nature (18 per cent). If there was ambiguity or the raters differed, both would go back to the respective article and discuss the issue until consensus was achieved. In this first stage, we achieved a 93 per cent initial inter-rater coding reliability.

In the second stage of the manual coding, the two authors, acting as independent raters, adapted the data coding process described in Brush et al. (2008) to the specific sample of 72 residual qualitative articles. Each article was read in detail and coded according to the author(s), title, the journal, the detailed applied methodological approach, the inference approach, the underlying paradigm and theory, the level of analysis and its relevancy with regard to the radical subjectivist disequilibrium perspective. The authors again compared and cross-checked the results of each single article, arriving at a >90 per cent inter-rater reliability.

To analyse our data, we applied a coding table following the example of Brush et al. (2008) and their interpretation of Astley and Van de Ven's (1983) classification of organizational theories. Since the review at hand was primarily meant as a basis for identifying the status quo of qualitative research methodology in entrepreneurship and for deducing a potential direction by applying the radical subjectivist paradigm, we considered the calculation of frequencies as sufficient. Figure 11.2 summarizes our review process.

This figure illustrates the refining steps we have undertaken and, furthermore, shows how they correspond to the elements of the review conduction process systematized by Brereton et al. (2007). In the next section, we present an overview of our review findings and the results of that coding process.

THE FINDINGS IN THE CONTEXT OF A LACHMANNIAN RESEARCH PARADIGM

Our initial sample, retrieved from the ISI Web of Knowledge Web of Science databank, resulted in 402 articles. After having coded this sample manually, 216 (54 per cent) articles were identified as being strictly quantitative in terms of their applied methodology, 114 (28 per cent) were more conceptual, review articles or teaching cases, and 72 utilized a qualitative methodology. The latter equalled 18 per cent of the original sample. Of these qualitative articles, 31 had some relevance to our Lachmannian paradigm, although none of them referred directly to a disequilibrium perspective or issues related to this paradigm shift in entrepreneurship research.

The refined sample therefore represents only 8 per cent of the original sample, but 43 per cent of the qualitative one, which could be an indication that potential references to a disequilibrium paradigm could be

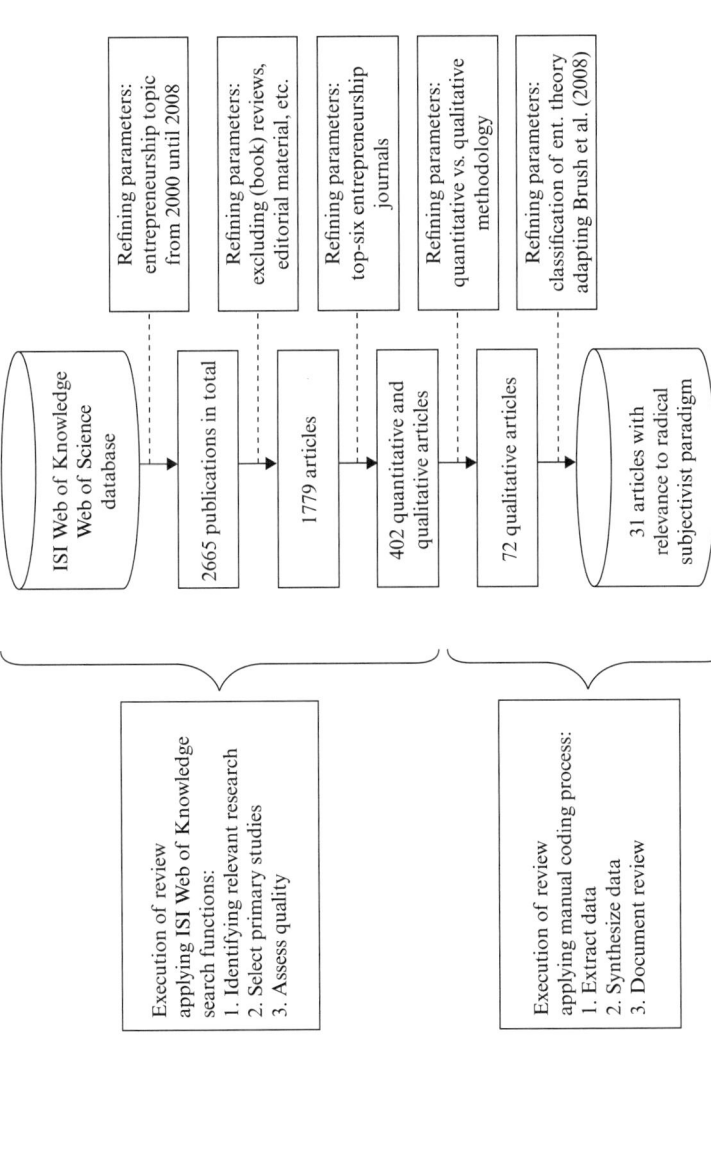

Refining parameters: entrepreneurship topic from 2000 until 2008

Refining parameters: excluding (book) reviews, editorial material, etc.

Refining parameters: top-six entrepreneurship journals

Refining parameters: quantitative vs. qualitative methodology

Refining parameters: classification of ent. theory adapting Brush et al. (2008)

ISI Web of Knowledge Web of Science database

2665 publications in total

1779 articles

402 quantitative and qualitative articles

72 qualitative articles

31 articles with relevance to radical subjectivist paradigm

Execution of review applying ISI Web of Knowledge search functions:
1. Identifying relevant research
2. Select primary studies
3. Assess quality

Execution of review applying manual coding process:
1. Extract data
2. Synthesize data
3. Document review

Figure 11.2   Overview of the systematic review process following Brereton et al. (2007)

disproportionally higher in articles applying a qualitative methodology than in the overall population. In the light of the works of Chiles et al. (2007), this finding is not surprising and supports their notion. Moreover, considering that this particular paradigm has only recently found its way into the field of entrepreneurship research, it is a surprisingly high number nonetheless. We believe that our coding process, as well as the overall rigour in terms of the underlying paradigms in entrepreneurship research explains this high number. Many articles did not explicitly state their underlying theories or they took many assumptions for granted without questioning them. We therefore needed to interpret their assumptions and theoretical background as accurately as possible during the coding process and to relate them to the disequilibrium approach.

Thus, our findings indicate that many contributors to qualitative entrepreneurship research are already applying assumptions that are actually Lachmannian in nature, but ignore the implications of this for their overall research approach and results. Provided these findings are correct, this would not only mean that entrepreneurship research is already adapting to the disequilibrium requirements of today's research environment, thus reflecting a strong need for this adaption, but it could also be interpreted as a strong plea to make theoretical assumptions in scientific contributions more explicit to allow findings to be interpreted in the right context.

Besides the simple distribution of article types, we also retrieved interesting data regarding the origin of publications in terms of institutions and countries, their chronological development, and their journal outlets. With regard to the original sample, it is interesting to note that the Max Planck Institute of Economics in Germany is the leading publishing organization (3.7 per cent of all publications), followed by the Erasmus University in the Netherlands (2.9 per cent), the University of Minnesota (2.7 per cent), and Babson College (2.5 per cent) in the US. There is a clear difference in the number of times each of these institutions is represented in the sample, although the share is relatively small due to the overall large number of organizations. This ranking is altered significantly if we only look at our refined samples: of the overall qualitative articles, the UK's De Montfort University, University of Lancaster, and Robert Gordon University are notable, with three publications each. This trend is consistent in the even further refined sample of 31 articles with Lachmannian relevance. In this case the University of Cambridge, the National University of Singapore, and the Royal Institute of Technology in Sweden also contribute, with two publications each.

The UK's dominance in terms of qualitative, as well as further refined publications, is also mirrored when calculating the overall number of contributions in terms of country of origin (see Figure 11.3).

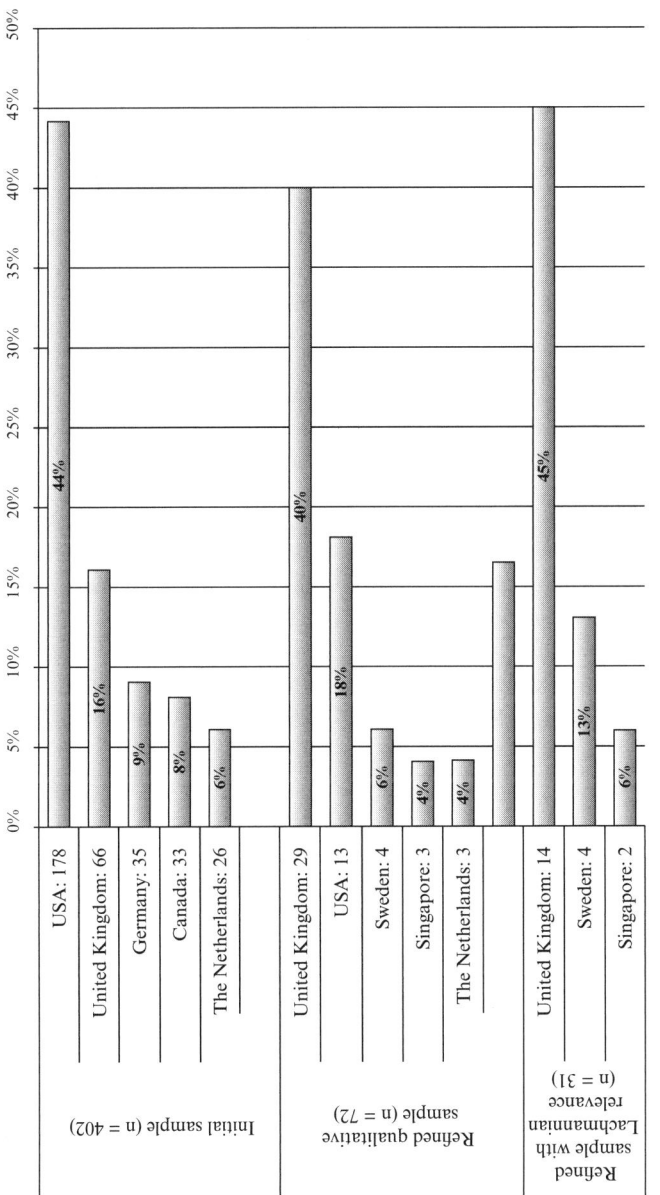

Note: Percentages are rounded.

Figure 11.3   Country of origin of articles in different samples (according to first author)

273

While the US clearly leads the field in the original sample, the result becomes more European-focused (due to the UK's dominance) the more the sample is refined. It is interesting to note that while the US is at least one of the leading countries of origin in terms of qualitative entrepreneurship research in general, it is actually not significantly represented in terms of relevance with regard to a disequilibrium paradigm.

When examining entrepreneurship research's chronological development during our timeframe of between 2000 and 2008, it is clear that in terms of our overall sample, there has been a continuous and significant increase in publications (Figure 11.4). Although not as constant and strong, a similar trend can be observed with regard to the qualitative article sample and, to a certain extent, the sample of articles relevant to the Lachmannian paradigm. While, in the latter case, we found no publications with such relevance in 2000 and 2001, there seems to be some indication of a peaking in interest in 2007 and 2008. If this is correct, it would support a strong plea for a paradigm shift in entrepreneurship research, since there already seems to be an approximation towards disequilibrium thinking.

As in the country of origin, an interesting shift in distribution occurs in terms of journal outlets when the sample levels of refinement are scrutinized. While in the original sample, the *Journal of Business Venturing* and *Small Business Economics* are ahead in numbers, in both the refined samples *Entrepreneurship and Regional Development* (ERD) leads (see Figure 11.5). This finding corresponds well with the residual findings, thus underlining a surprising UK dominance in our sample, as ERD is a UK-based journal.

Specific Findings

In terms of a comparison between the detailed entrepreneurship research approaches and the results presented in Brush et al. (2008), an exact comparison would obviously not be very accurate: These authors' sample comprises quantitative and qualitative articles, as well as review articles, thus exceeding our sample in scope, although more limited in focus. Nonetheless, Figure 11.6 summarizes our two refined samples in terms of the dimensions applied in Brush et al. (2008).

As can be seen in both cases, in terms of methods applied, the case study approach dominates, followed by interviews. Grounded and descriptive inference approaches were most frequently applied to analyse the collected data. Voluntaristic, firm-based theories, such as the resource-based view of the firm, strategic management theories or network theories, are significantly more common than deterministic ones.

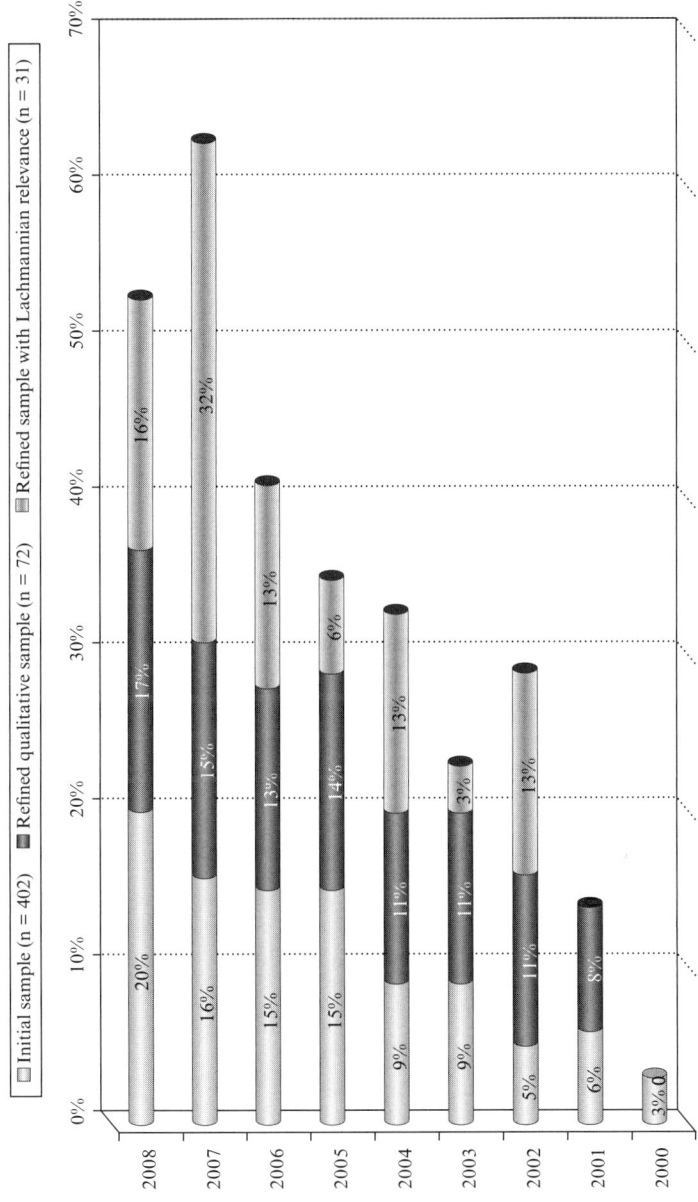

Legend:
☐ Initial sample (n = 402)   ▨ Refined qualitative sample (n = 72)   ▨ Refined sample with Lachmannian relevance (n = 31)

Note: Percentages are rounded.

Figure 11.4   Year of publication of articles in different samples

275

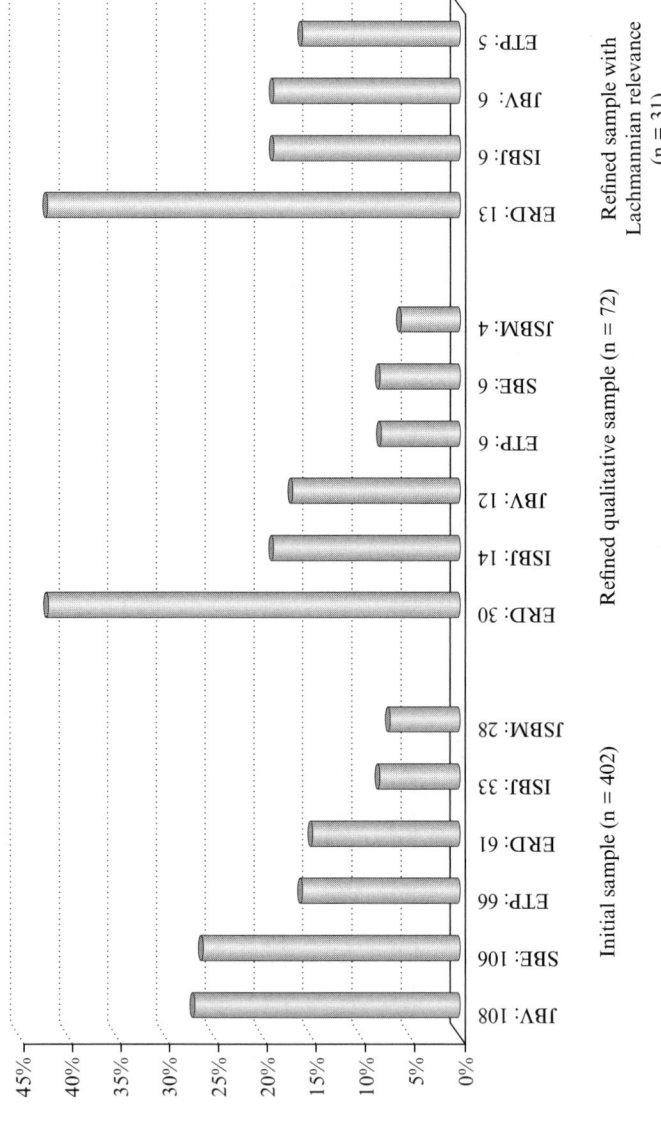

Note: Percentages are rounded.

Figure 11.5 Journal of publication of articles in different samples

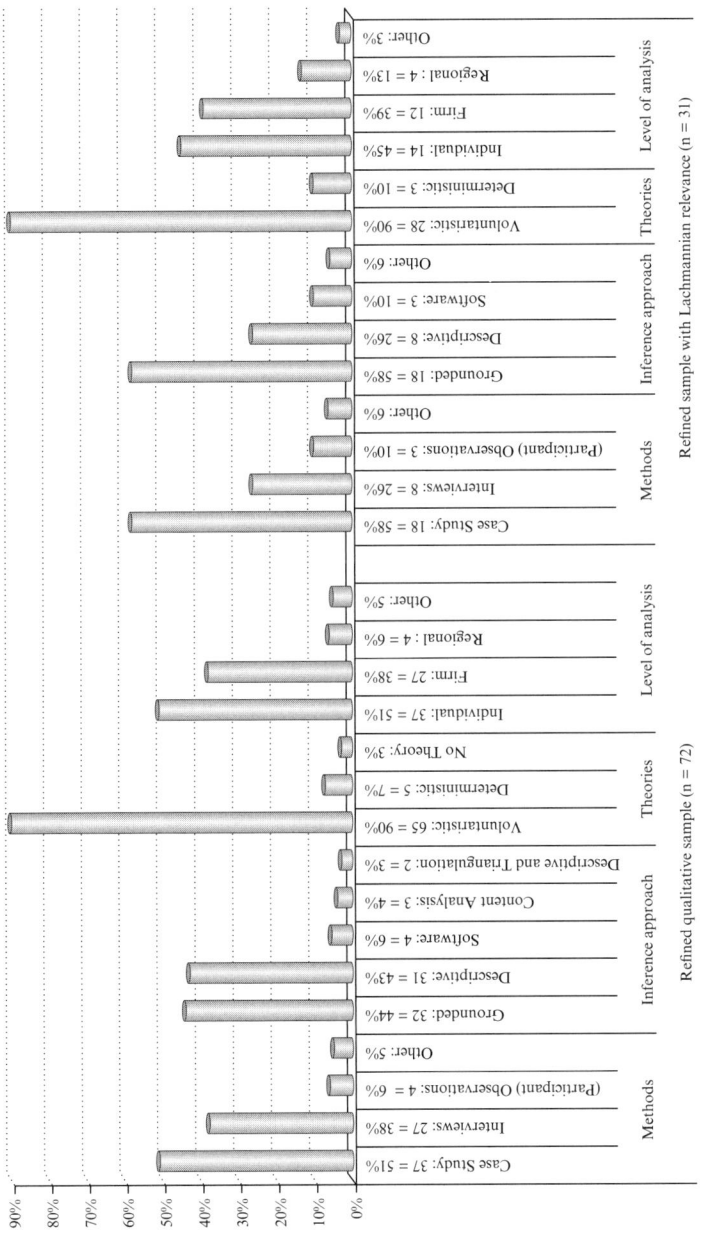

Note: Percentages are rounded.

Figure 11.6 Entrepreneurship research approaches following Brush et al. (2008)

Although, as mentioned above, these results cannot be directly compared to Brush et al. (2008), the similarities in terms of emphasis on firm-based voluntaristic approaches, case studies and interviews as the most frequently applied methods, and grounded and descriptive inference approaches – if their sample is only analysed in terms of qualitative methodology – convince us of the accuracy of our approach and support the reliability of our sample.

LIMITATIONS

We also have to emphasize the limitations of this approach. First of all, although we are sure that the six top journals in this sample do indeed reflect a reasonable consensus in terms of the top entrepreneurship outlets, the selection can be questioned. Most importantly, ERD's striking dominance in both our refined samples needs to be examined for bias and probably adjusted. The inclusion of this journal contributes significantly to the UK dominance within our samples. However, we think its inclusion is justified, since it is also ranked within the VHB JOURQUAL list and its importance highlighted in Katz (2003).

Secondly, after having applied the ISI Web of Knowledge Web of Science databank search to generate our initial sample and focusing only on publications explicitly indicated as articles, excluding reviews, and so on, there were still a significantly large number of conceptual and review articles and even teaching cases to eliminate from the sample during our manual coding. Since we cannot access the detailed search algorithms of the ISI Web of Knowledge databank service, we cannot guarantee that the search criteria were applied accurately, which might have affected the original sample's accuracy. This is also related to the rather broad search term 'entrepreneurship', which allows for focus, while it could simultaneously exclude less explicitly related articles. Nevertheless, due to the sufficient sample size (n = 402), we consider our sample as representative for this chapter's purposes. We mainly use the literature review results to prepare the basis for a discussion of methodological issues under a new paradigm and do not consider the review as a major finding in itself.

Finally, the reader also needs to consider the advantages and disadvantages of a manual coding process as described in this article. We addressed these by ensuring inter-rater reliability and a highly structured, reproducible review and coding protocol.

A HERMENEUTIC APPROACH TO QUALITATIVE METHODOLOGY IN ENTREPRENEURSHIP RESEARCH

Hermeneutics is a linguistic methodology that focuses on questions of how people interpret and understand texts (Prasad and Prasad, 2002). Though originally focused on biblical texts, hermeneutics has emerged as a powerful technique for interpreting the meanings of any text, including case studies, life stories, books, movies, emails and letters (Prasad and Mir, 2002). It recognizes that actors are not only born into and develop within an environment characterized by certain historical, social, and cultural institutions, but that they also reproduce and change this environment through their behaviours and actions (Garud and Karnoe, 2001). Not surprisingly, Lachmann (1990, p. 280) recommended hermeneutics as 'more congenial to the freedom of our wills and the requirements of a voluntaristic theory of action' than other methodologies.

Hermeneutics suggests that the various participants in a conversation jointly produce the understanding and meaning of a text (Prasad, 2002). It recognizes the existence of several different worldviews (or vantage points), which can differ to a greater or lesser degree from one another. Thus, the understanding of entrepreneurship is mutually constructed in conversations between entrepreneurs, lay people, media, commentators, and any other social participants who choose to join this conversation. The existence of these different worldviews must not be regarded as an obstacle to understanding, but should be seen as an opportunity to productively integrate diverse viewpoints to obtain a fresh perspective that may not otherwise have been possible.

Consider the movie *Pirates of Silicon Valley*, a popular movie about the early days of the PC–IT industry, which is frequently used in entrepreneurship courses around the world (Lunce and Smith, 2005). It is also the story of five men – Steve Jobs and Steve Wozniak (of Apple Computers) and Bill Gates, Paul Allen and Steve Ballmer (of Microsoft) – typical 'middle class white kids from good suburban homes'. The movie chronicles the early entrepreneurial days of these five men and how they created a new industry from nothing, an industry now 'the third largest industry in the world, somewhere between energy production and illegal drugs'. Was the PC–IT revolution –'a revolution that's changed the way we live, work and communicate' – the result of Bill Gates's vision ('A computer on every desk') as some accounts claim, or of Steve Jobs's charismatic leadership as many others argue, or did it just simply 'happen by accident because a bunch of disenfranchised nerds wanted to impress their friends'? The answer is not as clear as it should be.

The PC industry currently occupies an important place in public discourse about entrepreneurship and economic development. The success of people like Bill Gates and Steve Jobs has played an important role in making entrepreneurship a popular career choice for young people; nevertheless, scholarly understanding of the early emergence of firms such as Apple and Microsoft, as well as of the PC industry and Silicon Valley remains woefully inadequate. Though there have been some attempts to understand and explain the emergence of the PC industry (e.g., Hill and Deeds, 1996), we need much more research, using different theoretical lenses, to better understand how things turned out the way they did in this industry.

Hermeneutics emphasizes that understanding a text requires iterating between the interdependent meaning of parts and the whole that they form (Klein and Myers, 1999). Consider the sentence: 'Jo(e) is a successful entrepreneur'. The sentence must be understood by understanding the individual words in the sentence. At the same time, the meaning of individual words in the sentence only becomes clear when we understand what the sentence as a whole is trying to convey, or what the sentence is 'getting at', or what the 'direction' of the sentence is. Similarly, part or whole iterations are applicable to sentence–paragraph, paragraph–chapter, chapter–book, book–genre, and so on. This iteration between parts and the whole is well suited to address radical subjectivist questions on how entrepreneurs, firms and markets interact. Davidsson and Wiklund (2001) identified the individual, firm, industry and region as the major levels of analyses in entrepreneurship research. They encouraged entrepreneurship research to pursue research that is multi-level (examining multiple levels within the same study) as well as cross-level (understanding how different levels influence one another). Entrepreneurship researchers are well aware that entrepreneurship is inherently cross-level; the effect is that entrepreneurial action at one level can have important ramifications at other levels (Chiles et al., 2008). Hermeneutics is well suited to address the kinds of multi-level and cross-level questions that entrepreneurship researchers ask, or should ask (Sarasvathy, 2001).

Three additional issues deserve mention. First, a hermeneutic understanding of any text involves relating unique instances and occurrences found in this text to ideas and concepts that apply to multiple situations. The idiographic findings revealed in a text need to be related to theories and general concepts that describe the nature of human action and social systems. Thus, theory serves as a 'sensitizing device' to describe one's findings and draw conclusions from them (Klein and Myers, 1999).

Secondly, hermeneutics recognizes that preconceptions, assumptions and prejudices are inherent in any understanding of a text. For example, in recent years, several entrepreneurship researchers have acknowledged that scholarly understanding of entrepreneurial phenomena is through a North American lens. Consequently, the theories and methods we use to understand and describe entrepreneurship are based on an ethnocentric, limited understanding of what entrepreneurship does and how it acts (Thomas and Mueller, 2000). The North American bias favouring a particular understanding of entrepreneurship is certainly not limited to our field (Gupta and Fernandez, 2009), as a number of scholars have acknowledged that such biases are common in organizational research in general (Adler and Graham, 1989). Hofstede and Bond (1988) noted that even the most well–developed Western theories and tools may not adequately capture the various facets of organizational phenomenon. Hermeneutics acknowledges that readers bring their biases and prejudices to any understanding of a text. Entrepreneurship researchers would therefore do well to highlight their assumptions and preconceptions in their research endeavours.

Thirdly, hermeneutics encourages one to be suspicious of any text and to 'dig beneath' the surface to unveil and retrieve those meanings that often lie hidden. In entrepreneurship, recent research has unearthed the masculine social construction of entrepreneurship in Western society, and possibly around the world (Gupta, Turban, Wasti and Sikdar, 2009). Ahl (2006) reviewed several foundational books and articles on entrepreneurship. She defined foundational texts as 'those that scholars within any field build upon or openly argue against' (pp. 598–9). Her research reveals that major texts in our field construct entrepreneurship 'as something positive' and the entrepreneur is regarded as a masculine concept, that is it is not gender neutral. The inherently positive and masculine nature of the entrepreneur, which lies hidden beneath contemporary Western notions of who an entrepreneur is, may not be consistent with recent research. The newest research discusses the illegal (and, presumably, socially negative) aspects of entrepreneurship (Fadahunsi and Rosa, 2002), as well as the feminine construction of entrepreneurship in some cultures (Gupta, Turban and Pareek, 2009). Clearly, any investigation of entrepreneurs that builds on earlier scholarly work risks comparing them to a male-gendered, positive-valence archetype (Ahl, 2006), a fact that is not easily visible unless one is willing to dig deep into the meanings that underlie our texts.

CONCLUSION AND FURTHER RESEARCH

This chapter analyses publications in six leading entrepreneurship research journals between 2000 and 2008 with regard to their methodological orientations and relevance to the emerging disequilibrium paradigm according to Ludwig Lachmann. The key findings of this chapter prove that Lachmann's work represents a fundamental shift in entrepreneurship research: from the objectively anchored economic paradigms of Joseph Schumpeter and Israel Kirzner, to a thoroughly subjectivist paradigm based on the radical subjectivist notion of subjective ontology and epistemology. Not surprisingly, such a radical paradigm shift indicates new methodological directions, encouraging process-related, multilevel and historical research. However, relevant research efforts and appropriate methodological rigour is lacking. This article thus proposes hermeneutics as an exemplary approach that could address these deficiencies via narrative and pattern-matching strategies, while rejecting variance-theoretic models.

Despite our efforts, research on this issue is obviously still in its infancy. We believe that it will be necessary to expand our exemplary proposal in various dimensions such as those introduced, for example, by Davidsson and Wiklund (2001). Following these dimensions, this research should move beyond the focus on the voluntaristic individual and firm levels, towards the team, industry, regional and national perspectives. For example, the debate on the nature of entrepreneurship has attracted significant interest from scholars and researchers. It is possible to identify two distinct conceptions of entrepreneurship within the extant research literature, namely discovery theory and creation theory (Alvarez and Barney, 2007). They have very different conceptions of the market process: according to discovery theory, entrepreneurship is a function of the quality of alertness, that is when an alert individual is able to discover unexploited profit opportunities (Shane and Venkataraman, 2000). In contrast, creation theory views entrepreneurship as driven by the imaginative acts of forward-looking individuals who generate novelty *ex nihilo* (Chiles et al., 2007). Discovery theorists consider new opportunities as existing 'out there', ready to be discovered by a knowledgeable expert, whereas creation theorists perceive opportunities as generated when individuals imagine possible futures (Sarasvathy, 2001; Baker and Nelson, 2005). In the worldview of discovery theory, entrepreneurial opportunities exist objectively, but are not equally obvious to everyone. Creation theory regards the world as in-the-making and entrepreneurial opportunities as enacted through purposeful action.

We believe that changing our scientific understanding and knowledge of the two apparently opposing paradigms of discovery and creation can alter – for the better – the way we research entrepreneurial activities and teach entrepreneurship as well as policy-makers' encouragement of entrepreneurial activity (see Zahra, 2008). Nonetheless, conventional research methods have failed to achieve results. Therefore, we propose using hermeneutics as a research technique for such a study. Hermeneutics is an interpretive methodology (Phillips and Brown, 1993) that emphasizes the interpretation of 'events that make up the processes' researchers wish to understand. It is 'more congenial to the freedom of our wills and the requirements of a voluntaristic theory of action' than rival methodologies and is an appropriate methodology for the study of human behaviour, including entrepreneurial action (Chiles et al., 2007).

For the purpose of this chapter, it is enough to summarize that with respect to the radical subjectivist paradigm, entrepreneurship methodology still needs to be defined and developed. We consider this chapter a first humble attempt to head this effort and to provide first insights and potential solutions for the broader audience.

REFERENCES

Adler, N.J. and J.L. Graham (1989), 'Cross-cultural interaction: the international comparison fallacy?', *Journal of International Business Studies*, **20**(3), 515–37.

Ahl, H. (2006), 'Why research on women entrepreneurs needs new directions', *Entrepreneurship, Theory and Practice*, **30**, 595–621.

Ahl, H. (2007), 'Sex business in the toy store: a narrative analysis of a teaching case', *Journal of Business Venturing*, **22**(5), 673–93.

Allen, T. (2007), 'A toy store(y)', *Journal of Business Venturing*, **22**, 628–36.

Alvarez, S.A. and J.B. Barney (2007), 'Discovery and creation: alternative theories of entrepreneurial action', *Strategic Entrepreneurship Journal*, **1**, 11–26.Amit, R., L. Glosten and E. Mueller (1993), 'Challenges to theory development in entrepreneurship research', *Journal of Management Studies*, **30**(5), 815–34.

Astley, W. and A. Van de Ven (1983), 'Central perspectives and debates in organization theory', *Administrative Science Quarterly*, **28**(2), 245–73.

Baker, T. (2007), 'Resources in play: bricolage in the toy store(y)', *Journal of Business Venturing*, **22**(5), 694–711.

Baker, T. and R. Nelson (2005), 'Creating something from nothing: resource construction through entrepreneurial bricolage', *Administrative Science Quarterly*, **50**, 329–66.

Bird, B.J. and P.G. West (1997), 'Time and entrepreneurship', *Entrepreneurship Theory and Practice*, **22**(2), 5–9.

Bluedorn, A.C. (2002), *The Human Organization of Time*, Stanford, CA: Stanford University Press.

Boehm, S., I. Kirzner, R. Koppl, D. Lavoie, P. Lewin, C. Torr and L. Moss (2000), 'Remembrance and appreciation roundtable – Professor Ludwig M. Lachmann (1906–1990): Scholar, teacher, and Austrian school critic of late classical formalism in economics', *American Journal of Economics and Sociology*, **59**, 367–417.

Brereton, P., B. Kitchenham, D. Budgen, M. Turner and M. Khalil (2007), 'Lessons from applying the systematic literature review process within the software engineering domain', *Journal of Systems & Software*, **80**(4), 571–83.

Brush, C., T. Manolova and L. Edelman (2008), 'Separated by a common language? Entrepreneurship research across the Atlantic', *Entrepreneurship Theory and Practice*, **32**(2), 249–66.

Bruton, G., D. Ahlstrom and K. Obloj (2008), 'Entrepreneurship in emerging economies: where are we today and where should the research go in the future', *Entrepreneurship Theory and Practice*, **32**(1), 1–14.

Bruyat, C. and P.-A. Julien (2001), 'Defining the field of research in entrepreneurship', *Journal of Business Venturing*, **16**(2), 165–80.

Bygrave, W.D. (1989), 'The entrepreneurship paradigm (I): a philosophical look at its research methodologies', *Entrepreneurship Theory and Practice*, **14**(1), 7–26.

Chandler, G.N. and D.N. Lyon (2001), 'Issues of research design and construct measurement in entrepreneurship research: the past decade', *Entrepreneurship Theory and Practice*, **24**(4), 101–13.

Cheah, H.B. (1990), 'Schumpeterian and entrepreneurship: unity within duality', *Journal of Business Venturing*, **5**, 341–7.

Chiles, T.H. (2003), 'Process theorizing: too important to ignore in a kaleidic world', *Academy of Management Learning & Education*, **2**(3), 288–91.

Chiles, T.H. and V.K. Gupta (2004), 'Toward a new entrepreneurship paradigm: venturing beyond creative destruction and entrepreneurial discovery', presented at The Academy of Management Conference, New Orleans.

Chiles, T.H., A.C. Bluedorn and V.K. Gupta (2007), 'Beyond creative destruction and entrepreneurial discovery: a radical Austrian approach to entrepreneurship', *Organization Studies*, **28**(4), 467–93.

Chiles, T.H., V.K. Gupta and A.C. Bluedorn (2008), 'On Lachmannian and effectual entrepreneurship: a reply to Sarasvathy and Dew', *Organization Studies*, **29**(2), 247–53.

Chiles, T.H., D. Vultee, V.K. Gupta, D. Greening and C. Tuggle (2010), 'The philosophical foundations of a radical Austrian approach to entrepreneurship', *Journal of Management Inquiry*, 19(2), 138–64.

Cooper, A. (2003), 'Entrepreneurship: the past, the present, the future', in Z.J. Acs and D.B. Audretsch (eds), *Handbook of Entrepreneurship Research*, Boston, MA: Kluwer, pp. 21–34.

Coviello, N.E. and M.V. Jones (2004), 'Methodological issues in international entrepreneurship research', *Journal of Business Venturing*, **19**(4), 485–508.

Davidsson, P. and J. Wiklund (2001), 'Levels of analysis in entrepreneurship research: current research practice and suggestions for the future', *Entrepreneurship Theory and Practice*, **25**(4), 81–99.

Davidsson, P., M.B. Low and M. Wright (2001), 'Editor's introduction: Low and MacMillan ten years on: achievements and future directions for entrepreneurship research', *Entrepreneurship Theory and Practice*, **25**(4), 5–15.

Dean, M.A., C.L. Shook and G.T. Payne (2007), 'The past, present, and future of entrepreneurship research: data analytic trends and trends', *Entrepreneurship Theory and Practice*, **31**(4), 601–18.

Dew, N., S.R. Velamuri and S. Venkataraman (2004), 'Dispersed knowledge and an entrepreneurial theory of the firm', *Journal of Business Venturing*, **19**, 659–79.

Fadahunsi, A. and P. Rosa (2002), 'Entrepreneurship and illegality: insights from the Nigerian cross-border trade', *Journal of Business Venturing*, **17**, 397–429.

Fletcher, D. (2007), 'Toy story: the narrative world of entrepreneurship and the creation of interpretive communities', *Journal of Business Venturing*, **22**(5), 649–72.

Foss, N.J. and I. Ishikawa (2007), 'Towards a dynamic resource-based view:

insights from Austrian capital and entrepreneurship theory', *Organization Studies*, **28**, 749–72.

Foss, N.J., P.G. Klein, Y.Y. Kor and J.T. Mahoney (2008), 'Entrepreneurship, subjectivism, and the resource-based view: toward a new synthesis', *Strategic Entrepreneurship Journal*, **2**, 73–94.

Gartner, W.B. (2007), 'Entrepreneurial narrative and the science of imagination', *Journal of Business Venturing*, **22**, 613–27.

Gartner, W.B. and S. Birley (2002), 'Introduction to the special issue on qualitative methods in entrepreneurship research', *Journal of Business Venturing*, **17**, 385–95.

Gartner, W.B., B.J. Bird and J.A. Starr (1992), 'Acting as if: differentiating entrepreneurial from organizational behavior', *Entrepreneurship Theory and Practice*, **16**(3), 13–31.

Garud, R. and P. Karnoe (2001), 'Path creation as a process of mindful deviation', in R. Garud and P. Karnøe (eds), *Path Dependence and Creation*, Mahwah, NJ: Lawrence Erlbaum, pp. 1–38.

Gloria-Palermo, S. (1999), *The Evolution of Austrian Economics*, New York: Routledge.

Gupta, V.K. and C. Fernandez (2009), 'Cross-cultural similarities and differences in characteristics attributed to entrepreneurs: a three nation study', *Journal of Leadership & Organizational Studies*, **15**(3), 304–18.

Gupta, V.K. and A. Gupta (2009), 'Toward a theoretical paradigm for social entrepreneurship research: a new approach to social entrepreneurship from the radical Austrian school', presented at the *Eastern Academy of Management Conference*, Hartford, CT.

Gupta, V.K., D.B. Turban and N.M. Bhawe (2008), 'The effect of gender stereotype assimilation and reactance on entrepreneurial intentions', *Journal of Applied Psychology*, **93**(5), 1053–61.

Gupta, V.K., D.B. Turban and A. Pareek (2009), 'Exploiting an entrepreneurial opportunity: the effect of gender stereotype activation on Indian men and women', working paper.

Gupta, V.K., D.B. Turban, S.A. Wasti and A. Sikdar (2009), 'The role of gender stereotypes in perceptions of entrepreneurs and intentions to become an entrepreneur', *Entrepreneurship Theory and Practice*, **33**(2), 397–417.

Healy, M. and C. Perry (2000), 'Comprehensive criteria to judge validity and reliability of qualitative research within the realism paradigm', *Qualitative Market Research*, **3**(3), 118–26.

Hill, C.W.L. and D.L. Deeds (1996), 'The importance of industry structure for the determination of firm profitability: a neo-Austrian perspective', *Journal of Management Studies*, **33**(4), 429–51.

Hill, J. and P. McGowan (2001), 'Small business and enterprise development: questions about research methodology', *International Journal of Entrepreneurial Behavior & Research*, **5**(1), 5–18.

Hjorth, D. (2008), 'Nordic entrepreneurship research', *Entrepreneurship Theory and Practice*, **32**, 313–38.

Hoang, H. and B. Antoncic (2003), 'Network-based research in entrepreneurship', *Journal of Business Venturing*, **18**, 165–87.

Hofstede, G. and M.H. Bond (1988), 'The Confucius connection: from cultural roots to economic growth', *Organizational Dynamics*, **16**(4), 5–21.

Judge, T., D. Cable, A. Colbert and S. Rynes (2007), 'What causes a management article to be cited – article, author, or journal?', *Academy of Management Journal*, **50**(3), 491–506.

Katz, H. (2003), 'Core publications in entrepreneurship and related fields: a guide to getting published', available at http://eweb.slu.edu/booklist.htm, accessed 15 August 2010.

Kirzner, I.M. (1973), *Competition and Entrepreneurship*, Chicago, IL: University of Chicago Press.

Kirzner, I.M. (2000) 'Kirzner on the gallant warrior', in L.S. Moss (ed.), 'Remembrance and appreciation roundtable Professor Ludwig M. Lachmann (1906–1990): Scholar, teacher, and Austrian school critic of late classical formalism in economics, *American Journal of Economics and Sociology*, **59**, 367–419.

Klein, H.K. and M.D. Myers (1999), 'A set of principles for conducting and evaluating interpretive field studies in information systems', *MIS Quarterly*, **23**, 67–93.

Kor, Y.Y., J.T. Mahoney and S.C. Michael (2007), 'Resources, capabilities and entrepreneurial perceptions', *Journal of Management Studies*, **44**, 1187–212.

Kraus, S. and K. Gundolf (2008), 'Entrepreneurship: zur Genese eines Forschungsfeldes', in S. Kraus and K. Gundolf (eds), *Stand und Perspektiven der Deutschsprachigen Entrepreneurship- und KMU-Forschung*, Hannover/Stuttgart: Ibidem, pp. 8–28.

Kuratko, D. and D. Audretsch (2009), 'Strategic entrepreneurship: exploring different perspectives of an emerging concept', *Entrepreneurship Theory and Practice*, **33**, 1–17.

Lachmann, L.M. (1976), 'On the central concept of Austrian economics: market process', in E. Dolan (ed.), *Foundations of Modern Austrian Economics*, Kansas City, MO: Sheed and Ward, pp. 126–32.

Lachmann, L. (1977), *Capital, Expectations, and the Market Process: Essays on the Theory of the Market Economy*, Kansas City, MO: Sheed Andrews and Macmeel, Inc.

Lachmann, L.M. (1990), 'Austrian economics: a hermeneutic approach', in D. Lavoie (ed.), *Economics and Hermeneutics*, London: Routledge, pp. 134–46.

Lavoie, D. (1994), 'Introduction: expectations and the meaning of institutions', in D. Lavoie (ed.), *Expectaions and the Meaning of Institutions*, London: Routledge, PP. 1–19.

Lewin, P. (1997), 'Capital in disequilibrium: a reexamination of the capital theory of Ludwig M. Lachmann', *History of Political Economy*, **29**, 523–48.

Loasby, B.J. (2007), 'A cognitive perspective on entrepreneurship and the firm', *Journal of Management Studies*, **44**, 1078–106.

Lunce, S.E. and S. Smith (2005), 'Business in the media: a pedagogical approach to understanding basic business concepts', *International Journal of Innovation and Learning*, **2**(2), 210–22.

Meyer, A.D., V. Gaba and K.A. Colwell (2005), 'Organizing far from equilibrium: nonlinear change in organizational fields', *Organization Science*, **16**, 456–73.

Munir, K.A. and N. Phillips (2005), 'The birth of the "Kodak moment": institutional entrepreneurship and the adoption of new technologies', *Organization Studies*, **26**, 1665–87.

O'Connor, E.S. (2007), 'Reader beware: doing business with a store(y) of knowledge', *Journal of Business Venturing*, **22**(5), 637–48.

Phillips, N. and J.L. Brown (1993), 'Analyzing communication in and around organizations: a critical hermeneutic approach', *Academy of Management Journal*, **36**, 1547–76.

Prasad, A. (2002), 'The contest over meaning: hermeneutics as an interpretive methodology for understanding texts', *Organizational Research Methods*, **5**, 12–33.

Prasad, A. and R. Mir (2002), 'Digging deep for meaning: a critical hermeneutic analysis of CEO letters to shareholders in the oil industry', *Journal of Business Communication*, **39**(1), 92–116.

Prasad, A. and P. Prasad (2002), 'The coming of age of interpretive organizational research', *Organizational Research Methods*, **5**, 4–11.

Rauch, A., J. Wiklund, G. Lumpkin and M. Frese (2009), 'Entrepreneurial orientation and business performance: an assessment of past research and suggestions for the future', *Entrepreneurship Theory and Practice*, **33**(3), 761–87.

Sarason, Y., T. Dean and J.F. Dillard (2006), 'Entrepreneurship as the nexus of individual and opportunity: a structuration view', *Journal of Business Venturing*, **21**(3), 286–305.

Sarasvathy, S.D. (2001), 'Causation and effectuation: toward a theoretical shift from economic inevitability to entrepreneurial contingency', *Academy of Management Review*, **26**, 243–63.

Sarasvathy, S.D. (2003), 'The questions we ask and the questions we care about: reformulating some problems in entrepreneurship research', *Journal of Business Venturing*, **19**(5), 707–17.

Schumpeter, J. (1954), *The Theory of Economic Development*, Oxford: Oxford University Press.

Shackle, G.L.S. (1966), 'Policy, poetry and success', *Economic Journal*, **76**, 755–67.

Shane, S. and S. Venkataraman (2000), 'The promise of entrepreneurship as a field of research', *Academy of Management Review*, **25**, 217–26.

Steyaert, C. (2007), 'Of course that is not the whole (toy) story: entrepreneurship and the cat's cradle', *Journal of Business Venturing*, **22**(5), 733–51.

Thomas, A.S. and S.L. Mueller (2000), 'A case for comparative entrepreneurship: assessing the relevance of culture', *Journal of International Business Studies*, **31**(2), 287–301.

Ucbasaran, D., P. Westhead and M. Wright (2001), 'The focus of entrepreneurship research: contextual and process issues', *Entrepreneurship Theory and Practice*, **25**(4), 57–80.

Van de Ven, A.H. and R.M. Engleman (2004), 'Event- and outcome-driven explanations of entrepreneurship', *Journal of Business Venturing*, **19**, 343–58.

Vaughn, K.I. (1994), *Austrian Economics in America,* Cambridge, UK: Cambridge University Press.

Venkataraman, S. (1997) 'The distinctive domain of entrepreneurship research: an editor's perspective', in J. Katz and R. Brockhaus (eds), *Advances in Entrepreneurship, Firm Emergence, and Growth*, Greenwich, CT: JAI Press, pp. 119–38.

Welter, F. and F. Lasch (2008), 'Entrepreneurship research in Europe: taking stock and looking forward', *Entrepreneurship Theory and Practice*, **32**(2), 241–8.

Zahra, S.A. (2008), 'The virtuous circle of discovery and creation of entrepreneurial opportunities', *Strategic Entrepreneurship Journal*, **2**, 243–57.

Zahra, S.A. and G. Dess (2001), 'Entrepreneurship as a field of research: encouraging dialogue and debate', *Academy of Management Review*, **26**, 8–10.

Index